Y/A

The Britannica Guide to
Algebra and Trigonometry

MATH EXPLAINED

The Britannica Guide to
Algebra and
Trigonometry

EDITED BY WILLIAM L. HOSCH,
ASSOCIATE EDITOR, MATHEMATICS AND COMPUTER SCIENCES

Educational Publishing

IN ASSOCIATION WITH

EDUCATIONAL SERVICES

Published in 2011 by Britannica Educational Publishing
(a trademark of Encyclopædia Britannica, Inc.)
in association with Rosen Educational Services, LLC
29 East 21st Street, New York, NY 10010.

First Edition

Britannica Educational Publishing
Michael I. Levy: Executive Editor
J.E. Luebering: Senior Manager
Marilyn L. Barton: Senior Coordinator, Production Control
Steven Bosco: Director, Editorial Technologies
Lisa S. Braucher: Senior Producer and Data Editor
Yvette Charboneau: Senior Copy Editor
Kathy Nakamura: Manager, Media Acquisition
William L. Hosch: Associate Editor, Mathematics and Computer Sciences

Rosen Educational Services
Alexandra Hanson-Harding: Editor
Bethany Bryan: Editor
Nelson Sá: Art Director
Cindy Reiman: Photography Manager
Matthew Cauli: Designer, Cover Design
Introduction by John Strazzabosco

Library of Congress Cataloging-in-Publication Data

The Britannica guide to algebra and trigonometry / edited by William L. Hosch.
    p. cm. — (Math explained)
"In association with Britannica Educational Publishing, Rosen Educational Services."
Includes bibliographical references and index.
ISBN 978-1-61530-113-3 (lib. bdg.)
1. Algebra. 2. Trigonometry. I. Hosch, William L. II. Title: Algebra and trigonometry.
QA155.B75 2010
512—dc22

                                                                2009047905

Manufactured in the United States of America

CONTENTS

Introduction   12

Chapter 1: Algebra   **23**
  History of Algebra   23
    The Emergence of Formal Equations   23
      Problem Solving in Egypt and
      Babylon   25
      Greece and the Limits of
      Geometric Expression   27
      The Equation in India
      and China   31
      Islamic Contributions   32
      Commerce and Abacists in the
      European Renaissance   35
      Cardano and the Solving of
      Cubic and Quartic Equations 38
      Viète and the Formal Equation 40
      The Concept of Numbers   41
  Classical Algebra   43
    Analytic Geometry   43
    The Fundamental Theorem of
    Algebra   45
    Impasse with Radical Methods   47
    Galois Theory   48
    Applications of Group Theory   51
    Fundamental Concepts of
    Modern Algebra   54
    Systems of Equations   57
    Quaternions and Vectors   61
    The Close of the Classical Age   63
  Structural Algebra   63
    Precursors to the Structural
    Approach   64

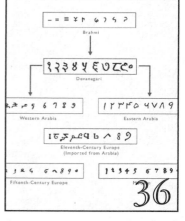

The Structural Approach
Dominates   66
Algebraic Superstructures   67
New Challenges and
Perspectives   69
Branches of Algebra   70
  Elementary Algebra   71
    Algebraic Quantities   71
    Algebraic Expressions   73
    Solving Algebraic Equations   75
    Solving Systems of Algebraic
    Equations   76
  Linear Algebra   78
    Vectors and Vector Spaces   78
    Linear Transformations and
    Matrices   81
    Eigenvectors   82
  Modern Algebra   83
    Basic Algebraic Structures   83
      Field Axioms   85
    Rings   86
    Group Theory   88

Chapter 2: Great Algebraists   **91**
Early Algebraists (Through the 16th
Century)   91
  Bhaskara II   91
  Brahmagupta   93
  Girolamo Cardano   94
  Diophantus of Alexandria   96
  Lodovico Ferrari   99
  Scipione Ferro   100
  al-Karaji   101
  al-Khwārizmī   102
  Liu Hui   103
  Mahavira   105
  Qin Jiushao   106

79

88

95

Classical Algebraists (17th–19th
Centuries)   107
    Niels Henrik Abel   107
    Bernhard Bolzano   110
    George Boole   111
    Arthur Cayley   113
    Évariste Galois   116
    Carl Friedrich Gauss   119
    Sir William Rowan Hamilton   124
    Charles Hermite   129
    Felix Klein   130
    Leopold Kronecker   131
    Ernst Eduard Kummer   132
    Sophus Lie   133
    Joseph Liouville   135
    Paolo Ruffini   137
    Seki Takakazu   138
    James Joseph Sylvester   140
    François Viète   142
Algebraists of the Structural Period
(20th Century–)   143
    Emil Artin   143
    Richard Ewen Borcherds   144
    Nicolas Bourbaki   144
    Richard Dagobert Brauer   145
    Élie-Joseph Cartan   146
    George Dantzig   147
    Leonard Eugene Dickson   148
    Jean Dieudonné   149
    Georg Frobenius   149
    Aleksandr Osipovich Gelfond   150
    David Hilbert   151
    Saunders Mac Lane   154
    Gregori Aleksandrovich Margulis   155
    Emmy Noether   156
    Daniel Gray Quillen   158
    Alfred Tarski   159

Hermann Weyl   160
Efim Isaakovich Zelmanov   161

Chapter 3: Algebraic Terms and Concepts   **163**

Algebraic Equation   163
Algebraic Number   163
Associative Law   164
Automorphism   164
Binomial Theorem   165
Boolean Algebra   166
Complex Number   168
Commutative Law   168
Cramer's Rule   168
Degree of Freedom   169
Determinant   170
Discriminant   171
Distributive Law   171
Eigenvalue   172
Equation   172
Factor   173
Fundamental Theorem of Algebra   173
Gauss Elimination   174
Group   175
Group Theory   175
Hodge Conjecture   176
Homomorphism   176
Ideal   178
Imaginary Number   179
Injection   179
Irrational Number   180
Linear Equation   180
Liouville Number   181
Matrix   182
Multinomial Theorem   186
Parameter   187
Pascal's Triangle   187

Polynomial   190
Quadratic Equation   191
Quaternion   192
Rational Number   192
Ring   193
Root   193
Square Root   195
Surjection   195
Synthetic Division   196
System of Equations   197
Variable   197
Vector   197
Vector Operations   200
Vector Space   200

Chapter 4: Trigonometry   **202**
History of Trigonometry   202
    Classical Trigonometry   202
        Ancient Egypt and the
        Mediterranean World   203
        India and the Islamic World   206
        Passage to Europe   207
    Modern Trigonometry   209
        From Geometric to Analytic
        Trigonometry   209
        Application to Science   212
Principles of Trigonometry   214
    Trigonometric Functions   214
        Trigonometric Functions of
        an Angle   216
        Tables of Natural Functions   219
    Plane Trigonometry   219
    Spherical Trigonometry   221
    Analytic Trigonometry   222
    Coordinates and Transformation
    of Coordinates   223

Polar Coordinates 223
Transformation of Coordinates 225

Chapter 5: Great Trigonometricians 227
Aryabhata I 227
al-Battānī 229
Abraham de Moivre 230
Leonhard Euler 231
James Gregory 234
Hipparchus 238
    Lover of Truth 238
    Solar and Lunar Theory 240
    Other Scientific Work 243
Menelaus of Alexandria 245
Ptolemy 246
    Astronomer 248
    Mathematician 250
    Geographer 251
Regiomontanus 252
Naṣīr al-Dīn al-Ṭūsī 256

**Chapter 6: Trigonometric Terms
and Concepts 259**
Alfonsine Tables 259
Almagest 259
Law of Cosines 262
Fourier Series 262
Hyperbolic Function 262
Law of Sines 263
Trigonometric Function 263
Trigonometry Table 264
Triangulation 266

Glossary 268
Bibliography 270
Index 273

INTRODUCTION

In this volume we meet the major discovering players in the recorded history of algebra and trigonometry. We also find detail that leads to revealing concepts, applications, connective strands, and explanations to enhance our understanding of what modern-day students affectionately refer to as algebra and trig. What is not lost are the human attributes of those who make great discoveries. The math, while consisting of incredible ingenuity in itself, has come from innovators who had stories of their own, people who dealt simultaneously with the same common mix that all humans share—desires, fears, profound joy, heartbreak, and agony—all delivered by life and carried to our work.

When the layers of mathematical discovery are peeled back, the fruit is sweet, though that conclusion might be debated by some. Math is not an easy pursuit, and so some are fascinated while others dread and even hate it.

Given the difficulties in learning about algebra and trigonometry, perhaps we might stand back in awe when we consider that some people actually originated these ideas, creating them from whole cloth—a daunting consideration when most of us have found difficulties with math even when shown the way. Somebody at one point said, for instance: Oh yes, here's a way to better investigate the problems of three-dimensional geometry. A question we mortals might ask is: What kind of person would do this? Adults? Children? Men? Women? Where would this person have come from? Europe? The Middle East? Asia?

The answer is, all of the above, and more.

Let's first consider a child learning Latin, Greek, and Hebrew by the age of five. That would be William Rowan Hamilton (1805–1865) of Ireland. Before he was 12, he had tacked on Arabic, Sanskrit, Persian, Syriac, French, and Italian. But that's language; what about algebra? Hamilton was reading Bartholomew Lloyd (analytic geometry),

Euclid (Euclidean geometry, of course), Isaac Newton, Pierre-Simon Laplace, Joseph-Louis Lagrange, and more by the time he was 16.

With hefty youthful pursuits such as Hamilton's, we can suspect that mental groundwork was being laid for notable achievement. The crescendo was actually reached for Hamilton suddenly. He was walking with his wife beside the Royal Canal to Dublin in 1843 when a grand thought occurred. We can only imagine the conversation on the path: "Dear, I just suddenly realized that the solution lies not in triplets but quadruplets, which could produce a noncommutative four-dimensional algebra."

"William, are you hallucinating?"

"We could call them quaternions."

Hamilton actually did engage in a similar dialogue with his wife, and they finished that walk but not before pausing at the bridge over the canal. There, Hamilton carved fundamentals of his discovery into the stone of the bridge. He spent the next 22 years on quaternion theory. His work further advanced algebra, dynamics, optics, and quantum mechanics. Notable among his achievements were his abilities in the languages of the world and his penchant for throwing those energetic years filled with that tireless strength called youth into mathematics that might later change the world.

Hamilton had to be thankful to some people when he reached his innovations. Though undoubtedly a mathematical genius, he hadn't started from scratch. At least he had the letters x, y, and z at his disposal when working out equations; not every mathematician since antiquity has had the luxury of math symbols. And for that matter, Hamilton had equations. Further, with his uncommon linguistic skills, he understood the languages of many other mathematicians. Hamilton had a structured algebraic system at his disposal that allowed him to work furiously at, for lack of a better expression, the guts of his math. What he took for granted, for example, were symbols in math at his fingertips, for where would algebra be without the *x*?

Actually, the *x* had been missing from math solutions for thousands of years.

The earliest texts (*c.* 1650 BCE) were in the Egyptian Rhind Papyrus scroll. There we find linear equations solved but without much use of symbols—it's all words. For example, take this problem from the Rhind Papyrus, also found later in the body of this volume:

- Method of calculating a quantity, multiplied by $1\frac{1}{2}$ added 4 it has come to 10.
- What is the quantity that says it?
- First you calculate the difference of this 10 to this 4. Then 6 results.
- Then you divide 1 by $1\frac{1}{2}$. Then $\frac{2}{3}$ results.
- Then you calculate $\frac{2}{3}$ of this 6. Then 4 results.
- Behold, it is 4, the quantity that said it.
- What has been found by you is correct.

If Sir William Rowan Hamilton were doing this problem, instead of writing the eight lines of verbiage and numbers above, he would have preferred the crisp:

$$1\frac{1}{2}x + 4 = 10$$

Then he would have solved that equation in a flash, as would most sixth- or seventh-grade math students today.

Verbal problems have traditionally made even capable algebra students squirm, but verbal *solutions* on top of the verbal problem? Especially when the teacher says, "And write down every step." One can hear the classroom full of groans. Not only was the solution so protracted in antiquity as to turn a rather simple modern-day math problem into a bear, the ancient numbers themselves were not so easy to tackle. For instance, in the Rhind Papyrus problem above, although a special case symbol existed for the fraction $^2/_3$, the Egyptians wrote all other fractions with only unit fractions, where the numerator must be 1. In other words, to write $^3/_4$ the sum they wrote $^1/_2 + ^1/_4$ instead.

We can see then why mathematical progress did not fly quickly when newly emerging from the cocoon; the tools of math simply were not there. Of course, what was required for full flight was the emergence of symbols and streamlined numbers.

But somebody first had to create them. Too late for the Rhind Papyrus scrolls, but in plenty of time for Hamilton, the Abacists gave introductory symbol usage a nudge.

Leonardo Pisano (better known as Fibonacci) in 1202 CE wrote *The Book of Abacus*, which communicated the sleek and manageable Hindu-Arabic numerals to a broader and receptive audience in the Latin world. This New Math of Italy gave merchants numbers and techniques that could be quickly used in calculating deals. What Pisano had bridged was the communication gap of different languages that had kept hidden useful math innovation.

Pisano's revelation of the Islamic numbers led to the Abacist school of thought, through which symbol use grew. Not only was equation solving enhanced, but the manageable numbers allowed higher math thought to emerge. Eventually negative numbers, complex numbers, and the great innovations that culminated in our modern technology followed.

Let's again step back to antiquity. As Pythagoras (*c.* 450 BCE) had neither letter symbols nor Arabic numerals, and was not privy to the algebraic structure to come — spurred much later greatly by his own contribution—he never saw his own equation regarding the sides and the hypotenuse of a right triangle, an equation known by heart to any middle-school student of the modern world, namely, $c^2 = a^2 + b^2$ (at least not in that form). One can only imagine Pythagoras's wonderment upon sitting down today before a calculator or a computer. His needs were simpler. In reality he probably would have given his left arm simply for the numbers, letters, symbols, and equation representations that would emerge 2,000 years later as the Abacist school of thought grew.

Évariste Galois (1811–1832) might've given *both* arms for a photocopier. First, it's worth mentioning his education. His father entered him into the Collège Royal de Louis-le-Grand, where Galois found his teachers, frankly, boring. The fault might have been the teachers', but it should also be noted that Galois was attempting to master the Collège Royal at the age of 11. Fortunately, he gained exposure to his fellow countrymen Lagrange and Legendre, whose brilliance he did not find mundane, and in 1829, at age 17, Galois submitted a memoir on the solvability of algebraic equations to the French Academy of Sciences. Here is where a photocopier might have prevented major angst. Galois's paper was lost (ironically by Augustin-Louis Cauchy, a brilliant mathematician and major contributor to the algebra discipline himself). Galois seems to have been devastated at his lost paper.

But he regrouped, and rewrote the paper from scratch, submitting it a year later, in 1830. This paper was lost, too, by Jean-Baptiste-Joseph Fourier, another brilliant contributor to the math world. He brought Galois's paper home but then died. The paper was never found. Galois, now age 19, rewrote the paper a *third* time and submitted it again, in 1831. This time he got consideration from still another brilliant pillar of math, Siméon-Denis Poisson. Unfortunately, Poisson rejected the paper and Galois's ideas. Even more unfortunate was Poisson's reason for the rejection. He thought it contained an error, but in fact, *he* was in error. Probably what contributed to the colossal oversight was Poisson's inability to consider that a brilliant young mind, a mere kid, if you will, was introducing a whole new way of looking at the math.

Galois never knew of his own ultimate mathematical success. He died at age 20 from wounds suffered in a duel, unaware that his math would reshape the discipline of algebra. Galois's manuscripts were finally published 15 years later in the *Journal de Mathématiques Pures et Appliquées*, but not until 1870, 38 years after Galois's death, would group theory become a fully established part of mathematics.

If clunky symbol use and multiple world languages resulted in sluggish though creative and ingenious algebra progress over time, we observe the same effects in trigonometry, where angles, arcs, ratios, and algebra together form a math that helped shrink the oceans. Spherical trigonometry was most useful early for navigation, cartography, and astronomy and thus important for global trade.

Early on, Hipparchus (190–120 BCE) was the first to construct a table of values of a trigonometric function. One must keep in mind that representations of those trigonometric functions were not yet appearing in the tight and uncomplicated symbols of modern times. The next major contributions to trigonometry would come from India and writing there called the *Aryabhatiya*, initiated a word that would undergo many translations and much later become very familiar. That word is "sine."

Most who have studied trigonometry, no matter how far removed from their schooling on the subject, can probably still hear the teacher's voice ringing in their memory from years past with mnemonic devices that might cement the sine, cosine, tangent, and ratios onto the student brain. For some, during the pressure-packed moments of a math examination, the ditty "Soh-Cah-Toa" has helped summon the memory that the sine was equal to the opposite side over the hypotenuse of a right triangle, from those clues an equation might spring up to solve a trigonometry problem.

Again we find that language differences result in time needed for evolution. Take the word "sine," the trigonometry ratio and trigonometry function. Aryabhata (*c.* 475–550 CE) coined *ardha-jya* (for "half-chord"), then turned it around to *jya-ardha* ("chord-half"), which was shortened over time to *jya* or *jiva*. With Muslim scholars *jiva* became *jaib* because it was easier to pronounce. The Latin translation was *sinus*. From this the term *sine* evolved and was spread through European math literature probably around the 12 century. *Sine's* abbreviation as *sin* was first used somewhat ironically by an English minister and cabinetmaker (Edmund Gunter, 1624). The other five trigonometric functions (cosine, tangent, cotangent, secant, and cosecant) followed shortly. But for *sine* to take about 1,000 years to travel from India to Europe relates an achingly slow journey compared to what we might expect today with e-mail, text messaging, and digital information spreading new ideas to hungry scholars by the nanosecond.

But good news was incapable of traveling fast in past centuries. The Alfonsine tables (based on the Ptolemac theory that the Earth was the centre of the universe) were prepared for King Alfonso of Spain in 1252. They were not widely known, but when a Latin version hit Paris some 80 years later, they sold like hotcakes and provided the best astronomical tables for two centuries. Copernicus learned from them and launched an improved work in the 1550s.

Around this time, algebra was spilling over into trigonometry, thanks in major part to the work of three French mathematical geniuses: François Viète, Pierre de Fermat, and René Descartes. Analytic trigonometry would now take the nutrients of algebraic applications, table values, and trigonometric ideas and make that garden grow into the mathematical language that supports our scientific discoveries and shapes our modern world.

Now that language, communication, and instant information are readily available for our modern mathematicians, the tools for new discovery in algebra and trigonometry hum, ready for action. What we know is that people will use those tools, but even modern-day people work while living their own lives. In the back of their minds, though, crackle the day-to-day of family problems, worries, fears, desires, love, absolute joy, and a plethora of other emotions. Mathematical discovery may happen faster but will nonetheless continue to be affected by what is in—and on—the mind of the innovator.

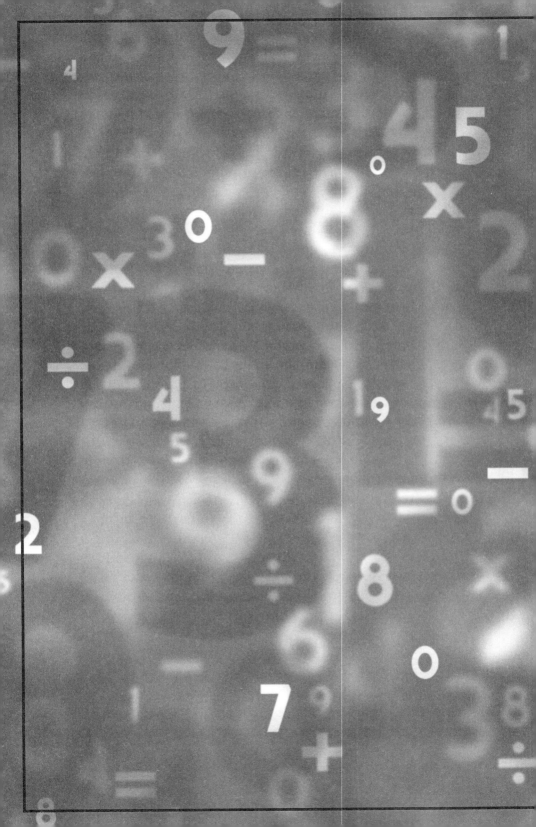

CHAPTER I

ALGEBRA

Algebra is the branch of mathematics in which arithmetical operations and formal manipulations are applied to abstract symbols, known as variables, rather than to specific numbers. Algebra is fundamental not only to all further mathematics and statistics but to the natural sciences, computer science, economics, and business. Along with writing, it is a cornerstone of modern scientific and technological civilization. Earlier civilizations—Babylonian, Greek, Indian, Chinese, and Islamic—all contributed in important ways to the development of algebra. It was left for Renaissance Europe, though, to develop an efficient system for representing all real numbers and a symbolism for representing unknowns, relations between them, and operations.

HISTORY OF ALGEBRA

The notion that there exists a distinct subdiscipline of mathematics that uses variables to stand for unspecified numbers, as well as the term *algebra* to denote this subdiscipline, resulted from a slow historical development. This chapter presents that history, tracing the evolution over time of the concept of the equation, number systems, symbols for conveying and manipulating mathematical statements, and the modern abstract structural view of algebra.

THE EMERGENCE OF FORMAL EQUATIONS

Perhaps the most basic notion in mathematics is the equation, a formal statement that two sides of a mathematical expression are equal—as in the simple equation $x + 3 = 5$—and that both sides of the equation can be simultaneously manipulated (by adding, dividing, taking roots, and so on to both sides) in order to "solve" the equation. Yet, as simple and natural as such a notion may appear today, its acceptance first required the development of numerous mathematical ideas, each of which took time to mature. In fact, it took until the late 16th century to consolidate the modern concept of an equation as a single mathematical entity.

Three main threads in the process leading to this consolidation deserve special attention:

1. Attempts to solve equations involving one or more unknown quantities. In describing the early history of algebra, the word *equation* is frequently used out of convenience to describe these operations, although early mathematicians would not have been aware of such a concept.
2. The evolution of the notion of exactly what qualifies as a legitimate number. Over time this notion expanded to include broader domains (rational numbers, irrational numbers, negative numbers, and complex numbers) that were flexible enough to support the abstract structure of symbolic algebra.
3. The gradual refinement of a symbolic language suitable for devising and conveying generalized algorithms, or step-by-step procedures for solving entire categories of mathematical problems.

These three threads are traced in this chapter, particularly as they developed in the ancient Middle East and Greece, the Islamic era, and the European Renaissance.

PROBLEM SOLVING IN EGYPT AND BABYLON

The earliest extant mathematical text from Egypt is the Rhind papyrus (c. 1650 BCE). It and other texts attest to the ability of the ancient Egyptians to solve linear equations in one unknown. A linear equation is a first-degree equation, or one in which all the variables are only to the first power. (In today's notation, such an equation in one unknown would be $7x + 3x = 10$.) Evidence from about 300 BCE indicates that the Egyptians also knew how to solve problems involving a system of two equations in two unknown quantities, including quadratic (second-degree, or squared unknowns) equations. For example, given that the perimeter of a rectangular plot of land is 100 units and its area is 600 square units, the ancient Egyptians could solve for the field's length l and width w. (In modern notation, they could solve the pair of simultaneous equations $2w + 2l = 100$ and $wl = 600$.) However, throughout this period there

The Rhind papyrus, shown above, is an ancient Egyptian scroll bearing mathematical tables and problems. It reveals a great deal about Egyptian mathematics, such as the ancient Egyptians' ability to solve linear equations. British Museum, London, UK/The Bridgeman Art Library/Getty Images

was no use of symbols—problems were stated and solved verbally. The following problem is typical:

- Method of calculating a quantity,
- multiplied by 1½ added 4 it has come to 10.
- What is the quantity that says it?
- First, you calculate the difference of this 10 to this 4. Then, 6 results.
- Then, you divide 1 by 1½. Then, ⅔ results.
- Then, you calculate ⅔ of this 6. Then, 4 results.
- Behold, it is 4, the quantity that said it.
- What has been found by you is correct.

Note that except for ⅔, for which a special symbol existed, the Egyptians expressed all fractional quantities using only unit fractions, that is, fractions bearing the numerator 1. For example, ¾ would be written as ½ + ¼.

Babylonian mathematics dates from as early as 1800 BCE, as indicated by cuneiform texts preserved in clay tablets. Babylonian arithmetic was based on a well-elaborated, positional sexagesimal system—that is, a system of base 60, as opposed to the modern decimal system, which is based on units of 10. The Babylonians, however, made no consistent use of zero. A great deal of their mathematics consisted of tables, such as for multiplication, reciprocals, squares (but not cubes), and square and cube roots.

In addition to tables, many Babylonian tablets contained problems that asked for the solution of some unknown number. Such problems explained a procedure to be followed for solving a specific problem, rather than proposing a general algorithm for solving similar problems. The starting point for a problem could be relations involving specific numbers and the unknown, or its square, or systems of such relations. The number sought could be the square root of a given number, the weight of a stone, or the length of the side of a triangle. Many of the questions were phrased in terms of concrete situations—such as partitioning a field among three pairs of brothers under certain constraints. Still, their artificial character made it clear that they were constructed for didactical purposes.

GREECE AND THE LIMITS OF GEOMETRIC EXPRESSION

The Pythagoreans and Euclid

A major milestone of Greek mathematics was the discovery by the Pythagoreans around 430 BCE that not all lengths are commensurable, that is, measurable by a common unit. This surprising fact became clear while investigating what appeared to be the most elementary ratio between geometric magnitudes, namely, the ratio between the side and the diagonal of a square. The Pythagoreans knew that for a unit square (that is, a square whose sides have a length of 1), the length of the diagonal must be $\sqrt{2}$—owing to the Pythagorean theorem, which states that the square on the diagonal of a triangle must equal the sum of the squares on the other two sides ($a^2 + b^2 = c^2$). The ratio between the two magnitudes thus deduced, 1 and $\sqrt{2}$, had the confounding property of not corresponding to the ratio of any two whole, or counting, numbers (1, 2, 3,. . .). This discovery of incommensurable quantities contradicted the basic metaphysics of Pythagoreanism, which asserted that all of reality was based on the whole numbers.

Attempts to deal with incommensurables eventually led to the creation of an innovative concept of proportion by Eudoxus of Cnidus (*c.* 400–350 BCE), which Euclid preserved in his *Elements* (*c.* 300 BCE). The theory of proportions remained an important component of mathematics well into the 17th century, by allowing the comparison of ratios of pairs of magnitudes of the same kind. Greek proportions, however, were very different from modern equalities, and no concept of equation could be based on it. For instance, a proportion could establish that the ratio between two line segments, say A and B, is the same as the ratio between two areas, say R and S. The Greeks would state this in strictly verbal fashion, since symbolic expressions, such as the much later $A:B::R:S$ (read, A is to B as R is to S), did not appear in Greek texts. The theory of proportions enabled significant mathematical results, yet it could not lead to the kind of results derived with modern equations. Thus, from $A:B::R:S$ the Greeks could deduce that (in modern terms) $A + B:A - B::R + S:R - S$, but they could not deduce in the same way that $A:R::B:S$. In fact, it did not even make sense to the Greeks to speak of a ratio between a line and an area since only like, or homogeneous, magnitudes were comparable. Their fundamental demand for homogeneity was strictly preserved in all Western mathematics until the 17th century.

When some of the Greek geometric constructions, such as those that appear in Euclid's *Elements*, are suitably translated into modern algebraic language, they establish algebraic identities, solve quadratic equations, and produce related results. However, not only were symbols of this kind never used in classical Greek works, but such a translation would be completely alien to their spirit. Indeed, the Greeks not only lacked an abstract language for performing general symbolic manipulations, but they even lacked the concept of an equation to support such an algebraic interpretation of their geometric constructions.

For the classical Greeks, especially as shown in Books VII–XI of the *Elements*, a number was a collection of units, and hence they were limited to the counting numbers. Negative numbers were obviously out of this picture, and zero could not even start to be considered. In fact, even the status of 1 was ambiguous in certain texts, since it did not really constitute a collection as stipulated by Euclid. Such a numerical limitation, coupled with the strong geometric orientation of Greek mathematics, slowed the development and full acceptance of more elaborate and flexible ideas of number in the West.

Diophantus

A somewhat different, and idiosyncratic, orientation to solving mathematical problems can be found in the work of a later Greek, Diophantus of Alexandria (fl. *c.* 250 CE), who developed original methods for solving problems that, in retrospect, may be seen as linear or quadratic equations. Yet even Diophantus, in line with the basic Greek conception of mathematics, considered only positive rational solutions; he called a problem "absurd" whose only solutions were negative numbers. Diophantus solved specific problems using ad hoc methods convenient for the problem at hand, but he did not provide general solutions. The problems that he solved sometimes had more than one (and in some cases even infinitely many) solutions, yet he always stopped after finding the first one. In problems involving quadratic equations, he never suggested that such equations might have two solutions.

On the other hand, Diophantus was the first to introduce some kind of systematic symbolism for polynomial equations. A polynomial equation is composed of a sum of terms, in which each term is the product of some constant and a nonnegative power of the variable or variables. Because of their great generality, polynomial equations can express a large proportion of the mathematical relationships that occur in nature—for example, problems involving area, volume, mixture, and motion. In modern notation, polynomial equations in one variable take the form

$$a_n x^n + a_{n-1} x^{n-1} + \ldots + a_2 x^2 + a_1 x + a_0 = 0,$$

where the a_i are known as coefficients and the highest power of n is known as the degree of the equation (for example, 2 for a quadractic, 3 for a cubic, 4 for a quartic, 5 for a quintic, and so on). Diophantus's symbolism was a kind of shorthand, though, rather than a set of freely manipulable symbols. A typical case was:

$$\Delta^v \Delta \bar{\beta} \zeta \, \bar{\delta} M \bar{\beta} \pitchfork K^v \bar{\beta} \bar{a}^v \bar{\gamma}$$

(meaning: $2x^4 - x^3 - 3x^2 + 4x + 2$). Here M represents units, ζ the unknown quantity, K^v its square, and so forth. Since there were no negative coefficients, the terms that corresponded to the unknown and its third power appeared to the right of the special symbol $\pitchfork$. This symbol did not function like the equals sign of a modern equation, however. There was nothing like the idea of moving terms from one side of the symbol to the other. Also, since all of the Greek letters were used to represent specific numbers, there was no simple and unambiguous method of representing abstract coefficients in an equation.

A typical Diophantine problem would be: "Find two numbers such that each, after receiving from the other a given number, will bear to the remainder a given relation." In modern terms, this problem would be stated $(x + a)/(y - a) = r$, $(y + b)/(x - b) = s$.

Diophantus always worked with a single unknown quantity ζ. In order to solve this specific problem, he assumed as given certain values that allowed him a smooth solution: $a = 30$, $r = 2$, $b = 50$, $s = 3$. Now the two numbers sought were $\zeta + 30$ (for y) and $2\zeta - 30$ (for x), so that the first ratio was an identity, $2\zeta/\zeta = 2$, that was fulfilled for any nonzero value of ζ. For the modern reader, substituting these values in the second ratio would result in (ζ + 80) (2ζ - 80) = 3. By applying his solution techniques, Diophantus was led to z = 64. The two required numbers were therefore 98 and 94.

The Equation in India and China

Indian mathematicians, such as Brahmagupta (598–670 CE) and Bhaskara II (1114–1185 CE), developed nonsymbolic, yet very precise, procedures for solving first- and second-degree equations and equations with more than one variable. However, the main contribution of Indian mathematicians was the elaboration of the decimal, positional numeral system. A full-fledged decimal, positional system certainly existed in India by the 9th century, yet many of its central ideas had been transmitted well before that time to China and the Islamic world. Indian arithmetic, moreover, developed consistent and correct rules for operating with positive and negative numbers and for treating zero like any other number, even in problematic contexts such as division. Several hundred years passed before European mathematicians fully integrated such ideas into the developing discipline of algebra.

Chinese mathematicians during the period parallel to the European Middle Ages developed their own methods for classifying and solving quadratic equations by radicals — solutions that contain only combinations of the most tractable operations: addition, subtraction, multiplication, division, and taking roots. They were unsuccessful, however, in their attempts to obtain exact solutions to higher-degree equations. Instead, they developed approximation methods of high accuracy, such as those described in Yang Hui's *Yang Hui suanfa* (1275; "Yang Hui's Mathematical Methods"). The calculational advantages afforded by their expertise with the abacus may help explain why Chinese mathematicians gravitated to numerical analysis methods.

ISLAMIC CONTRIBUTIONS

Islamic contributions to mathematics began around 825 CE, when the Baghdad mathematician Muḥammad ibn Mūsā al-Khwārizmī wrote his famous treatise *al-Kitab al-mukhtasar fi hisab al-jabr wa'l-muqabala* (translated into Latin in the 12th century as *Algebra et Almucabal*, from which the modern term *algebra* is derived).

By the end of the 9th century, a significant Greek mathematical corpus, including works of Euclid, Archimedes (*c.* 285–212/211 BCE), Apollonius of Perga (*c.* 262–190 BCE), Ptolemy (fl. 127–145 CE), and Diophantus, had been translated into Arabic. Similarly, ancient Babylonian and Indian mathematics, as well as more recent contributions by Jewish sages, were available to Islamic scholars. This unique background allowed the creation of a whole new kind of mathematics that was much more than a mere amalgamation of these earlier traditions. A systematic study of methods for solving quadratic equations constituted a central concern of Islamic mathematicians. A no less central contribution was related to the Islamic reception and transmission of ideas related to the Indian system of numeration, to which they added decimal fractions (fractions such as 0.125, or $^1/_8$).

Al-Khwārizmī's algebraic work embodied much of what was central to Islamic contributions. He declared that his book was intended to be of "practical" value, yet this definition hardly applies to its contents. In the first part of his book, al-Khwārizmī presented the procedures for solving six types of equations: squares equal roots, squares equal numbers, roots equal numbers, squares and roots equal numbers, squares and numbers equal roots, and roots and numbers equal squares. In modern

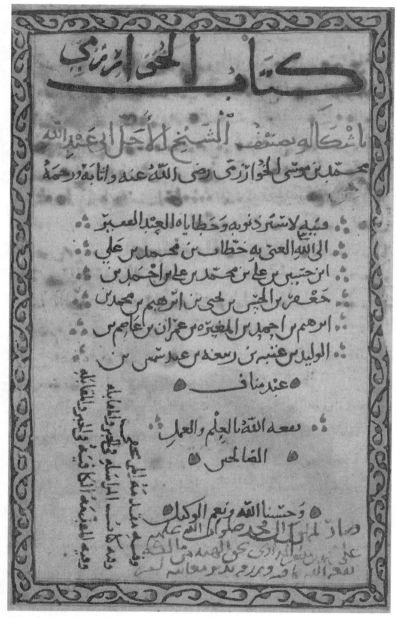

The frontispiece of Muḥammad ibn Mūsā al-Khwārizmī's al-Kitab al-mukhtasar fi hisab al-jabr wa'l-muqabala, *a seminal work on algebra, which was also novel in its incorporation of Euclid's geometric concepts.* The Bodleian Library, University of Oxford, MS. Huntington 214, title page notation, these equations would be stated $ax^2 = bx$, $ax^2 = c$, $bx = c$, $ax^2 + bx = c$, $ax^2 + c = bx$, and $bx + c = ax^2$, respectively. Only positive numbers were considered legitimate coefficients or solutions to equations. Moreover, neither symbolic representation nor abstract symbol manipulation appeared in these problems—even the quantities were written in words rather than in symbols. In fact, all procedures were described verbally. This is nicely illustrated by the following typical problem (recognizable as the modern method of completing the square):

> *What must be the square which, when increased by 10 of its own roots, amounts to 39? The solution is this: You halve the number of roots, which in the present instance yields 5. This you multiply by itself; the product is 25. Add this to 39; the sum is 64. Now take the root of this, which is 8, and subtract from it half the number of the roots, which is 5; the remainder is 3. This is the root of the square which you sought.*

In the second part of his book, al-Khwārizmī used propositions taken from Book II of Euclid's *Elements* in order to provide geometric justifications for his procedures. As remarked above, in their original context these were purely geometric propositions. Al-Khwārizmī directly connected them for the first time, however, to the solution of quadratic equations. His method was a hallmark of the Islamic approach to solving equations—systematize all cases and then provide a geometric justification, based on Greek sources. Typical of this approach was the Persian mathematician and poet Omar Khayyam's *Risalah fī'l-barahin 'ala masa'il al-jabr wa'l-muqabalah* (c. 1070; "Treatise on Demonstration of Problems of Algebra"), in which Greek knowledge concerning conic sections (ellipses, parabolas, and hyperbolas) was applied to questions involving cubic equations.

The use of Greek-style geometric arguments in this context also led to a gradual loosening of certain traditional Greek constraints. In particular, Islamic mathematics allowed, and indeed encouraged, the unrestricted combination of commensurable and incommensurable magnitudes within the same framework, as well as the simultaneous manipulation of magnitudes of different dimensions as part of the solution of a problem. For example, the Egyptian mathematician Abu Kamil (c. 850–930) treated the solution of a quadratic equation as a number rather than as a line segment or an area. Combined with the decimal system, this approach was fundamental in developing a more abstract and general conception of number, which was essential for the eventual creation of a full-fledged abstract idea of an equation.

COMMERCE AND ABACISTS IN THE EUROPEAN RENAISSANCE

Greek and Islamic mathematics were basically "academic" enterprises, having little interaction with day-to-day matters involving building, transportation, and commerce. This situation first began to change in Italy in the 13th and 14th centuries. In particular, the rise of Italian mercantile companies and their use of modern financial instruments for trade with the East, such as letters of credit, bills of exchange, promissory notes, and interest calculations, led to a need for improved methods of bookkeeping.

Leonardo Pisano, known to history as Fibonacci, studied the works of Kamil and other Arabic mathematicians as a boy while accompanying his father's trade mission to North Africa on behalf of the merchants of Pisa. In 1202, soon after his return to Italy, Fibonacci wrote *Liber Abbaci* ("Book of the Abacus"). Although it contained no specific innovations, and although it strictly followed the Islamic

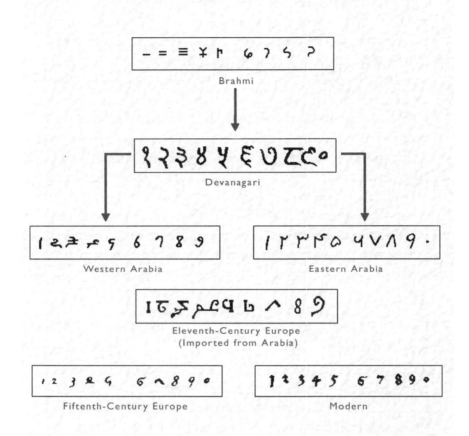

Hindu-Arabic numerals, the evolution of which is shown above, are used throughout the world today, though they originated in India and were first introduced to the Europeans by Arab mathematicians. Modified from Karl Menninger, *Number Words and Number Symbols: A Cultural History of Numbers*, Cambridge, MA: The MIT Press, 1969

tradition of formulating and solving problems in purely rhetorical fashion, it was instrumental in communicating the Hindu-Arabic numerals to a wider audience in the Latin world. Early adopters of the "new" numerals became known as abacists, regardless of whether they used the numerals for calculating and recording transactions or employed an abacus for doing the actual calculations.

Soon numerous abacist schools sprang up to teach the sons of Italian merchants the "new math."

The abacists first began to introduce abbreviations for unknowns in the 14th century—another important milestone toward the full-fledged manipulation of abstract symbols. For instance, *c* stood for *cossa* ("thing"), *ce* for *censo* ("square"), *cu* for *cubo* ("cube"), and *R* for *Radice* ("root"). Even combinations of these symbols were introduced for obtaining higher powers. This trend eventually led to works such as the first French algebra text, Nicolas Chuquet's *Triparty en la science des nombres* (1484; "The Science of Numbers in Three Parts"). As part of a discussion on how to use the Hindu-Arabic numerals, *Triparty* contained relatively complicated symbolic expressions, such as

$$R^2 14 p R^2 180$$

(meaning: $\sqrt{14 + \sqrt{180}}$).

Chuquet also introduced a more flexible way of denoting powers of the unknown—i.e., 12^2 (for 12 squares) and even $m12^m$ (to indicate $-12x^{-2}$). This was, in fact, the first time that negative numbers were explicitly used in European mathematics. Chuquet could now write an equation as follows:

$$.3.^2 p .12 \ egaulx \ a \ .9.^1$$

(meaning: $3x^2 + 12 = 9x$).

Following the ancient tradition, coefficients were always positive, and thus the above was only one of several possible equations involving an unknown and squares of it. Indeed, Chuquet would say that the above was an impossible equation, since its solution would involve the square root of -63. This illustrates the difficulties involved in reaching a more general and flexible concept of number: the same mathematician would allow negative numbers in a certain context and even introduce a useful notation for dealing with them, but he would completely avoid their use in a different, albeit closely connected, context.

In the 15th century, the German-speaking countries developed their own version of the abacist tradition: the Cossists, including mathematicians such as Michal Stiffel, Johannes Scheubel, and Christoff Rudolff. There, one finds the first use of specific symbols for the arithmetic operations, equality, roots, and so forth. The subsequent process of standardizing symbols was, nevertheless, lengthy and involved.

CARDANO AND THE SOLVING OF CUBIC AND QUARTIC EQUATIONS

Girolamo Cardano was a famous Italian physician, an avid gambler, and a prolific writer with a lifelong interest in mathematics.

His widely read *Ars Magna* (1545; "Great Work") contains the Renaissance era's most systematic and comprehensive account of solving cubic and quartic equations. Cardano's presentation followed the Islamic tradition of solving one instance of every possible case and then giving geometric justifications for his procedures, based on propositions from Euclid's *Elements*. He also followed the Islamic tradition of expressing all coefficients as positive numbers, and his presentation was fully rhetorical, with no real symbolic manipulation. Nevertheless, he did expand the use of symbols as a kind of shorthand for stating problems and describing solutions. Thus, the Greek geometric perspective still dominated—for instance, the solution of an equation was always a line segment, and the cube was the cube built on such a segment. Still, Cardano could write a cubic equation to be solved as *cup p*: 6 *reb aequalis* 20

(meaning: $x^3 + 6x = 20$) and present the solution as

R.V: cu.R. 108 *p*: 10 *m: R.V: cu. R.* 108*m*: 10,

meaning

$$x = \sqrt[3]{\sqrt{108} + 10} - \sqrt[3]{\sqrt{108} - 10}.$$

Because Cardano refused to view negative numbers as possible coefficients in equations, he could not develop a notion of a general third-degree equation. This meant that he had to consider 13 "different" third-degree equations. Similarly, he considered 20 different cases for fourth-degree equations, following procedures developed by his student Ludovico Ferrari. However, Cardano was sometimes willing to consider the possibility of negative (or "false") solutions. This allowed him to formulate some general rules, such as that in an equation with three real roots (including even negative roots), the sum of the roots must, except for sign, equal the coefficient of the square's term.

In spite of his basic acceptance of traditional views on numbers, the solution of certain problems led Cardano to consider more radical ideas. For instance, he demonstrated that 10 could be divided into two parts whose product was 40. The answer, $5 + \sqrt{-15}$ and $5 - \sqrt{-15}$, however, required the use of imaginary, or complex numbers — that is, numbers involving the square root of a negative number. Such a solution made Cardano uneasy, but he finally accepted it, declaring it to be "as refined as it is useless."

The first serious and systematic treatment of complex numbers had to await the Italian mathematician Rafael Bombelli, particularly the first three volumes of his unfinished *L'Algebra* (1572). Nevertheless, the notion of a number whose square is a negative number left most mathematicians uncomfortable. Where, exactly, in nature could one point to the existence of a negative or imaginary quantity? Thus, the acceptance of numbers beyond the positive rational numbers was slow and reluctant.

VIÈTE AND THE FORMAL EQUATION

It is in the work of the French mathematician François Viète that the first consistent, coherent, and systematic conception of an algebraic equation in the modern sense appeared. A main innovation of Viète's *In artem analyticam isagoge* (1591; "Introduction to the Analytic Art") was its use of well-chosen symbols of one kind (vowels) for unknowns and of another kind (consonants) for known quantities. This allowed not only flexibility and generality in solving linear and quadratic equations but also something absent from all his predecessors' work, namely, a clear analysis of the relationship between the forms of the solutions and the values of the coefficients of the original equation. Viète saw his contribution as developing a "systematic way of thinking" leading to general solutions, rather than just a "bag of tricks" to solve specific problems.

By combining existing usage with his own innovations, Viète was able to formulate equations clearly and to provide rules for transposing factors from one side of an equation to the other in order to find solutions. An example of an equation would be:

A cubus + C plano in A aequatus D solido

(meaning: $x^3 + cx = d$).

Note that each of the terms involved was one-dimensional, that is, after canceling powers, the remaining terms on each side of the equation are to the first power. Thus, on the left-hand side, the two-dimensional magnitude Z *plano* (a square) was divided by the one-dimensional variable G, leaving one dimension. On the right-hand side, a sum of two three-dimensional magnitudes (a third power) was divided by a product of two one-dimensional variables (which make a square), leaving one dimension. Thus, Viète did not break the important Greek tradition whereby the terms equated must always be of the same dimension. Nevertheless, for the first time it became possible, in the framework of an equation, to multiply or divide both sides by a certain magnitude. The result was a new equation, homogeneous in itself yet not homogeneous with the original one.

Viète showed how to transform given equations into others, already known. For example, in modern notation, he could transform $x^3 + ax^2 = b^2x$ into $x^2 + ax = b^2$. He thus reduced the number of cases of cubic equations from the 13 given by Cardano and Bombelli. Nevertheless, since he still did not use negative or zero coefficients, he could not reduce all the possible cases to just one.

Viète applied his methods to solve, in a general, abstract-symbolic fashion, problems similar to those in the Diophantine tradition. However, very often he also rephrased his answers in plain words — as if to reassure his contemporaries, and perhaps even himself, of the validity of his new methods.

THE CONCEPT OF NUMBERS

The work of Viète, described above, contained a clear, systematic, and coherent conception of the notion of equation that served as a broadly accepted starting point for later developments. No similar single reference point exists for the general conception of number, however. Some significant milestones may nevertheless be mentioned, and prominent among them was *De Thiende* (*Disme: The Art of Tenths*), an influential booklet published in 1585 by the Flemish mathematician Simon Stevin. *De Thiende* was intended as a practical manual aimed at teaching the essentials of operating with decimal fractions, but it also contained many conceptual innovations. It was the first mathematical text where the all-important distinction between number and magnitude, going back to the ancient Greeks, was explicitly and totally abolished. Likewise, Stevin declared that 1 is a number just like any other and that the root of a number is a number as well. Stevin also showed how one single idea of number, expressed as decimal fractions, could be used equally in such separate contexts as land surveying, volume measurement, and astronomical and financial computations. The very need for an explanation of this kind illuminates how far Stevin's contemporaries and predecessors were from the modern notion of numbers.

Indeed, throughout the 17th century, lively debates continued among mathematicians over the legitimacy of using various numbers. For example, concerning the irrationals, some prominent mathematicians—such as the Frenchman Blaise Pascal and the Britons Isaac Barrow and Isaac Newton—were willing only to grant them legitimacy as geometric magnitudes. The negative numbers were sometimes seen as even more problematic, and in many cases negative solutions of equations were still considered by many to be "absurd" or "devoid of interest." Finally, the complex numbers were still ignored by many mathematicians, even though Bombelli had given precise rules for working with them.

All these discussions dwindled away as the 18th century approached. A new phase in the development of the concept of number began, involving a systematization and search for adequate foundations for the various systems.

CLASSICAL ALGEBRA

François Viète's work at the close of the 16th century, as described earlier in the chapter, marks the start of the classical discipline of algebra. Further developments included several related trends, among which the following deserve special mention: the quest for systematic solutions of higher order equations, including approximation techniques; the rise of polynomials and their study as autonomous mathematical entities; and the increased adoption of the algebraic perspective in other mathematical disciplines, such as geometry, analysis, and logic. During this same period, new mathematical objects arose that eventually replaced polynomials as the main focus of algebraic study.

ANALYTIC GEOMETRY

The creation of what came to be known as analytic geometry can be attributed to two great 17th-century French thinkers: Using algebraic techniques developed by Viète and Girolamo Cardano, as described earlier in this chapter, Pierre de Fermat and René Descartes, French mathematicians, tackled geometric problems that had remained unsolved since the time of the classical Greeks. The new kind of organic connection that they established between algebra and geometry was a major breakthrough, without which the subsequent development of mathematics in general—and geometry and calculus in particular—would be unthinkable.

In his famous book *La Géométrie* (1637), Descartes established equivalences between algebraic operations and geometric constructions. In order to do so, he introduced a unit length that served as a reference for all other lengths and for all operations among them. For example, suppose that Descartes was given a segment *AB* and was asked to find its square root. He would draw the straight line DB, where DA was defined as the unit length. Then, he would bisect DB at C, draw the semicircle on the diameter DB with centre C, and finally draw the perpendicular from A to E on the semicircle. Elementary properties of the circle imply that $\angle DEB = 90°$, which in turn implies that $\angle ADE = \angle AEB$ and $\angle DEA = \angle EBA$. Thus, $\triangle DEA$ is similar to $\triangle EBA$, or in other words, the ratio of corresponding sides is equal. Substituting x, 1, and y for AB, DA, and AE, respectively, one obtains $x/y = y/1$. Simplifying, $x = y^2$, or y is the square root of x. Thus, in what might appear to be an ordinary application of classical Greek techniques, Descartes demonstrated that he could find the square root of any given number, as represented by a line segment. The key step in his construction was the introduction of the unit length DA. This seemingly trivial move, or anything similar to it, had never been done before, and it had enormous repercussions for what could thereafter be done by applying algebraic reasoning to geometry.

Descartes also introduced a notation that allowed great flexibility in symbolic manipulation. For instance, he would write

$$\sqrt{C.a^3 - b^3 + abb}$$

to denote the cubic root of this algebraic expression. This was a direct continuation (with some improvement) of techniques and notations introduced by Viète. Descartes also introduced a new idea with truly far-reaching consequences when he explicitly eliminated the demand for homogeneity among the terms in an equation—although for convenience he tried to stick to homogeneity wherever possible.

Descartes's program was based on the idea that certain geometric loci (straight lines, circles, and conic sections) could be characterized in terms of specific kinds of equations involving magnitudes that were taken to represent line segments. However, he did not envision the equally important, reciprocal idea of finding the curve that corresponded to an arbitrary algebraic expression. Descartes was aware that much information about the properties of a curve—such as its tangents and enclosed areas—could be derived from its equation, but he did not elaborate.

On the other hand, Descartes was the first to discuss, separately and systematically, the algebraic properties of polynomial equations. This included his observations on the correspondence between the degree of an equation and the number of its roots, the factorization of a polynomial with known roots into linear factors, the rule for counting the number of positive and negative roots of an equation, and the method for obtaining a new equation whose roots were equal to those of a given equation, though increased or diminished by a given quantity.

The Fundamental Theorem of Algebra

Descartes's work was the start of the transformation of polynomials into an autonomous object of intrinsic mathematical interest. To a large extent, algebra became identified with the theory of polynomials. A clear notion of a polynomial equation, together with existing techniques for solving some of them, allowed coherent and systematic reformulations of many questions that had previously been dealt with in a haphazard fashion. High on the agenda remained the problem of finding general algebraic solutions for equations of degree higher than four. Closely related to this was the question of the kinds of numbers that should count as legitimate solutions, or roots, of equations. Attempts to deal with these two important problems forced mathematicians to realize the centrality of another pressing question, namely, the number of solutions for a given polynomial equation.

The answer to this question is given by the fundamental theorem of algebra, first suggested by the French-born mathematician Albert Girard in 1629, and which asserts that every polynomial with real number coefficients could be expressed as the product of linear and quadratic real number factors or, alternatively, that every polynomial equation of degree n with complex coefficients had n complex roots. For example, $x^3 + 2x^2 - x - 2$ can be decomposed into the quadratic factor $x^2 - 1$ and the linear factor $x + 2$, that is, $x^3 + 2x^2 - x - 2 = (x^2-1)(x+2)$. The mathematical beauty of having n solutions for n-degree equations overcame most of the remaining reluctance to consider complex numbers as legitimate.

Although every single polynomial equation had been shown to satisfy the theorem, the essence of mathematics since the time of the ancient Greeks has been to establish universal principles. Therefore, leading mathematicians throughout the 18th century sought the honour of being the first to prove the theorem. The flaws in their proofs were generally related to the lack of rigorous foundations for polynomials and the various number systems. Indeed, the process of criticism and revision that accompanied successive attempts to formulate and prove some correct version of the theorem contributed to a deeper understanding of both.

The first complete proof of the theorem was given by the German mathematician Carl Friedrich Gauss in his doctoral dissertation of 1799. Subsequently, Gauss provided three additional proofs. A remarkable feature of all these proofs was that they were based on methods and ideas from calculus and geometry, rather than algebra. The theorem was fundamental in that it established the most basic concept around which the discipline as a whole was built. The theorem was also fundamental from the historical point of view, since it contributed to the consolidation of the discipline, its main tools, and its main concepts.

IMPASSE WITH RADICAL METHODS

A major breakthrough in the algebraic solution of higher-degree equations was achieved by the Italian-French mathematician Joseph-Louis Lagrange in 1770.

Rather than trying to find a general solution for quintic equations directly, Lagrange attempted to clarify first why all attempts to do so had failed by investigating the known solutions of third- and fourth-degree equations. In particular, he noticed how certain algebraic expressions connected with those solutions remained invariant when the coefficients of the equations were permuted (exchanged) with one another. Lagrange was certain that a deeper analysis of this invariance would provide the key to extending existing solutions to higher-degree equations.

Using ideas developed by Lagrange, in 1799 the Italian mathematician Paolo

Joseph-Louis Lagrange. SSPL/Getty Images

47

Ruffini was the first to assert the impossibility of obtaining a radical solution for general equations beyond the fourth degree. He adumbrated in his work the notion of a group of permutations of the roots of an equation and worked out some basic properties. Ruffini's proofs, however, contained several significant gaps.

Between 1796 and 1801, in the framework of his seminal number-theoretical investigations, Gauss systematically dealt with cyclotomic equations: $x^p - 1 = 0$ ($p > 2$ and prime). Although his new methods did not solve the general case, Gauss did demonstrate solutions for these particular higher-degree equations.

In 1824 the Norwegian mathematician Niels Henrik Abel provided the first valid proof of the impossibility of obtaining radical solutions for general equations beyond the fourth degree. However, this did not end polynomial research. Rather, it opened an entirely new field of research since, as Gauss's example showed, some equations were indeed solvable. In 1828 Abel suggested two main points for research in this regard: to find all equations of a given degree solvable by radicals, and to decide if a given equation can be solved by radicals. His early death in complete poverty, two days before receiving an announcement that he had been appointed professor in Berlin, prevented Abel from undertaking this program.

GALOIS THEORY

Rather than establishing whether specific equations can or cannot be solved by radicals, as Abel had suggested, the French mathematician Évariste Galois (1811–32) pursued the somewhat more general problem of defining necessary and sufficient conditions for the solvability of any given equation. Although Galois's life was short and exceptionally turbulent—he was arrested several times for supporting republican causes, and he died at the age of 20 from wounds incurred in a duel—his work reshaped the discipline of algebra.

Galois's Work on Permutations

Prominent among Galois's seminal ideas was the clear realization of how to formulate precise solvability conditions for a polynomial in terms of the properties of its group of permutations. A permutation of a set, say the elements a, b, and c, is any re-ordering of the elements, and it is usually denoted as follows:

$$\begin{pmatrix} a & b & c \\ c & a & b \end{pmatrix}$$

This particular permutation takes a to c, b to a, and c to b. For three elements, as here, there are six different possible permutations. In general, for n elements there are $n!$ permutations to choose from. (Where $n! = n(n - 1)(n - 2) \cdots 2 \cdot 1$.) Furthermore, two permutations can be combined to produce a third permutation in an operation known as composition. (The set of permutations are closed under the operation of composition.) For example,

$$\begin{pmatrix} a & b & c \\ c & a & b \end{pmatrix} * \begin{pmatrix} a & b & c \\ a & c & b \end{pmatrix} = \begin{pmatrix} a & b & c \\ b & a & c \end{pmatrix}$$

Here a goes first to c (in the first permutation) and then from c to b (in the second permutation), which is equivalent to a going directly to b, as given by the permutation to the right of the equation. Composition is associative—given three permutations P, Q, and R, then $(P * Q) * R = P * (Q * R)$. Also, there exists an identity permutation that leaves the elements unchanged:

$$I = \begin{pmatrix} a & b & c \\ a & b & c \end{pmatrix}$$

Finally, for each permutation there exists another permutation, known as its inverse, such that their composition results in the identity permutation. The set of permutations for n elements is known as the symmetric group S_n.

The concept of an abstract group developed somewhat later. It consisted of a set of abstract elements with an operation defined on them such that the conditions given above were satisfied: closure, associativity, an identity element, and an inverse element for each element in the set.

This abstract notion is not fully present in Galois's work. Like some of his predecessors, Galois focused on the permutation group of the roots of an equation. Through some beautiful and highly original mathematical ideas, Galois showed that a general polynomial equation was solvable by radicals if and only if its associated symmetric group was "soluble." Galois's result, it must be stressed, referred to conditions for a solution to exist. It did not provide a way to calculate radical solutions in those cases where they existed.

Acceptance of Galois Theory

Galois's work was both the culmination of a main line of algebra—solving equations by radical methods—and the beginning of a new line—the study of abstract structures. Work on permutations, started by Lagrange and Ruffini, received further impetus in 1815 from the leading French mathematician, Augustin-Louis Cauchy. In a later work of 1844, Cauchy systematized much of this knowledge and introduced basic concepts. For instance, the permutation

$$\begin{pmatrix} a & b & c & d & e \\ b & a & e & c & d \end{pmatrix}$$

was denoted by Cauchy in cycle notation as $(ab)(ced)$, meaning that the permutation was obtained by the disjoint cycles a to b (and back to a) and c to e to d (and back to c).

A series of unusual and unfortunate events involving the most important contemporary French mathematicians prevented Galois's ideas from being published for a long time. It was not until 1846 that Joseph Liouville edited and published for the first time, in his prestigious *Journal de Mathématiques Pures et Appliquées*, the important memoire in which Galois had presented his main ideas and that the Paris Academy had turned down in 1831. In Germany, Leopold Kronecker applied some of these ideas to number theory in 1853, and Richard Dedekind lectured on Galois theory in 1856. At this time, however, the impact of the theory was still minimal.

A major turning point came with the publication of *Traité des substitutions et des équations algebriques* (1870; "Treatise on Substitutions and Algebraic Equations") by the French mathematician Camille Jordan. In his book and papers, Jordan elaborated an abstract theory of permutation groups, with algebraic equations merely serving as an illustrative application of the theory. In particular, Jordan's treatise was the first group theory book and it served as the foundation for the conception of Galois theory as the study of the interconnections between extensions of fields and the related Galois groups of equations—a conception that proved fundamental for developing a completely new abstract approach to algebra in the 1920s. Major contributions to the development of this point of view for Galois theory came variously from Enrico Betti (1823–92) in Italy and from Dedekind, Henrich Weber (1842–1913), and Emil Artin (1898–1962) in Germany.

APPLICATIONS OF GROUP THEORY

Galois theory arose in direct connection with the study of polynomials, and thus the notion of a group developed from within the mainstream of classical algebra. However, it also found important applications in other mathematical disciplines throughout the 19th century, particularly geometry and number theory.

Geometry

In 1872 Felix Klein suggested in his inaugural lecture at the University of Erlangen, Germany, that group theoretical ideas might be fruitfully put to use in the context of geometry. Since the beginning of the 19th century, the study of projective geometry had attained renewed impetus, and later on non-Euclidean geometries were introduced and increasingly investigated. This proliferation of geometries raised pressing questions concerning both the interrelations among them and their relationship with the empirical world. Klein suggested that these geometries could be classified and ordered within a conceptual hierarchy. For instance, projective geometry seemed particularly fundamental because its properties were also relevant in Euclidean geometry, while the main concepts of the latter, such as length and angle, had no significance in the former.

A geometric hierarchy may be expressed in terms of which transformations leave the most relevant properties of a particular geometry unchanged. It turned out that these sets of transformations were best understood as forming a group. Klein's idea was that the hierarchy of geometries might be reflected in a hierarchy of groups whose properties would be easier to understand. An example from Euclidean geometry illustrates the basic idea. The set of rotations in the plane has closure: if rotation I rotates a figure by an angle α, and rotation J by an angle β, then rotation $I*J$ rotates it by an angle $\alpha + \beta$. The rotation operation is obviously associative, $\alpha + (\beta + \gamma) = (\alpha + \beta) + \gamma$.

The identity element is the rotation through an angle of 0 degrees, and the inverse of the rotation through angle α is the angle -α. Thus, the set of rotations of the plane is a group of invariant transformations for Euclidean geometry. The groups associated with other kinds of geometries is somewhat more involved, but the idea remains the same.

In the 1880s and 1890s, Klein's friend, the Norwegian Sophus Lie, undertook the enormous task of classifying all possible continuous groups of geometric transformations, a task that eventually evolved into the modern theory of Lie groups and Lie algebras. At roughly the same time, the French mathematician Henri Poincaré studied the groups of motions of rigid bodies, a work that helped to establish group theory as one of the main tools in modern geometry.

Number Theory

The notion of a group also started to appear prominently in number theory in the 19th century, especially in Gauss's work on modular arithmetic. In this context, he proved results that were later reformulated in the abstract theory of groups—for instance (in modern terms), that in a cyclic group (all elements generated by repeating the group operation on one element) there always exists a subgroup of every order (number of elements) dividing the order of the group.

In 1854 Arthur Cayley, one of the most prominent British mathematicians of his time, was the first explicitly to realize that a group could be defined abstractly—without any reference to the nature of its elements and only by specifying the properties of the operation defined on them. Generalizing on Galois's ideas, Cayley took a set of meaningless symbols 1, α, β,. . . with an operation defined on them as shown in the table below.

	1	a	b	---
1	1	a	b	---
a	a	a^2	ab	---
b	b	ba	b^2	---
---	---	---	---	---

Cayley demanded only that the operation be closed with respect to the elements on which it was defined, while he assumed implicitly that it was associative and that each element had an inverse. He correctly deduced some basic properties of the group, such as that if the group has n elements, then $\theta^n = 1$ for each element θ. Nevertheless, in 1854 the idea of permutation groups was rather new, and Cayley's work had little immediate impact.

FUNDAMENTAL CONCEPTS OF MODERN ALGEBRA

Prime Factorization

Some other fundamental concepts of modern algebra also had their origin in 19th-century work on number theory, particularly in connection with attempts to generalize the theorem of (unique) prime factorization beyond the natural numbers. This theorem asserted that every natural number could be written as a product of its prime factors in a unique way, except perhaps for order (e.g., $24 = 2\cdot2\cdot2\cdot3$). This property of the natural numbers was known, at least implicitly, since the time of Euclid. In the 19th century, mathematicians sought to extend some version of this theorem to the complex numbers.

One should not be surprised, then, to find the name of Gauss in this context. In his classical investigations on arithmetic, Gauss was led to the factorization properties of numbers of the type $a + ib$ (a and b integers and $i = -1$), sometimes called Gaussian integers. In doing so, Gauss not only used complex numbers to solve a problem involving ordinary integers—a fact remarkable in itself—but he also opened the way to the detailed investigation of special subdomains of the complex numbers.

In 1832 Gauss proved that the Gaussian integers satisfied a generalized version of the factorization theorem where the prime factors had to be especially defined in this domain. In the 1840s the German mathematician Ernst Eduard Kummer extended these results to other, even more general domains of complex numbers, such as numbers of the form $a + \theta b$, where $\theta^2 = n$ for n a fixed integer, or numbers of the form $a + \rho b$, where $\rho^n = 1$, $\rho \neq 1$, and $n > 2$. Although Kummer did prove interesting results, it finally turned out that the prime factorization theorem was not valid in such general domains. The following example illustrates the problem.

Consider the domain of numbers of the form $a + b\sqrt{-5}$ and, in particular, the number $21 = 21 + 0\sqrt{-5}$. 21 can be factored as both $3 \cdot 7$ and as $(4 + \sqrt{-5})(4 - \sqrt{-5})$. It can be shown that none of the numbers 3, 7, $4 \pm \sqrt{-5}$ could be further decomposed as a product of two different numbers in this domain. Thus, in one sense they were prime. However, at the same time, they violated a property of prime numbers known from the time of Euclid: if a prime number p divides a product ab, then it either divides a or b. In this instance, 3 divides 21 but neither of the factors $4 + \sqrt{-5}$ or $4 - \sqrt{-5}$.

This situation led to the concept of indecomposable numbers. In classical arithmetic any indecomposable number is a prime (and vice versa), but in more general domains a number may be indecomposable, such as 3 here, yet not prime in the earlier sense. The question thus remained open which domains the prime factorization theorem was valid in and how properly to formulate a generalized version of it. This problem was undertaken by Dedekind in a series of works spanning over 30 years, starting in 1871.

Dedekind's general methodological approach promoted the introduction of new concepts around which entire theories could be built. Specific problems were then solved as instances of the general theory.

Fields

A main question pursued by Dedekind was the precise identification of those subsets of the complex numbers for which some generalized version of the theorem made sense. The first step toward answering this question was the concept of a field, defined as any subset of the complex numbers that was closed under the four basic arithmetic operations (except division by zero). The largest of these fields was the whole system of complex numbers, whereas the smallest field was the rational numbers. Using the concept of field and some other derivative ideas, Dedekind identified the precise subset of the complex numbers for which the theorem could be extended. He named that subset the algebraic integers.

Ideals

Finally, Dedekind introduced the concept of an ideal. A main methodological trait of Dedekind's innovative approach to algebra was to translate ordinary arithmetic properties into properties of sets of numbers. In this case, he focused on the set I of multiples of any given integer and pointed out two of its main properties:

1. If n and m are two numbers in I, then their difference is also in I.
2. If n is a number in I and a is any integer, then their product is also in I.

As he did in many other contexts, Dedekind took these properties and turned them into definitions. He defined a collection of algebraic integers that satisfied these properties as an ideal in the complex numbers. This was the concept that allowed him to generalize the prime factorization theorem in distinctly set-theoretical terms.

In ordinary arithmetic, the ideal generated by the product of two numbers equals the intersection of the ideals generated by each of them. For instance, the set of multiples of 6 (the ideal generated by 6) is the intersection of the ideal generated by 2 and the ideal generated by 3. Dedekind's generalized versions of the theorem were phrased precisely in these terms for general fields of complex numbers and their related ideals. He distinguished among different types of ideals and different types of decompositions, but the generalizations were all-inclusive and precise. More important, he reformulated what were originally results on numbers, their factors, and their products as far more general and abstract results on special domains, special subsets of numbers, and their intersections.

Dedekind's results were important not only for a deeper understanding of factorization. He also introduced the set-theoretical approach into algebraic research, and he defined some of the most basic concepts of modern algebra that became the main focus of algebraic research throughout the 20th century. Moreover, Dedekind's ideal-theoretical approach was soon successfully applied to the factorization of polynomials as well, thus connecting itself once again to the main focus of classical algebra.

SYSTEMS OF EQUATIONS

In spite of the many novel algebraic ideas that arose in the 19th century, solving equations and studying properties of polynomial forms continued to be the main focus of algebra. The study of systems of equations led to the notion of a determinant and matrix theory.

Determinants

Given a system of n linear equations in n unknowns, its determinant was defined as the result of a certain combination of multiplication and addition of the coefficients of the equations that allowed the values of the unknowns to be calculated directly. For example, given the system

$$a_1 x + b_1 y = c_1$$

$$a_2 x + b_2 y = c_2$$

the determinant Δ of the system is the number $\Delta = a_1 b_2 - a_2 b_1$, and the values of the unknowns are given by

$$x = (c_1 b_2 - c_2 b_1)/D$$

$$y = (a_1 c_2 - a_2 c_1)/D.$$

Historians agree that the 17th-century Japanese mathematician Seki Kowa was the earliest to use methods of this kind systematically. In Europe, credit is usually given to his contemporary, the German coinventor of calculus, Gottfried Wilhelm Leibniz.

In 1815 Cauchy published the first truly systematic and comprehensive study of determinants, and he was the one who coined the name. He introduced the notation $(a_{i,n})$ for the system of coefficients of the system and demonstrated a general method for calculating the determinant.

Matrices

Closely related to the concept of a determinant was the idea of a matrix as an arrangement of numbers in lines and columns. That such an arrangement could be taken as an autonomous mathematical object, subject to special rules that allow for manipulation like ordinary numbers, was first conceived in the 1850s by Cayley and his good friend the attorney and mathematician James Joseph Sylvester. Determinants were a main, direct source for this idea, but so were ideas contained in previous work on number theory by Gauss and by the German mathematician Ferdinand Gotthold Max Eisenstein (1823–52).

Given a system of linear equations:

$$\xi = \alpha x + \beta y + \gamma z + \ldots$$

$$h = \alpha \phi x + \beta' y + \gamma' z + \ldots$$

$$z = \alpha^2 x + \beta'' y + \gamma'' z + \ldots$$

$$\ldots = \ldots + \ldots + \ldots + \ldots$$

Cayley represented it with a matrix as follows:

$$(\xi, \eta, \zeta, \ldots) = \begin{pmatrix} \alpha & \beta & \gamma & \ldots \\ \alpha' & \beta' & \gamma' & \ldots \\ \alpha'' & \beta'' & \gamma'' & \ldots \\ \ldots & \ldots & \ldots & \ldots \end{pmatrix} (x, y, z, \ldots)$$

The solution could then be written as:

$$(x, y, z, \ldots) = \begin{pmatrix} \alpha & \beta & \gamma & \ldots \\ \alpha' & \beta' & \gamma' & \ldots \\ \alpha'' & \beta'' & \gamma'' & \ldots \\ \ldots & \ldots & \ldots & \ldots \end{pmatrix}^{-1} (\xi, \eta, \zeta, \ldots)$$

The matrix bearing the -1 exponent was called the inverse matrix, and it held the key to solving the original system of equations. Cayley showed how to obtain the inverse matrix using the determinant of the original matrix. Once this matrix is calculated, the arithmetic of matrices allowed him to solve the system of equations by a simple analogy with linear equations: $ax = b \rightarrow x = a^{-1}b$.

Cayley was joined by other mathematicians—such as the Irish William Rowan Hamilton, the German Georg Frobenius, and Camille Jordan—in developing the theory of matrices, which soon became a fundamental tool in analysis, geometry, and especially in the emerging discipline of linear algebra. A further important point was that matrices enlarged the range of algebraic notions. In particular, matrices embodied a new, mathematically significant instance of a system with a well-elaborated arithmetic, whose rules departed from traditional number systems in the important sense that multiplication was not generally commutative.

In fact, matrix theory was naturally connected after 1830 with a central trend in British mathematics developed by George Peacock and Augustus De Morgan, among others. In trying to overcome the last reservations about the legitimacy of the negative and complex numbers, these mathematicians suggested that algebra be conceived as a purely formal, symbolic language, irrespective of the nature of the objects whose laws of combination it stipulated. In principle, this view allowed for new, different kinds of arithmetic, such as matrix arithmetic. The British tradition of symbolic algebra was instrumental in shifting the focus of algebra from the direct study of objects (numbers, polynomials, and the like) to the study of operations among abstract objects. Still, in most respects, Peacock and De Morgan strove to gain a deeper understanding of the objects of classical algebra rather than to launch a new discipline.

Another important development in Britain concerned the elaboration of an algebra of logic. De Morgan and George Boole—and somewhat later Ernst Schröder in

Germany—were instrumental in transforming logic from a purely metaphysical into a mathematical discipline. They also added to the growing realization of the immense potential of algebraic thinking, freed from its narrow conception as the discipline of polynomial equations and number systems.

QUATERNIONS AND VECTORS

Remaining doubts about the legitimacy of complex numbers were finally dispelled when their geometric interpretation became widespread among mathematicians. This interpretation—initially and independently conceived by the Norwegian surveyor Caspar Wessel and the French bookkeeper Jean-Robert Argand—was made known to a larger audience of mathematicians mainly through its explicit use by Gauss in his 1848 proof of the fundamental theorem of algebra. Under this interpretation, every complex number appeared as a directed segment on the plane, characterized by its length and its angle of inclination with respect to the x-axis. The number i thus corresponded to the segment of length 1 that was perpendicular to the x-axis. Once a proper arithmetic was defined on these numbers, it turned out that $i^2 = -1$, as expected.

An alternative interpretation, very much within the spirit of the British school of symbolic algebra, was published in 1837 by William Rowan Hamilton. Hamilton defined a complex number $a + bi$ as a pair (a, b) of real numbers and gave the laws of arithmetic for such pairs. For example, he defined multiplication as:

$$(a, b)(c, d) = (ac - bd, bc + ad).$$

In Hamilton's notation $i = (0, 1)$ and by the above definition of complex multiplication $(0, 1)(0, 1) = (-1, 0)$—that is, $i^2 = -1$ as desired. This formal interpretation obviated the need to give any essentialist definition of complex numbers.

Starting in 1830, Hamilton pursued intensely, and unsuccessfully, a scheme to extend his idea to triplets (a, b, c), which he expected to be of great utility in mathematical physics. His difficulty lay in defining a consistent multiplication for such a system, which in hindsight is known to be impossible. In 1843 Hamilton finally realized that the generalization he was looking for had to be found in the system of quadruplets (a, b, c, d), which he named quaternions. He wrote them, in analogy with the complex numbers, as $a + bi + cj + dk$, and his new arithmetic was based on the rules: $i^2 = j^2 = k^2 = ijk = -1$ and $ij = k, ji = -k, jk = i$, $kj = -i$, $ki = j$, and $ik = -j$. This was the first example of a coherent, significant mathematical system that preserved all of the laws of ordinary arithmetic, with the exception of commutativity.

In spite of Hamilton's initial hopes, quaternions never really caught on among physicists, who generally preferred vector notation when it was introduced later. Nevertheless, his ideas had an enormous influence on the gradual introduction and use of vectors in physics. Hamilton used the name *scalar* for the real part a of the quaternion, and the term *vector* for the imaginary part $bi + cj + dk$, and defined what are now known as the scalar (or dot) and vector (or cross) products. It was through successive work in the 19th century of the Britons Peter Guthrie Tait, James Clerk Maxwell, and Oliver Heaviside and the American Josiah Willard Gibbs that an autonomous theory of vectors was first established while developing on Hamilton's initial ideas. In spite of physicists' general lack of interest in quaternions, they remained important inside mathematics, although mainly as an example of an alternate algebraic system.

THE CLOSE OF THE CLASSICAL AGE

The last major algebra textbook in the classical tradition was Heinrich Weber's *Lehrbuch der Algebra* (1895; "Textbook of Algebra"), which codified the achievements and current dominant views of the subject and remained highly influential for several decades. At its centre was a well-elaborated, systematic conception of the various systems of numbers, built as a rigorous hierarchy from the natural numbers up to the complex numbers. Its primary focus was the study of polynomials, polynomial equations, and polynomial forms, and all relevant results and methods derived in the book directly depended on the properties of the systems of numbers. Radical methods for solving equations received a great deal of attention, but so did approximation methods, which are now typically covered instead in analysis and numerical analysis textbooks. Recently developed concepts, such as groups and fields, as well as methods derived from Galois's work, were treated in Weber's textbook, but only as useful tools to help deal with the main topic of polynomial equations.

To a large extent, Weber's textbook was a very fine culmination of a long process that started in antiquity. Fortunately, rather than bringing this process to a conclusion, it served as a catalyst for the next stage of algebra.

STRUCTURAL ALGEBRA

At the turn of the 20th century, algebra reflected a very clear conceptual hierarchy based on a systematically elaborated arithmetic, with a theory of polynomial equations built on top of it. Finally, a well-developed set of conceptual tools, most prominently the idea of groups, offered a comprehensive means of investigating algebraic properties. Then, in 1930 a textbook was published that presented a totally new image of the discipline. This was *Moderne Algebra*, by the Dutch mathematician Bartel van der Waerden, who since 1924 had attended lectures in Germany by Emmy Noether at Göttingen and by Emil Artin at Hamburg. Van der Waerden's new image of the discipline inverted the conceptual hierarchy of classical algebra. Groups, fields, rings, and other related concepts became the main focus, based on the implicit realization that all of these concepts were, in fact, instances of a more general, underlying idea: the idea of an algebraic structure. Thus, the main task of algebra became the elucidation of the properties of each of these structures and of the relationships among them. Similar questions were now asked about all these concepts, and similar concepts and techniques were used where possible. The main tasks of classical algebra became ancillary. The systems of real numbers, rational numbers, and polynomials were studied as particular instances of certain algebraic structures. The properties of these systems depended on what was known about the general structures of which they were instances, rather than the other way round.

PRECURSORS TO THE STRUCTURAL APPROACH

Van der Waerden's book did not contain many new results or concepts. Its innovation lay in the unified picture it presented of the discipline of algebra. Van der Waerden brought together, in a surprisingly illuminating manner, algebraic research that had taken place over the previous three decades, and in doing so, he combined the contributions of several leading German algebraists from the beginning of the 20th century.

Hilbert and Steinitz

Of these German mathematicians, few were more important than David Hilbert. Among his important contributions, his work in the 1890s on the theory of algebraic number fields was decisive in establishing the conceptual approach promoted by Dedekind as dominant for several decades. As the undisputed leader of mathematics at Göttingen—then the world's premiere research institution—Hilbert's influence propagated through the 68 doctoral dissertations he directed as well as through the many students and mathematicians who attended his lectures. To a significant extent, the structural view of algebra was the product of some of Hilbert's innovations, yet he basically remained a representative of the classical discipline of algebra. It is likely that the kind of algebra that developed under the influence of van der Waerden's book had no direct appeal for Hilbert.

In 1910 Ernst Steinitz published an influential article on the abstract theory of fields that was an important milestone on the road to the structural image of algebra. His work was highly structural in that he first established the simplest kinds of subfields that any field contains and established a classification system. He then investigated how properties were passed from a field to any extension of it or to any of its subfields. In this way, he was able to characterize all possible fields abstractly. To a great extent, van der Waerden extended to the whole discipline of algebra what Steinitz accomplished for the more restricted domain of fields.

Noether and Artin

The greatest influence behind the consolidation of the structural image of algebra was no doubt Emmy Noether, who became the most prominent figure in Göttingen in the 1920s. Noether synthesized the ideas of Dedekind, Hilbert, Steinitz, and others in a series of articles in which the theory of factorization of algebraic numbers and of polynomials was masterly and succinctly subsumed under a single theory of abstract rings. She also contributed important papers to the theory of hypercomplex systems (extensions, such as the quaternions, of complex numbers to higher dimensions) that followed a similar approach, further demonstrating the potential of the structural approach.

The last significant influence on van der Waerden's structural image of algebra was by Artin, above all for the latter's reformulation of Galois theory. Rather than speaking of the Galois group of a polynomial equation with coefficients in a particular field, Artin focused on the group of automorphisms of the coefficients' splitting field (the smallest extension of the field such that the polynomial could be factored into linear terms). Galois theory could then be seen as the study of the interrelations between the extensions of a field and the possible subgroups of the Galois group of the original field. In this typical structural reformulation of a classical 19th-century theory of algebra, the problem of solvability of equations by radicals appeared as a particular application of an abstract general theory.

THE STRUCTURAL APPROACH DOMINATES

After the late 1930s, it was clear that algebra—and in particular the structural approach within it—had become one of the most dynamic areas of research in mathematics. Structural methods, results, and concepts were actively pursued by algebraists in Germany, France, the United States, Japan, and elsewhere. The structural approach was also successfully applied to redefine other mathematical disciplines. An important early example of this was the thorough reformulation of algebraic geometry in the hands of van der Waerden, André Weil in France, and the Russian-born Oscar Zariski in Italy and the United States. In particular, they used the concepts and approach developed in ring theory by Noether and her successors. Another important example was the work of the American Marshall Stone, who in the late 1930s defined Boolean algebras, bringing under a purely algebraic framework ideas stemming from logic, topology, and algebra itself.

Over the following decades, algebra textbooks appeared around the world along the lines established by van der Waerden. Prominent among these was *A Survey of Modern Algebra* (1941) by Saunders Mac Lane and Garret Birkhoff, a book that was fundamental for the next several generations of mathematicians in the United States. Nevertheless, it must be stressed that not all algebraists felt, at least initially, that the new direction implied by *Moderne Algebra* was paramount. More classically oriented research was still being carried out well beyond the 1930s. The research of Georg Frobenius and his former student Issai Schur—who were the most outstanding representatives of the Berlin mathematical school at the beginning of the 20th century—and of Hermann Weyl, one of Hilbert's most prominent students, merit special mention.

ALGEBRAIC SUPERSTRUCTURES

Although the structural approach had become prominent in many mathematical disciplines, the notion of structure remained more a regulative, informal principle than a real mathematical concept for independent investigation. It was only natural that sooner or later the question would arise how to define structures in such a way that the concept could be investigated. For example, Noether brought new and important insights into certain rings (algebraic numbers and polynomials) previously investigated under separate frameworks by studying their underlying structures. Similarly, it was expected that a general metatheory of structures, or superstructures, would prove fruitful for studying other related concepts.

Bourbaki

Attempts to develop such a metatheory were undertaken starting in the 1940s. The first one came from a group of young French mathematicians working under the common pseudonym of Nicolas Bourbaki. The founders of the group included Weil, Jean Dieudonné, and Henri Cartan. Over the next few decades, the group published a collection of extremely influential textbooks, *Eléments de mathématique*, that covered several central mathematical disciplines, particularly from a structural perspective. Yet, to the extent that Bourbaki's mathematics was structural, it was so in a general, informal way. As van der Waerden extended to all of algebra the structural approach that Steinitz introduced in the theory of fields, so Bourbaki's *Eléments* extended this approach to a truly broad range of mathematical disciplines. Although Bourbaki did define a formal concept of structure in the first book of the collection, their concept turned out to be quite cumbersome and was not pursued further.

Category Theory

The second attempt to formalize the notion of structure developed within category theory. The first paper on the subject was published in the United States in 1942 by Mac Lane and Samuel Eilenberg. The idea behind their approach was that the essential features of any particular mathematical domain (a category) could be identified by focusing on the interrelations among its elements, rather than looking at the behaviour of each element in isolation. For example, what characterized the category of groups were the properties of its homomorphisms (mappings between groups that preserve algebraic operations) and comparisons with morphisms for other categories, such as homeomorphisms for topological spaces. Another important concept of Mac Lane and Eilenberg was their formulation of "functors," a generalization of the idea of function that enabled them to connect different categories. For example, in algebraic topology functors associated topological spaces with certain groups such that their topological properties could be expressed as algebraic properties of the groups—a process that enabled powerful algebraic tools to be used on previously intractable problems.

Although category theory did not become a universal language for all of mathematics, it did become the standard formulation for algebraic topology and homology. Category theory also led to new approaches in the study of the foundations of mathematics by means of Topos theory. Some of these developments were further enhanced between 1956 and 1970 through the intensive work of Alexandre Grothendieck and his collaborators in France, using still more general concepts based on categories.

NEW CHALLENGES AND PERSPECTIVES

The enormous productivity of research in algebra over the second half of the 20th century precludes any complete synopsis. Nevertheless, two main issues deserve some comment. The first was a trend toward abstraction and generalization as embodied in the structural approach. This trend was not exclusive, however. Researchers moved back and forth, studying general structures as well as classical entities such as the real and rational numbers. The second issue was the introduction of new kinds of proofs and techniques. The following examples are illustrative.

A subgroup H of a group G is called a normal group if for every element g in G and h in H, $g^{-1}hg$ is an element of H. A group with no normal subgroups is known as a simple group. Simple groups are the basic components of group theory, and since Galois's time, it was known that the general quintic was unsolvable by radicals because its Galois group was simple. However, a full characterization of simple groups remained unattainable until a major breakthrough in 1963 by two Americans, Walter Feit and John G. Thomson. They proved an old conjecture of the British mathematician William Burnside, namely, that the order of noncommutative finite simple groups is always even. Their proof was long and involved, but it reinforced the belief that a full classification of finite simple groups might, after all, be possible. The completion of the task was announced in 1983 by the American mathematician Daniel Gorenstein, following the contributions of hundreds of individuals over thousands of pages. Although this classification seems comprehensive, it is anything but clear-cut and systematic, since simple groups appear in all kinds of situations and under many guises. Thus, there seems to be no single individual who can boast of knowing all of its details. This kind of very large, collective theorem is certainly a novel mathematical phenomenon.

Another example concerns the complex and involved question of the use of computers in proving and even formulating new theorems. This now incipient trend will certainly receive increased attention in the 21st century.

Finally, probabilistic methods of proof in algebra, and in particular for solving difficult, open problems in group theory, have been introduced. This trend began with a series of papers by the Hungarian mathematicians Paul Erdös and Paul Turán, both of whom introduced probabilistic methods into many other branches of mathematics as well.

BRANCHES OF ALGEBRA

The principles and main functions of the three main branches of algebra are described below. These branches are elementary algebra, linear algebra, and modern algebra.

ELEMENTARY ALGEBRA

Elementary algebra deals with the general properties of numbers and the relations between them. More specifically, it is concerned with the following topics:

1. Real and complex numbers, constants, and variables — collectively known as algebraic quantities.
2. Rules of operation for such quantities.
3. Geometric representations of such quantities.
4. Formation of expressions involving algebraic quantities.
5. Rules for manipulating such expressions.
6. Formation of sentences, also called equations, involving algebraic expressions.
7. Solution of equations and systems of equations.

ALGEBRAIC QUANTITIES

The principal distinguishing characteristic of algebra is the use of simple symbols to represent numerical quantities and mathematical operations. Following a system that originated with the 17th-century French thinker René Descartes, letters near the beginning of the alphabet $(a, b, c, ...)$ typically represent known, but arbitrary, numbers in a problem, while letters near the end of the alphabet, especially x, y, and z, represent unknown quantities, or variables. The + and - signs indicate addition and subtraction of these quantities, but multiplication is simply indicated by adjacent letters. Thus, ax represents the product of a by x. This simple expression can be interpreted, for example, as the interest earned in one year by a sum of *a* dollars invested at an annual rate of *x*. It can also be interpreted as the distance traveled in *a* hours by a car moving at *x* miles per hour. Such flexibility of representation is what gives algebra its great utility.

Another feature that has greatly increased the range of algebraic applications is the geometric representation of algebraic quantities. For instance, to represent the real numbers, a straight line is imagined that is infinite in both directions. An arbitrary point *O* can be chosen as the origin, representing the number o, and another arbitrary point *U* chosen to the right of *O*. The segment *OU* (or the point *U*) then represents the unit length, or the number 1. The rest of the positive numbers correspond to multiples of this unit length—so that 2, for example, is represented by a segment *OV*, twice as long as *OU* and extended in the same direction. Similarly, the negative real numbers extend to the left of *O*. A straight line whose points are thus identified with the real numbers is called a number line. Many earlier mathematicians realized there was a relationship between all points on a straight line and all real numbers, but it was the German mathematician Richard Dedekind who made this explicit as a postulate in his *Continuity and Irrational Numbers* (1872).

In the Cartesian coordinate system (named for Descartes) of analytic geometry, one horizontal number line (usually called the *x*-axis) and one vertical number line (the *y*-axis) intersect at right angles at their common origin to provide coordinates for each point in the plane. For example, the point on a vertical line through some particular *x* on the *x*-axis and on the horizontal line through some *y* on the *y*-axis is represented by the pair of real numbers (x, y). A similar geometric representation exists for the complex numbers, where the horizontal axis corresponds to the real numbers and the vertical axis corresponds to the imaginary numbers (where the imaginary unit i is equal to the square root of -1). The algebraic form of complex numbers is $x + iy$, where x represents the real part and iy the imaginary part.

This pairing of space and number gives a means of pairing algebraic expressions, or functions, in a single variable with geometric objects in the plane, such as straight lines and circles. The result of this pairing may be thought of as the graph of the expression for different values of the variable.

Algebraic Expressions

Any of the quantities mentioned so far may be combined in expressions according to the usual arithmetic operations of addition, subtraction, and multiplication. Thus, $ax + by$ and $axx + bx + c$ are common algebraic expressions. However, exponential notation is commonly used to avoid repeating the same term in a product, so that one writes x^2 for xx and y^3 for yyy. (By convention $x^0 = 1$.) Expressions built up in this way from the real and complex numbers, the algebraic quantities a, b, c, . . ., x, y, z, and the three above operations are called polynomials—a word introduced in the late 16th century by the French mathematician François Viète from the Greek *polys* ("many") and the Latin *nominem* ("name" or "term"). One way of characterizing a polynomial is by the number of different unknown, or variable, quantities in it. Another way of characterizing a polynomial is by its degree. The degree of a polynomial in one unknown is the largest power of the unknown appearing in it. The expressions $ax + b$, $ax^2 + bx + c$, and $ax^3 + bx^2 + cx + d$ are general polynomials in one unknown (x) of degrees 1, 2, and 3, respectively. When only one unknown is involved, it does not matter which letter is used for it. One could equally well write the above polynomials as $ay + b$, $az^2 + bz + c$, and $at^3 + bt^2 + ct + d$.

Because some insight into complicated functions can be obtained by approximating them with simpler functions, polynomials of the first degree were investigated early on. In particular, $ax + by = c$, which represents a straight line, and $ax + by + cz = e$, which represents a plane in three-dimensional space, were among the first algebraic equations studied.

Polynomials can be combined according to the three arithmetic operations of addition, subtraction, and multiplication, and the result is again a polynomial. To simplify expressions obtained by combining polynomials in this way, one uses the distributive law, as well as the commutative and associative laws for addition and multiplication. Until very recently a major drawback of algebra was the extreme tedium of routine manipulation of polynomials, but now a number of symbolic algebra programs make this work as easy as typing the expressions into a computer.

By extending the operations on polynomials to include division, or ratios of polynomials, one obtains the rational functions. Examples of such rational functions are $2/3x$ and $(a + bx^2)/(c + dx^2 + ex^5)$. Working with rational functions allows one to introduce the expression $1/x$ and its powers, $1/x^2, 1/x^3, \ldots$ (often written $x^{-1}, x^{-2}, x^{-3}, \ldots$). When the degree of the numerator of a rational function is at least as large as that of its denominator, it is possible to divide the numerator by the denominator much as one divides one integer by another. In this way one can write any rational function as the sum of a polynomial and a rational function in which the degree of the numerator is less than that of the denominator. For example,

$$(x^8 - x^5 + 3x^3 + 2)/(x^3 - 1) = x^5 + 3 + 5/(x^3 - 1).$$

Since this process reduces the degrees of the terms involved, it is especially useful for calculating the values of rational functions and for dealing with them when they arise in calculus.

SOLVING ALGEBRAIC EQUATIONS

For theoretical work and applications, one often needs to find numbers that, when substituted for the unknown, make a certain polynomial equal to zero. Such a number is called a "root" of the polynomial. For example, the polynomial

$$-16t^2 + 88t + 48$$

represents the height above Earth at t seconds of a projectile thrown straight up at 88 feet per second from the top of a tower 48 feet high. (The 16 in the formula comes from one-half the acceleration of gravity, 32 feet per second per second.) By setting the equation equal to zero and factoring it as $(4t - 24)(-4t - 2) = 0$, the equation's one positive root is found to be 6, meaning that the object will hit the ground about 6 seconds after it is thrown. (This problem also illustrates the important algebraic concept of the zero factor property: if $ab = 0$, then either $a = 0$ or $b = 0$.)

The theorem that every polynomial has as many complex roots as its degree is known as the fundamental theorem of algebra and was first proved in 1799 by Carl Friedrich Gauss.

Simple formulas exist for finding the roots of the general polynomials of degrees one and two, and much less simple formulas exist for polynomials of degrees three and four. The French mathematician Évariste Galois discovered, shortly before his death in 1832, that no such formula exists for a general polynomial of degree greater than four. Many ways exist, however, of approximating the roots of these polynomials.

SOLVING SYSTEMS OF ALGEBRAIC EQUATIONS

An extension of the study of single equations involves multiple equations that are solved simultaneously—so-called systems of equations. For example, the intersection of two straight lines, $ax + by = c$ and $Ax + By = C$, can be found algebraically by discovering the values of x and y that simultaneously solve each equation. The earliest systematic development of methods for solving systems of equations occurred in ancient China. An adaptation of a problem from the 1st-century-CE Chinese classic *Nine Chapters on the Mathematical Procedures* illustrates how such systems arise. Imagine there are two kinds of wheat and that you have four sheaves of the first type and five sheaves of the second type. Although neither of these is enough to produce a bushel of wheat, you can produce a bushel by adding three sheaves of the first type to five of the second type, or you can produce a bushel by adding four sheaves of the first type to two of the second type. What fraction of a bushel of wheat does a sheaf of each type of wheat contain?

Using modern notation, suppose we have two types of wheat, respectively, and x and y represent the number of bushels obtained per sheaf of the first and second types, respectively. Then the problem leads to the system of equations:

$$3x + 5y = 1 \text{ (bushel)}$$

$$4x + 2y = 1 \text{ (bushel)}$$

A simple method for solving such a system is first to solve either equation for one of the variables. For example, solving the second equation for y yields $y = 1/2 - 2x$. The right side of this equation can then be substituted for y in the first equation ($3x + 5y = 1$), and then the first equation can be solved to obtain x (= $3/14$). Finally, this value of x can be substituted into one of the earlier equations to obtain y (= $1/14$). Thus, the first type yields $3/14$ bushels per sheaf and the second type yields $1/14$. Note that the solution ($3/14, 1/14$) would be difficult to discern by graphing techniques. In fact, any precise value based on a graphing solution may be only approximate. For example, the point ($0.0000001, 0$) might look like ($0, 0$) on a graph, but even such a small difference could have drastic consequences in the real world.

Rather than individually solving each possible system of two equations in two unknowns, the general system can be solved. To return to the general equations given above:

$$ax + by = c$$

$$Ax + By = C$$

The solutions are given by $x = (Bc - bC)/(aB - Ab)$ and $y = (Ca - cA)/(aB - Ab)$. Note that the denominator of each solution, $(aB - Ab)$, is the same. It is called the determinant of the system, and systems in which the denominator is equal to zero have either no solution (in which case the equations represent parallel lines) or infinitely many solutions (in which case the equations represent the same line).

One can generalize simultaneous systems to consider m equations in n unknowns. In this case, one usually uses subscripted letters $x_1, x_2, \ldots, x_n$ for the unknowns and $a_{1,1}, \ldots, a_{1,n}; a_{2,1}, \ldots, a_{2,n}; \ldots; a_{m,1}, \ldots, a_{m,n}$ for the coefficients of each equation, respectively. When $n = 3$ one is dealing with planes in three-dimensional space, and for higher values of n one is dealing with hyperplanes in spaces of higher dimension. In general, n equations in m unknowns have infinitely many solutions when $m < n$ and no solutions when $m > n$. The case $m = n$ is the only case where there can exist a unique solution.

Large systems of equations are generally handled with matrices, especially as implemented on computers. Matrices are discussed below in the context of linear algebra.

LINEAR ALGEBRA

Linear algebra is a mathematical discipline that deals with vectors and matrices and, more generally, with vector spaces and linear transformations. Unlike other parts of mathematics that are frequently invigorated by new ideas and unsolved problems, linear algebra is very well understood. Its value lies in its many applications, from mathematical physics to modern algebra and coding theory.

VECTORS AND VECTOR SPACES

Linear algebra usually starts with the study of vectors, which are understood as quantities having both magnitude and direction. Vectors lend themselves readily to physical applications. For example, consider a solid object that is free to move in any direction. When two forces act at the same time on this object, they produce a combined effect that is the same as a single force. To picture this, represent the two forces v and w as arrows; the direction of each arrow gives the direction of the force, and its length gives the magnitude of the force. The single force that results from combining v and w is called their sum, written $v + w$. In the figure on page 79, $v + w$ corresponds to the diagonal of the parallelogram formed from adjacent sides represented by v and w.

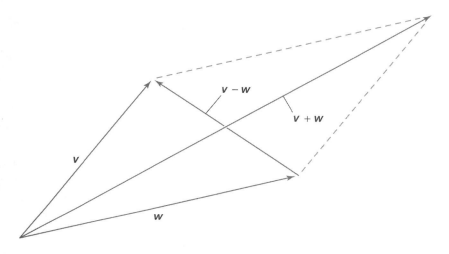

One method of adding and subtracting vectors is to place their tails together and then supply two more sides to form a parallelogram. The vector from their tails to the opposite corner of the parallelogram is equal to the sum of the original vectors. The vector between their heads (starting from the vector being subtracted) is equal to their difference. Encyclopædia Britannica, Inc.

Vectors are often expressed using coordinates. For example, in two dimensions a vector can be defined by a pair of coordinates (a_1, a_2) describing an arrow going from the origin (o, o) to the point (a_1, a_2). If one vector is (a_1, a_2) and another is (b_1, b_2), then their sum is $(a_1 + b_1, a_2 + b_2)$. This gives the same result as the parallelogram (*see* the figure on page 80).

In three dimensions a vector is expressed using three coordinates (a_1, a_2, a_3), and this idea extends to any number of dimensions.

Representing vectors as arrows in two or three dimensions is a starting point, but linear algebra has been applied in contexts where this is no longer appropriate. For example, in some types of differential equations the sum of two solutions gives a third solution, and any constant multiple

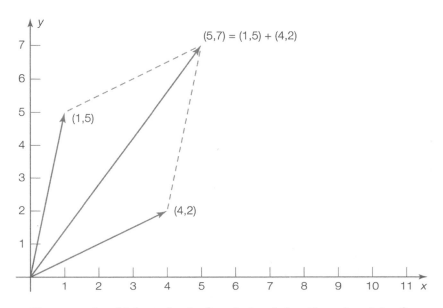

Vectors can be added together by first placing their tails at the origin of a coordinate system such that their lengths and directions are unchanged. Then, the coordinates of their heads are added pairwise; e.g., in two dimensions, their x-coordinates and their y-coordinates are added separately to obtain the resulting vector sum. As shown by the dotted lines, this vector sum coincides with one diagonal of the parallelogram formed with the original vectors. Encyclopædia Britannica, Inc.

of a solution is also a solution. In such cases the solutions can be treated as vectors, and the set of solutions is a vector space in the following sense. In a vector space, any two vectors can be added together to give another vector, and vectors can be multiplied by numbers to give "shorter" or "longer" vectors. The numbers are called scalars because in early examples they were ordinary numbers that altered the scale, or length, of a vector. For example, if v is a vector and 2 is a scalar, then $2v$ is a vector in the same direction as v but twice as long. In many modern applications of linear algebra, scalars are no longer ordinary real numbers, but the important thing is that they can be combined among themselves by addition, subtraction, multiplication, and division. For example, the scalars may be complex numbers, or they may be elements of a finite field such as the field having only the two elements 0 and 1, where 1 + 1 = 0. The coordinates of a vector are scalars, and when these scalars are from the field of two elements, each coordinate is 0 or 1, so each vector can be viewed as a particular sequence of 0s and 1s. This is very useful in digital processing, where such sequences are used to encode and transmit data.

LINEAR TRANSFORMATIONS AND MATRICES

Vector spaces are one of the two main ingredients of linear algebra—the other being linear transformations (or "operators" in the parlance of physicists). Linear transformations are functions that send, or "map," one vector to another vector. The simplest example of a linear transformation sends each vector to c times itself, where c is some constant. Thus, every vector remains in the same direction, but all lengths are multiplied by c. Another example is a rotation, which leaves all lengths the same but alters the directions of the vectors. *Linear* refers to the fact that the transformation preserves vector addition and scalar multiplication. This means that if T is a linear transformation sending a vector v to $T(v)$, then for any vectors v and w, and any scalar c, the transformation must satisfy the properties $T(v + w) = T(v) + T(w)$ and $T(cv) = cT(v)$.

When doing computations, linear transformations are treated as matrices. A matrix is a rectangular arrangement of scalars, and two matrices can be added or multiplied. The product of two matrices shows the result of doing one transformation followed by another (from right to left), and if the transformations are done in reverse order the result is usually different. Thus, the product of two matrices depends on the order of multiplication. If S and T are square matrices (matrices with the same number of rows as columns) of the same size, then ST and TS are rarely equal. The matrix for a given transformation is found using coordinates. For example, in two dimensions a linear transformation T can be completely determined simply by knowing its effect on any two vectors v and w that have different directions. Their transformations $T(v)$ and $T(w)$ are given by two coordinates. Therefore, only four coordinates, two for $T(v)$ and two for $T(w)$, are needed to specify T. These four coordinates are arranged in a 2-by-2 matrix. In three dimensions, three vectors u, v, and w are needed, and to specify $T(u)$, $T(v)$, and $T(w)$, one needs three coordinates for each. This results in a 3-by-3 matrix.

Eigenvectors

When studying linear transformations, it is extremely useful to find nonzero vectors whose direction is left unchanged by the transformation. These are called eigenvectors (also known as characteristic vectors). If v is an eigenvector for the linear transformation T, then $T(v) = \lambda v$ for some scalar λ. This scalar is called an eigenvalue. The eigenvalue of greatest absolute value, along with its associated eigenvector, have special significance for many physical applications. This is because whatever process is represented by the linear transformation often acts repeatedly—feeding output from the last transformation back into another transformation—which results in every arbitrary (nonzero) vector converging on the eigenvector associated with the largest eigenvalue, though rescaled by a power of the eigenvalue. In other words, the long-term behaviour of the system is determined by its eigenvectors.

Finding the eigenvectors and eigenvalues for a linear transformation is often done using matrix algebra, first developed in the mid-19th century by the English mathematician Arthur Cayley. His work formed the foundation for modern linear algebra.

MODERN ALGEBRA

Modern algebra, also called abstract algebra, is concerned with the general algebraic structure of various sets (such as real numbers, complex numbers, matrices, and vector spaces), rather than rules and procedures for manipulating their individual elements.

During the second half of the 19th century, various important mathematical advances led to the study of sets in which any two elements can be added or multiplied together to give a third element of the same set. The elements of the sets concerned could be numbers, functions, or some other objects. As the techniques involved were similar, it seemed reasonable to consider the sets, rather than their elements, to be the objects of primary concern. A definitive treatise, *Modern Algebra*, was written in 1930 by the Dutch mathematician Bartel van der Waerden, and the subject has had a deep effect on almost every branch of mathematics.

BASIC ALGEBRAIC STRUCTURES

Fields

In itself a set is not very useful, being little more than a well-defined collection of mathematical objects. However, when a set has one or more operations (such as addition and multiplication) defined for its elements, it becomes very useful. If the operations satisfy familiar arithmetic rules (such as associativity, commutativity, and distributivity) the set will have a particularly "rich" algebraic structure. Sets with the richest algebraic structure are known as fields. Familiar examples of fields are the rational numbers (fractions a/b where a and b are positive or negative whole numbers), the real numbers (rational and irrational numbers), and the complex numbers (numbers of the form $a + bi$ where a and b are real numbers and $i^2 = -1$). Each of these is important enough to warrant its own special symbol: null for the rationals, null for the reals, and null for the complex numbers. The term *field* in its algebraic sense is quite different from its use in other contexts, such as vector fields in mathematics or magnetic fields in physics. Other languages avoid this conflict in terminology. For example, a field in the algebraic sense is called a *corps* in French and a *Körper* in German, both words meaning "body."

In addition to the fields mentioned above, which all have infinitely many elements, there exist fields having only a finite number of elements (always some power of a prime number), and these are of great importance, particularly for discrete mathematics. In fact, finite fields motivated the early development of abstract algebra. The simplest finite field has only two elements, 0 and 1, where $1 + 1 = 0$. This field has applications to coding theory and data communication.

Structural Axioms

A set that satisfies all 10 of the basic rules, or axioms, for addition and multiplication, as shown in the table of field axioms, is called a field. A set satisfying only axioms 1–7 is called a ring, and if it also satisfies axiom 9 it is called a ring with unity. A ring satisfying the commutative law of multiplication (axiom 8) is known as a commutative ring. When axioms 1–9 hold and there are no proper divisors of zero (i.e., whenever $ab = 0$ either $a = 0$ or $b = 0$), a set is called an integral domain. For example, the set of integers $\{\ldots, -2, -1, 0, 1, 2, \ldots\}$ is a commutative ring with unity, but it is not a field, because axiom 10 fails. When only axiom 8 fails, a set is known as a division ring or skew field.

FIELD AXIOMS	
AXIOM 1	Closure: the combination (hereafter indicated by addition or multiplication) of any two elements in the set produces an element in the set.
AXIOM 2	Addition is commutative: $a + b = b + a$ for any elements in the set.
AXIOM 3	Addition is associative: $a + (b + c) = (a + b) + c$ for any elements in the set.
AXIOM 4	Additive identity: there exists an element 0 such that $a + 0 = a$ for every element in the set.
AXIOM 5	Additive inverse: for each element a in the set, there exists an element $-a$ such that $a + (-a) = 0$.
AXIOM 6	Multiplication is associative: $a(bc) = (ab)c$ for any elements in the set.
AXIOM 7	Distributive law: $a(b + c) = ab + ac$ and $(a + b)c = ac + bc$ for any elements in the set.
AXIOM 8	Multiplication is commutative: $ab = ba$ for any elements in the set.
AXIOM 9	Multiplicative identity: there exists an element 1 such that $1a = a$ for any element in the set.
AXIOM 10	Multiplicative inverse: for each element a in the set, there exists an element a^{-1} such that $aa^{-1} = 1$.

Quaternions and Abstraction

The discovery of rings having noncommutative multiplication was an important stimulus in the development of modern algebra. For example, the set of n-by-n matrices is a noncommutative ring, but since there are nonzero matrices without inverses, it is not a division ring. The first example of a noncommutative division ring was the quaternions. These are numbers of the form $a + bi + cj + dk$, where $a, b, c,$

and d are real numbers and their coefficients 1, i, j, and k are unit vectors that define a four-dimensional space. Quaternions were invented in 1843 by the Irish mathematician William Rowan Hamilton to extend complex numbers from the two-dimensional plane to three dimensions in order to describe physical processes mathematically. Hamilton defined the following rules for quaternion multiplication: $i^2 = j^2 = k^2 = -1$, $ij = k = -ji$, $jk = i = -kj$, and $ki = j = -ik$.

After struggling for some years to discover consistent rules for working with his higher-dimensional complex numbers, inspiration struck while he was strolling in his hometown of Dublin, and he stopped to inscribe these formulas on a nearby bridge. In working with his quaternions, Hamilton laid the foundations for the algebra of matrices and led the way to more abstract notions of numbers and operations.

RINGS

Rings in Number Theory

In another direction, important progress in number theory by German mathematicians such as Ernst Kummer, Richard Dedekind, and Leopold Kronecker used rings of algebraic integers. (An algebraic integer is a complex number satisfying an algebraic equation of the form $x^n + a_1 x^{n-1} + \ldots + a^n = 0$ where the coefficients $a_1, \ldots, a^n$ are integers.) Their work introduced the important concept of an ideal in such rings, so called because it could be represented by "ideal elements" outside the ring concerned. In the late 19th century, the German mathematician David Hilbert used ideals to solve an old problem about polynomials (algebraic expressions using many variables $x_1, x_2, x_3, \ldots$). The problem was to take a finite number of variables and decide which ideals could be generated by at most finitely many polynomials. Hilbert's method solved the problem and brought an end to further investigation by showing that they all had this property. His abstract "hands off" approach led the German mathematician Paul Gordon to exclaim *"Das ist nicht Mathematik, das ist Theologie!"* ("That is not mathematics, that is theology!"). The power of modern algebra had arrived.

Rings can arise naturally in solving mathematical problems, as shown in the following example: Which whole numbers can be written as the sum of two squares? In other words, when can a whole number n be written as $a^2 + b^2$? To solve this problem, it is useful to factor n into prime factors, and it is also useful to factor $a^2 + b^2$ as $(a + bi)$ $(a - bi)$, where $i^2 = -1$. The question can then be rephrased in terms of numbers $a + bi$ where a and b are integers. This set of numbers forms a ring, and, by considering factorization in this ring, the original problem can be solved. Rings of this sort are very useful in number theory.

Rings in Algebraic Geometry

Rings are used extensively in algebraic geometry. Consider a curve in the plane given by an equation in two variables such as $y^2 = x^3 + 1$. The curve shown in the figure on page 88 consists of all points (x, y) that satisfy the equation. For example, $(2, 3)$ and $(-1, 0)$ are points on the curve. Every algebraic function in two variables assigns a value to every point of the curve. For example, $xy + 2x$ assigns the value 10 to the point $(2, 3)$ and -2 to the point $(-1, 0)$. Such functions can be added and multiplied together, and they form a ring that can be used to study the original curve. Functions such as y^2 and $x^3 + 1$ that agree with each other at every point of the curve are treated as the same function, and this allows the curve to be recovered from the ring.

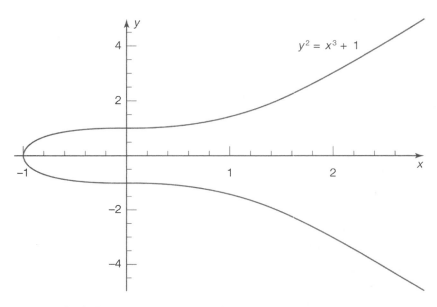

A simple algebraic curve. Encyclopædia Britannica, Inc.

Geometric problems can therefore be transformed into algebraic problems, solved using techniques from modern algebra, and then transformed back into geometric results.

The development of these methods for the study of algebraic geometry was one of the major advances in mathematics during the 20th century. Pioneering work in this direction was done in France by the mathematicians André Weil in the 1950s and Alexandre Grothendieck in the 1960s.

GROUP THEORY

In addition to developments in number theory and algebraic geometry, modern algebra has important applications to symmetry by means of group theory. The word *group* often refers to a group of operations, possibly preserving the symmetry of some object or an arrangement of like objects. In the latter case the operations are called permutations, and one talks of a group of permutations, or simply a permutation group. If α and β are operations, their composite (α followed by β) is usually written αβ, and their composite in the opposite order (β followed by α) is written βα. In general, αβ and βα are not equal. A group can also be defined axiomatically as a set with multiplication that satisfies the axioms for closure, associativity, identity element, and inverses (axioms 1, 6, 9, and 10). In the special case where αβ and βα are equal for all α and β, the group is called commutative, or Abelian; for such Abelian groups, operations are sometimes written α + β instead of αβ, using addition in place of multiplication.

The first application of group theory was by the French mathematician Évariste Galois to settle an old problem concerning algebraic equations. The question was to decide whether a given equation could be solved using radicals (meaning square roots, cube roots, and so on, together with the usual operations of arithmetic). By using the group of all "admissible" permutations of the solutions, now known as the Galois group of the equation, Galois showed whether or not the solutions could be expressed in terms of radicals. His was the first important use of groups, and he was the first to use the term in its modern technical sense. It was many years before his work was fully understood, in part because of its highly innovative character and in part because he was not around to explain his ideas—due to his death in a duel at the age of 20. The subject is now known as Galois theory.

Group theory developed first in France and then in other European countries during the second half of the 19th century. One early and essential idea was that many groups, and in particular all finite groups, could be decomposed into simpler groups in an essentially unique way. These simpler groups could not be decomposed further, and so they were called "simple," although their lack of further decomposition often makes them rather complex.

This is rather like decomposing a whole number into a product of prime numbers or a molecule into atoms.

In 1963 a landmark paper by the American mathematicians Walter Feit and John Thompson showed that if a finite simple group is not merely the group of rotations of a regular polygon, then it must have an even number of elements. This result was immensely important because it showed that such groups had to have some elements x such that $x^2 = 1$. Using such elements enabled mathematicians to get a handle on the structure of the whole group. The paper led to an ambitious program for finding all finite simple groups that was completed in the early 1980s. It involved the discovery of several new simple groups, one of which, the "Monster," cannot operate in fewer than 196,883 dimensions. The Monster still stands as a challenge today because of its intriguing connections with other parts of mathematics.

CHAPTER 2
GREAT ALGEBRAISTS

The discipline of algebra can be seen as passing through three periods in its history. Early algebraists—from ancient Egyptian and Babylonian scribes through the great Greek and Islamic mathematicians to the thinkers of the European Renaissance—laboured to produce what are today commonly accepted notions of mathematics, such as number, the solvable equation, and the use of symbols to represent unknown quantities. The classical discipline of algebra began at the end of the 16th century with the work of the French mathematician François Viète, who presented the first consistent, coherent, and systematic conception of an algebraic equation. Finally, around 1930 the Dutch mathematician Bartel Van der Waerden presented a new image of algebra focused on the properties of algebraic structures and the relationships among these structures. Mathematicians who contributed to these three periods are presented in this chapter.

EARLY ALGEBRAISTS (THROUGH THE 16TH CENTURY)

BHASKARA II
(b. 1114, Biddur, India—d. c. 1185, probably Ujjain)

Bhaskara II (also called Bhaskaracarya, or Bhaskara The Learned), the leading mathematician of the 12th century, wrote the first work with full and systematic use of the decimal number system.

Bhaskara II was the lineal successor of the noted Indian mathematician Brahmagupta (598–c. 665) as head of an astronomical observatory at Ujjain, the leading mathematical centre of ancient India.

In his mathematical works—particularly *Lilavati* ("The Beautiful") and *Bijaganita* ("Seed Counting")—he not only used the decimal system but also compiled problems from Brahmagupta and others. He filled many of the gaps in Brahmagupta's work, especially in obtaining a general solution to the Pell equation ($x^2 = 1 + py^2$) and in giving many particular solutions. Bhaskara II anticipated the modern convention of signs (minus by minus makes plus, minus by plus makes minus) and evidently was the first to gain some understanding of the meaning of division by zero, for he specifically stated that the value of $3/0$ is an infinite quantity. However, his understanding seems to have been limited, for he also stated wrongly that $\frac{a}{0} \times 0 = a$. Bhaskara II used letters to represent unknown quantities, much as in modern algebra, and solved indeterminate equations of 1st and 2nd degrees. He reduced quadratic equations to a single type and solved them and investigated regular polygons up to those having 384 sides, thus obtaining a good approximate value of $\pi = 3.141666$.

In other of his works, notably *Siddhantasiromani* ("Head Jewel of Accuracy") and *Karanakutuhala* ("Calculation of Astronomical Wonders"), he wrote on his astronomical observations of planetary positions, conjunctions, eclipses, cosmography, geography, and the mathematical techniques and astronomical equipment used in these studies. Bhaskara II was also a noted astrologer, and tradition has it that he named his first work, *Lilavati*, after his daughter in order to console her. His astrological meddling coupled with an unfortunate twist of fate is said to have deprived her of her only chance for marriage and happiness.

BRAHMAGUPTA

(b. 598—d. *c.* 665, possibly Bhillamala [modern Bhinmal],
Rajasthan, India)

Brahmagupta was one of the most accomplished of the
ancient Indian astronomers. He also had a profound and
direct influence on Islamic and Byzantine astronomy.

Brahmagupta was an orthodox Hindu, and his religious views—particularly the Hindu yuga system of
measuring the ages of mankind—influenced his work. He
severely criticized Jain cosmological views and other
heterodox ideas, such as the view of Aryabhata I (b. 476)
that the Earth is a spinning sphere, a view that was widely
disseminated by Brahmagupta's contemporary and rival
Bhaskara I.

Brahmagupta's fame rests mostly on his *Brahma-
sphuta-siddhanta* (628; "Correctly Established Doctrine of
Brahma"), an astronomical work that he probably wrote
while living in Bhillamala, then the capital of the Gurjara-
Pratihara dynasty. It was translated into Arabic in Baghdad
about 771 and had a major impact on Islamic mathematics
and astronomy. Late in his life, Brahmagupta wrote
Khandakhadyaka (665; "A Piece Eatable"), an astronomical
handbook that employed Aryabhata's system of starting
each day at midnight.

In addition to expounding on traditional Indian
astronomy in his books, Brahmagupta devoted several
chapters of *Brahma-sphuta-siddhanta* to mathematics. In
chapters 12 and 18 in particular, he laid the foundations of
the two major fields of Indian mathematics, *pati-ganita*
("mathematics of procedures," or algorithms) and *bijaganita* ("mathematics of seeds," or equations), which
roughly correspond to arithmetic (including mensuration)
and algebra, respectively. Chapter 12 is simply named
"Mathematics," probably because the "basic operations,"

such as arithmetic operations and proportions, and the "practical mathematics," such as mixture and series, treated there occupied the major part of the mathematics of Brahmagupta's milieu. He stressed the importance of these topics as a qualification for a mathematician, or calculator (*ganaka*). Chapter 18, "Pulverizer," is named after the first topic of the chapter, probably because no particular name for this area (algebra) existed yet.

Among his major accomplishments, Brahmagupta defined zero as the result of subtracting a number from itself and gave rules for arithmetical operations among negative numbers ("debts") and positive numbers ("property"), as well as surds. He also gave partial solutions to certain types of indeterminate equations of the second degree with two unknown variables. Perhaps his most famous result was a formula for the area of a cyclic quadrilateral (a four-sided polygon whose vertices all reside on some circle) and the length of its diagonals in terms of the length of its sides. He also gave a valuable interpolation formula for computing sines.

GIROLAMO CARDANO

(b. Sept. 24, 1501, Pavia, duchy of Milan [Italy]—d. Sept. 21, 1576, Rome)

Girolamo Cardano (known in English as Jerome Cardan) was an Italian physician, mathematician, and astrologer who gave the first clinical description of typhus fever and whose book *Ars magna* (*The Great Art*; or, *The Rules of Algebra*) is one of the cornerstones in the history of algebra.

Educated at the universities of Pavia and Padua, Cardano received his medical degree in 1526. In 1534 he moved to Milan, where he lived in great poverty until he became a lecturer in mathematics. Admitted to the college of physicians in 1539, he soon became rector. His fame as a physician grew rapidly, and many of Europe's crowned heads solicited his services; however, he valued his independence too much to become a court physician. In 1543 he accepted a professorship in medicine in Pavia.

Cardano was the most outstanding mathematician of his time. In 1539 he published two books on arithmetic embodying his popular lectures, the more important being *Practica arith-*

Girolamo Cardano. SSPL/Getty Images

metica et mensurandi singularis ("Practice of Mathematics and Individual Measurements"). His *Ars magna* (1545) contained the solution of the cubic equation, for which he was indebted to the Venetian mathematician Niccolò Tartaglia, and also the solution of the quartic equation found by Cardano's former servant, Lodovico Ferrari. His *Liber de ludo aleae* ("The Book on Games of Chance") presents the first systematic computations of probabilities, a century before Blaise Pascal and Pierre de Fermat. Cardano's popular fame was based largely on books dealing with scientific and philosophical questions, especially *De subtilitate rerum* ("The Subtlety of Things"), a collection of physical experiments and inventions, interspersed with anecdotes.

Cardano's favourite son, having married a disreputable girl, poisoned her and was executed in 1560. Cardano never recovered from the blow. From 1562 he was a professor in Bologna, but in 1570 he was suddenly arrested on the accusation of heresy. After several months in jail, he was permitted to abjure privately, but he lost his position and the right to publish books. Before his death he completed his autobiography, *De propria vita* (*The Book of My Life*).

DIOPHANTUS OF ALEXANDRIA
(fl. *c.* 250 CE)

Diophantus was a Greek mathematician, famous for his work in algebra.

What little is known of Diophantus's life is circumstantial. From the appellation "of Alexandria" it seems that he worked in the main scientific centre of the ancient Greek world. Because he is not mentioned before the 4th century, it seems likely that he flourished during the 3rd century. An arithmetic epigram from the *Anthologia Graeca* of late antiquity, purported to retrace some landmarks of his life (marriage at 33, birth of his son at 38, death of his son four years before his own at 84), may well be contrived. Two works have come down to us under his name, both incomplete. The first is a small fragment on polygonal numbers (a number is polygonal if that same number of dots can be arranged in the form of a regular polygon). The second, a large and extremely influential treatise upon which all the ancient and modern fame of Diophantus reposes, is his *Arithmetica*. Its historical importance is twofold: it is the first known work to employ algebra in a modern style, and it inspired the rebirth of number theory.

The *Arithmetica* begins with an introduction addressed to Dionysius — arguably St. Dionysius of Alexandria. After some generalities about numbers, Diophantus explains his symbolism—he uses symbols for the unknown (corresponding to our x) and its powers, positive or negative, as well as for some arithmetic operations—most of these symbols are clearly scribal abbreviations. This is the first and only occurrence of algebraic symbolism before the 15th century. After teaching multiplication of the powers of the unknown, Diophantus explains the multiplication of positive and negative terms and then how to reduce an equation to one with only positive terms (the standard form preferred in antiquity). With these preliminaries out of the way, Diophantus proceeds to the problems. Indeed, the *Arithmetica* is essentially a collection of problems with solutions, about 260 in the part still extant.

The introduction also states that the work is divided into 13 books. Six of these books were known in Europe in the late 15th century, transmitted in Greek by Byzantine scholars and numbered from I to VI. Four other books were discovered in 1968 in a 9th-century Arabic translation by Qusta ibn Luqa. However, the Arabic text lacks mathematical symbolism, and it appears to be based on a later Greek commentary—perhaps that of Hypatia (*c.* 370–415)—that diluted Diophantus's exposition. We now know that the numbering of the Greek books must be modified: the *Arithmetica* thus consists of Books I to III in Greek, Books IV to VII in Arabic, and, presumably, Books VIII to X in Greek (the former Greek Books IV to VI). Further renumbering is unlikely. It is fairly certain that the Byzantines knew only the six books they transmitted and the Arabs no more than Books I to VII in the commented version.

The problems of Book I are not characteristic, being mostly simple problems used to illustrate algebraic reckoning. The distinctive features of Diophantus's problems appear in the later books: they are indeterminate (having more than one solution), are of the second degree or are reducible to the second degree (the highest power on variable terms is 2, i.e., x^2), and end with the determination of a positive rational value for the unknown that will make a given algebraic expression a numerical square or sometimes a cube. (Throughout his book Diophantus uses "number" to refer to what are now called positive, rational numbers.; thus, a square number is the square of some positive, rational number.) Books II and III also teach general methods. In three problems of Book II it is explained how to represent: (1) any given square number as a sum of the squares of two rational numbers; (2) any given nonsquare number, which is the sum of two known squares, as a sum of two other squares; and (3) any given rational number as the difference of two squares. While the first and third problems are stated generally, the assumed knowledge of one solution in the second problem suggests that not every rational number is the sum of two squares. Diophantus later gives the condition for an integer: the given number must not contain any prime factor of the form $4n + 3$ raised to an odd power, where n is a non-negative integer. Such examples motivated the rebirth of number theory. Although Diophantus is typically satisfied to obtain one solution to a problem, he occasionally mentions in problems that an infinite number of solutions exists.

In Books IV to VII Diophantus extends basic methods such as those outlined above to problems of higher degrees that can be reduced to a binomial equation of the first or second degree. The prefaces to these books state that their purpose is to provide the reader with "experience and skill." While this recent discovery does not increase knowledge of Diophantus's mathematics, it does alter the appraisal of his pedagogical ability. Books VIII and IX (presumably Greek Books IV and V) solve more difficult problems, even if the basic methods remain the same. For instance, one problem involves decomposing a given integer into the sum of two squares that are arbitrarily close to one another. A similar problem involves decomposing a given integer into the sum of three squares; in it, Diophantus excludes the impossible case of integers of the form $8n + 7$ (again, n is a non-negative integer). Book X (presumably Greek Book VI) deals with right-angled triangles with rational sides and subject to various further conditions.

The contents of the three missing books of the *Arithmetica* can be surmised from the introduction, where — after saying that the reduction of a problem should "if possible" conclude with a binomial equation — Diophantus adds that he will "later on" treat the case of a trinomial equation, a promise not fulfilled in the extant part.

Although he had limited algebraic tools at his disposal, Diophantus managed to solve a great variety of problems, and the *Arithmetica* inspired Arabic mathematicians such as al-Karaji (*c.* 980–1030) to apply his methods. The most famous extension of Diophantus's work was by Pierre de Fermat (1601–65), the founder of modern number theory. In the margins of his copy of the *Arithmetica*, Fermat wrote various remarks, proposing new solutions, corrections, and generalizations of Diophantus's methods — as well as some conjectures such as Fermat's last theorem, which occupied mathematicians for generations to come. Indeterminate equations restricted to integral solutions have come to be known, though inappropriately, as Diophantine equations.

LODOVICO FERRARI

(b. Feb. 2, 1522, Bologna, Papal States [Italy] — d. Oct. 5, 1565, Bologna)

Italian mathematician Lodovico Ferrari (also spelled Ludovico Ferraro) was the first to find an algebraic solution to the biquadratic, or quartic, equation (an algebraic equation that contains the fourth power of the unknown quantity but no higher power).

From a poor family, Ferrari was taken into the service of the noted Italian mathematician Gerolamo Cardano as an errand boy at the age of 15. By attending Cardano's lectures, he learned Latin, Greek, and mathematics. In 1540 he succeeded Cardano as public mathematics lecturer in Milan, at which time he found the solution of the quartic equation, later published in Cardano's *Ars magna* (1545; "Great Art"). The publication of *Ars magna* brought Ferrari into a celebrated controversy with the noted Italian mathematician Niccolò Tartaglia over the solution of the cubic equation. After six printed challenges and counter-challenges, Ferrari and Tartaglia met in Milan on Aug. 10, 1548, for a public mathematical contest, of which Ferrari was declared the winner. This success brought him immediate fame, and he was deluged with offers for various positions. He accepted that from Cardinal Ercole Gonzaga, regent of Mantua, to become supervisor of tax assessments, an appointment that soon made him wealthy. Later, ill health and a quarrel with the cardinal forced him to give up his lucrative position. He then accepted a professorship in mathematics at the University of Bologna, where he died shortly thereafter.

SCIPIONE FERRO

(b. 1465, Bologna—d. 1526, Bologna, Papal States)

Scipione Ferro (also called Dal Ferro) was an Italian mathematician who is believed to have found a solution to the cubic equation $x^3 + px = q$ where p and q are positive numbers.

Ferro attended the University of Bologna and, in 1496, accepted a position at the university as a lecturer in arithmetic and geometry. He remained at the university until his death. Although none of his work survives, he is known to have influenced the study of fractions with irrational denominators.

AL-KARAJI

(b. *c.* 980, most likely Karaj, Persia, rather than Karkh, near Baghdad, Iraq—d. *c.* 1030)

Abu Bakr ibn Muhammad ibn al-Husayn al-Karaji was a mathematician and engineer who held an official position in Baghdad (*c.* 1010–1015), perhaps culminating in the position of vizier. During this time he wrote his three main works, *al-Fakhri fi'l-jabr wa'l-muqabala* ("Glorious on Algebra"), *al-Badi' fi'l-hisab* ("Wonderful on Calculation"), and *al-Kāfī fi'l-hisāb* ("Sufficient on Calculation"). A now lost work of his contained the first description of what later became known as Pascal's triangle.

Al-Karaji combined tradition and novelty in his mathematical exposition. Like his Arabic predecessors, he did not use symbolism—even writing numbers as words rather than using Indian numerals (except for large numbers and in numerical tables). However, with his writings Arabic algebra began to free itself from the early tradition of illustrating formulas and the resolutions of equations with geometric diagrams.

As part of his official duties, al-Karaji composed his *Sufficient*, an arithmetic textbook for civil servants on calculating with integers and fractions (in both base 10 and base 60), extracting square roots, and determining areas and volumes. He also composed a small and very elementary compendium of basic algebra.

The *Glorious* and the *Wonderful* are more advanced algebraic texts and contain a large collection of problems. In particular, the *Wonderful* contains a useful introduction to the basic algebraic methods of Diophantus of Alexandria (fl. *c.* 250).

Although much of his work was taken from others' writings, there is no doubt that al-Karaji was an able mathematician, and traces of his influence were frequent in the following centuries. However, the quality of his work was uneven. He seems to have worked too hastily at times, as he confessed in the closing words of the *Sufficient*.

After leaving Baghdad for Persia, al-Karaji wrote an engineering work on drilling wells and building aqueducts.

AL-KHWĀRIZMĪ

(b. *c.* 780, Baghdad, Iraq—d. *c.* 850)

Muḥammad ibn Mūsā al-Khwārizmī was a Muslim mathematician and astronomer whose major works introduced Hindu-Arabic numerals and the concepts of algebra into European mathematics. Latinized versions of his name and of his most famous book title live on in the terms *algorithm* and *algebra*.

Al-Khwārizmī lived in Baghdad, where he worked at the "House of Wisdom" (*Dar al-Hikma*) under the caliphate of al-Ma'mun. (The House of Wisdom acquired and translated scientific and philosophic treatises, particularly Greek, as well as publishing original research.) Al-Khwārizmī's work on elementary algebra, *al-Kitab al-mukhtasar fi hisab al-jabr wa'l-muqabala* ("The Compendious Book on Calculation by Completion and Balancing"), was translated into Latin in the 12th century, from which the title and term *Algebra* derives. *Algebra*, as was described in chapter 1, is a compilation of rules, together with demonstrations, for finding solutions of linear and quadratic equations based on intuitive geometric arguments—rather than the abstract notation now associated with the subject. Its systematic, demonstrative approach distinguishes it from earlier treatments of the subject. It also contains sections on calculating areas and volumes of geometric figures and on the use of algebra to solve inheritance problems according to proportions prescribed by Islamic law. Elements within the work can be traced from Babylonian mathematics of the early 2nd millennium BCE through Hellenistic, Hebrew, and Hindu treatises.

In the 12th century, a second work by al-Khwārizmī introduced Hindu-Arabic numerals and their arithmetic to the West. It is preserved only in a Latin translation, *Algoritmi de numero Indorum* ("Al-Khwarizmi Concerning the Hindu Art of Reckoning"). From the name of the author, rendered in Latin as *algoritmi*, originated the term *algorithm*.

A third major book was his *Kitab surat al-ard* ("The Image of the Earth"; translated as *Geography*), which presented the coordinates of localities in the known world based, ultimately, on those in the *Geography* of Ptolemy (fl. 127–145 CE) but with improved values for the length of the Mediterranean Sea and the location of cities in Asia and Africa. He also assisted in the construction of a world map for al-Ma'mun and participated in a project to determine the circumference of the Earth, which had long been known to be spherical, by measuring the length of a degree of a meridian through the plain of Sinjar in Iraq.

Finally, al-Khwārizmī also compiled a set of astronomical tables (*Zīj*), based on a variety of Hindu and Greek sources. This work included a table of sines, evidently for a circle of radius 150 units. Like his treatises on algebra and Hindu-Arabic numerals, this astronomical work (or an Andalusian revision thereof) was translated into Latin.

LIU HUI
(fl. *c.* 263 CE, China)

All that is known about the life of Chinese mathematician Liu Hui is that he lived in the northern Wei kingdom during the 3rd century CE. His fame rests on the commentary he completed in 263 on *Jiuzhang suanshu* (*The Nine Chapters on the Mathematical Art*)—a mathematical canon of the 1st century BCE or CE that played a similar role in the East to Euclid's *Elements* in the West. Liu's commentary on *The Nine Chapters* proved the correctness of its algorithms. These proofs are the earliest-known Chinese proofs in the contemporary sense. However, in contrast to authors of ancient Greek mathematical texts, Liu did not set out to prove theorems so much as to establish the correctness of algorithms. For example, he rigorously proved algorithms for determining the area of circles and the volume of pyramids by dissecting the regions into infinitely many pieces. He also proved algorithms for arithmetic and algebraic operations, such as adding fractions and solving systems of simultaneous linear equations.

An analysis of Liu's proofs reveals some recurring procedures. For instance, he regularly used what can be called algebraic proofs within an algorithmic context, perhaps a contribution to the emergence of this specific kind of proof in world mathematics. In all these cases, it appears that he aimed to show that a small number of fundamental operations underlie all the algorithms in *The Nine Chapters*, thereby reducing their diversity.

In his preface to the *The Nine Chapters*, Liu noted a gap in its procedures that did not allow one to tackle problems involving celestial distances. He thus appended surveying problems and algorithms that amounted to a kind of trigonometry to fill this gap. These problems were gathered, probably in the 7th century, in an independent book, *Haidao suanjing* ("Sea Island Mathematical Manual"), ascribed to him.

A certain philosophical perspective permeates the mathematical work of Liu. He quotes a great variety of ancient philosophical texts, such as the Confucian canons, prominently the *Yijing* (*I Ching; Book of Changes*); Daoist key texts, such as the *Zhuangzi*; and Mohist texts. Moreover, his commentary regularly echoes contemporary philosophical developments. It can be argued that he considered an algorithm to be that which, in mathematics, embodies the transformations that are at play everywhere in the cosmos—thus his philosophical reflections on mathematics related to the concept of "change" as a main topic of inquiry in China.

MAHAVIRA
(fl. *c.* 850, Karnataka, India)

Mahavira was an Indian mathematician who made significant contributions to the development of algebra.

All that is known about Mahavira's life is that he was a Jain (he perhaps took his name to honour the great Jainism reformer Mahavira [*c.* 599–527 BCE]) and that he wrote *Ganitasarasangraha* ("Compendium of the Essence of Mathematics") during the reign of Amoghavarsha (*c.* 814–878) of the Rashtrakuta dynasty. The work comprises more than 1,130 versified rules and examples divided in nine chapters: the first chapter for "terminology" and the rest for "mathematical procedures" such as basic operations, reductions of fractions, miscellaneous problems involving a linear or quadratic equation with one unknown, the rule of three (involving proportionality), mixture problems, geometric computations with plane figures, ditches (solids), and shadows (similar right-angled triangles).

At the beginning of his work, Mahavira stresses the importance of mathematics in both secular and religious life and in all kinds of disciplines, including love and cooking. While giving rules for zero and negative quantities, he explicitly states that a negative number has no square root because it is not a square (of any "real number"). Besides mixture problems (interest and proportions), he treats various types of linear and quadratic equations (where he admits two positive solutions) and improves on the methods of Aryabhata I (b. 476). He also treats various arithmetic and geometric, as well as complex, series. For rough computations, Mahavira used 3 as an approximation for π, while for more exact computations he used the traditional Jain value of 10. He also included rules for permutations and combinations and for the area of a conchlike plane figure (two unequal semicircles stuck together along their diameters), all traditional Jain topics.

QIN JIUSHAO
(b. c. 1202, Puzhou [modern Anyue, Sichuan province], China—d. c. 1261, Meizhou [modern Meixian, Guangdong province])

Qin Jiushao (in Wade-Giles spelling, Ch'in Chiu-Shao) was a Chinese mathematician who developed a method of solving simultaneous linear congruences.

In 1219 Qin joined the army as captain of a territorial volunteer unit and helped quash a local rebellion. In 1224–25 Qin studied astronomy and mathematics in the capital Lin'an (modern Hangzhou) with functionaries of the Imperial Astronomical Bureau and with an unidentified hermit. In 1233 Qin began his official mandarin (government) service. He interrupted his government career for three years beginning in 1244 because of his mother's death. During the mourning period, he wrote his only mathematical book, now known as *Shushu jiuzhang* (1247; "Mathematical Writings in Nine Sections"). He later rose to the position of provincial governor of Qiongzhou (in modern Hainan), but charges of corruption and bribery brought his dismissal in 1258. Contemporary authors mention his ambitious and cruel personality.

His book is divided into nine "categories," each containing nine problems related to calendrical computations, meteorology, surveying of fields, surveying of remote objects, taxation, fortification works, construction works, military affairs, and commercial affairs. Categories concern indeterminate analysis, calculation of the areas and volumes of plane and solid figures, proportions, calculation of interest, simultaneous linear equations, progressions, and solution of higher-degree polynomial equations in one unknown. Every problem is followed by a numerical answer, a general solution, and a description of the calculations performed with counting rods.

The two most important methods found in Qin's book are for the solution of simultaneous linear congruences $N \equiv r_1 \pmod{m_1} \equiv r_2 \pmod{m_2} \equiv \ldots \equiv r_n \pmod{m_n}$ and an algorithm for obtaining a numerical solution of higher-degree polynomial equations based on a process of successively better approximations. This method was rediscovered in Europe about 1802 and was known as the Ruffini-Horner method. Although Qin's is the earliest surviving description of this algorithm, most scholars believe that it was widely known in China before this time.

CLASSICAL ALGEBRAISTS (17TH–19TH CENTURIES)

NIELS HENRIK ABEL

(b. Aug. 5, 1802, island of Finnøy, near Stavanger, Nor.—d. April 6, 1829, Froland)

Norwegian mathematician Niels Henrik Abel was a pioneer in the development of several branches of modern mathematics.

Niels Henrik Abel, painting by Johan Gorbitz, 1826. Mathematics Institute, University of Oslo/The Abel Prize/The Norwegian Academy of Science and Letters

Abel's father was a poor Lutheran minister who moved his family to the parish of Gjerstad, near the town of Risør in southeast Norway, soon after Niels Henrik was born. In 1815 Niels entered the cathedral school in Oslo, where his mathematical talent was recognized in 1817 with the arrival of a new mathematics teacher, Bernt Michael Holmboe, who introduced him to the classics in mathematical literature and proposed original problems for him to solve. Abel studied the mathematical works of the 17th-century Englishman Sir Isaac Newton, the 18th-century German Leonhard Euler, and his contemporaries the Frenchman Joseph-Louis Lagrange and the German Carl Friedrich Gauss in preparation for his own research.

Abel's father died in 1820, leaving the family in straitened circumstances, but Holmboe contributed and raised funds that enabled Abel to enter the University of Christiania (Oslo) in 1821. Abel obtained a preliminary degree from the university in 1822 and continued his studies independently with further subsidies obtained by Holmboe.

Abel's first papers, published in 1823, were on functional equations and integrals. He was the first person to formulate and solve an integral equation. His friends urged the Norwegian government to grant him a fellowship for study in Germany and France. In 1824, while waiting for a royal decree to be issued, he published at his own expense his proof of the impossibility of solving algebraically the general equation of the fifth degree, which he hoped would bring him recognition. He sent the pamphlet to Gauss, who dismissed it, failing to recognize that the famous problem had indeed been settled.

Abel spent the winter of 1825–26 with Norwegian friends in Berlin, where he met August Leopold Crelle, civil engineer and self-taught enthusiast of mathematics, who became his close friend and mentor. With Abel's warm encouragement, Crelle founded the *Journal für die reine und angewandte Mathematik* ("Journal for Pure and Applied Mathematics"), commonly known as *Crelle's Journal*. The first volume (1826) contains papers by Abel, including a more elaborate version of his work on the quintic equation. Other papers dealt with equation theory, calculus, and theoretical mechanics. Later volumes presented Abel's theory of elliptic functions, which are complex functions that generalize the usual trigonometric functions.

In 1826 Abel went to Paris, then the world centre for mathematics, where he called on the foremost mathematicians and completed a major paper on the theory of integrals of algebraic functions. His central result, known as Abel's theorem, is the basis for the later theory of Abelian integrals and Abelian functions—a generalization of elliptic function theory to functions of several variables. However, Abel's visit to Paris was unsuccessful in securing him an appointment, and the memoir he submitted to the French Academy of Sciences was lost.

Abel returned to Norway heavily in debt and suffering from tuberculosis. He subsisted by tutoring, supplemented by a small grant from the University of Christiania and, beginning in 1828, by a temporary teaching position. His poverty and ill health did not decrease his production. He wrote a great number of papers during this period, principally on equation theory and elliptic functions. Among them are the theory of polynomial equations with Abelian groups. He rapidly developed the theory of elliptic functions in competition with the German Carl Gustav Jacobi. By this time Abel's fame had spread to all mathematical centres, and strong efforts were made to secure a suitable position for him by a group from the French Academy, who addressed King Bernadotte of Norway-Sweden. Crelle also worked to secure a professorship for him in Berlin.

In the fall of 1828, Abel became seriously ill, and his condition deteriorated on a sled trip at Christmastime to visit his fiancée at Froland, where he died. The French Academy published his memoir in 1841.

Bernhard Bolzano

(b. Oct. 5, 1781, Prague, Bohemia, Austrian Habsburg domain [now in Czech Republic]—d. Dec. 18, 1848, Prague)

Bohemian mathematician and theologian Bernhard Bolzano provided a more detailed proof for the binomial theorem in 1816 and suggested the means of distinguishing between finite and infinite classes.

Bolzano graduated from the University of Prague as an ordained priest in 1805 and was immediately appointed professor of philosophy and religion at the university. Within a matter of years, however, Bolzano alienated many faculty and church leaders with his teachings of the social waste of militarism and the needlessness of war. He urged a total reform of the educational, social, and economic systems that would direct the nation's interests toward peace rather than toward armed conflict between nations. Upon his refusal to recant his beliefs, Bolzano was dismissed from the university in 1819 and at that point devoted his energies to his writings on social, religious, philosophical, and mathematical matters.

Bolzano held advanced views on logic, mathematical variables, limits, and continuity. In his studies of the physical aspects of force, space, and time, he proposed theories counter to those suggested by the German philosopher Immanuel Kant. Much of his work remained unpublished during his lifetime and did not have wide impact until the late 19th and early 20th centuries, when a number of his conclusions were arrived at independently.

Bolzano's published works include *Der binomische Lehrsatz* (1816; "The Binomial Theorem"), *Rein analytischer Beweis* (1817; "Pure Analytic Proof"), *Functionenlehre* (1834; "Functions Model"), *Wissenschaftslehre,* 4 vol. (1834; "Scientific Model"), *Versuch einer neuen Darstellung der Logik,* 4 vol. (1837; "An Attempt at a New Presentation of Logic"), and *Paradoxien des Unendlichen* (1851; "Paradoxes of Infinity").

GEORGE BOOLE

(b. Nov. 2, 1815, Lincoln, Lincolnshire, Eng.—d. Dec. 8, 1864, Ballintemple, County Cork, Ire.)

English mathematician George Boole helped establish modern symbolic logic. His algebra of logic, now called Boolean algebra, is basic to the design of digital computer circuits.

Boole was given his first lessons in mathematics by his father, a tradesman, who also taught him to make optical instruments. Aside from his father's help and a few years at local schools, however, Boole was self-taught in mathematics. When his father's business declined, George had to work to support the family. From the age of 16, he taught in village schools in the West Riding of Yorkshire, and he opened his own school in Lincoln when he was 20. During scant leisure time, he read mathematics journals in the Lincoln's Mechanics Institute. There he also read Isaac Newton's *Principia*, Pierre-Simon Laplace's *Traité de mécanique céleste*, and Joseph-Louis Lagrange's *Mécanique analytique* and began to solve advanced problems in algebra.

Boole submitted a stream of original papers to the new *Cambridge Mathematical Journal*, beginning in 1839 with his "Researches on the Theory of Analytical Transformations." These papers were on differential equations and the algebraic problem of linear transformation, emphasizing the concept of invariance. In 1844, in an important paper in the *Philosophical Transactions of the Royal Society* for which he was awarded the Royal Society's first gold medal for mathematics, he discussed how methods of algebra and calculus might be combined. Boole soon saw that his algebra could also be applied in logic.

Developing novel ideas on logical method and confident in the symbolic reasoning he had derived from his mathematical investigations, he published in 1847 a pamphlet, "Mathematical Analysis of Logic," in which he argued persuasively that logic should be allied with mathematics, not philosophy. He won the admiration of the English logician Augustus De Morgan, who published *Formal Logic* the same year. On the basis of his publications, Boole in 1849 was appointed professor of mathematics at Queen's College, County Cork, even though he had no university degree. In 1854 he published *An Investigation into the Laws of Thought, on Which Are Founded the Mathematical Theories of Logic and Probabilities*, which he regarded as a mature statement of his ideas. The next year he married Mary Everest, niece of Sir George Everest, for whom the mountain is named. The Booles had five daughters.

One of the first Englishmen to write on logic, Boole pointed out the analogy between algebraic symbols and those that can represent logical forms and syllogisms, showing how the symbols of quantity can be separated from those of operation. With Boole's influence, in 1847 and 1854 the algebra of logic, or what is now called Boolean algebra, began. Boole's original and remarkable general symbolic method of logical inference, fully stated in *Laws of Thought* (1854), enables one, given any propositions involving any number of terms, to draw conclusions that are logically contained in the premises. He also attempted a general method in probabilities, which would make it possible from the given probabilities of any system of events to determine the consequent probability of any other event logically connected with the given events.

In 1857 Boole was elected a fellow of the Royal Society. The influential *Treatise on Differential Equations* appeared in 1859 and was followed the next year by its sequel, *Treatise on the Calculus of Finite Differences*. Used as textbooks for many years, these works embody an elaboration of Boole's more important discoveries. Boole's abstruse reasoning has led to applications of which he never dreamed: for example, telephone switching and electronic computers use binary digits and logical elements that rely on Boolean logic for their design and operation.

ARTHUR CAYLEY

(b. Aug. 16, 1821, Richmond, Surrey, Eng. — d. Jan. 26, 1895, Cambridge, Cambridgeshire)

Arthur Cayley was an English mathematician and leader of the British school of pure mathematics that emerged in the 19th century.

Although Cayley was born in England, his first seven years were spent in St. Petersburg, Russia, where his parents lived in a trading community affiliated with the Muscovy Company. On the family's permanent return to England in 1828, he was educated at a small private school in Blackheath, followed by the three-year course at King's College, London. Cayley entered Trinity College, Cambridge, in 1838 and emerged as the champion student of 1842, the "Senior Wrangler" of his year. A fellowship enabled him to stay on at Cambridge, but in 1846 he left the university to study the law at Lincoln's Inn in London. Cayley practised law in London from 1849 until 1863, while writing more than 300 mathematical papers in his spare time. In recognition of his mathematical work, he was elected to the Royal Society in 1852 and presented with its Royal Medal seven years later. In 1863 he accepted the Sadleirian professorship in mathematics at Cambridge — sacrificing his legal career in order to devote himself full-time to mathematical research. In that same year, he married Susan Moline, the daughter of a country banker.

Cayley's manner was diffident but decisive. He was a capable administrator who quietly and effectively discharged his academic duties. He was an early supporter of women's higher education and steered Newnham College, Cambridge (founded in 1871), during the 1880s. Despite aiding the careers of a few students who naturally took to pure mathematics, Cayley never established a full-fledged research school of mathematics at Cambridge.

In mathematics Cayley was an individualist. He handled calculations and symbolic manipulations with formidable skill, guided by a deep intuitive understanding of mathematical theories and their interconnections. His ability to keep abreast of current work while seeing the wider view enabled him to perceive important trends and to make valuable suggestions for further investigation.

Cayley made important contributions to the algebraic theory of curves and surfaces, group theory, linear algebra, graph theory, combinatorics, and elliptic functions. He formalized the theory of matrices. Among Cayley's most important papers were his series of 10 "Memoirs on Quantics" (1854–78). A quantic, known today as an algebraic form, is a polynomial with the same total degree for each term. For example, every term in the following polynomial has a total degree of 3: $x^3 + 7x^2y - 5xy^2 + y^3$.

Alongside work produced by his friend James Joseph Sylvester, Cayley's study of various properties of forms that are unchanged (invariant) under some transformation, such as rotating or translating the coordinate axes, established a branch of algebra known as invariant theory.

In geometry Cayley concentrated his attention on analytic geometry, for which he naturally employed invariant theory. For example, he showed that the order of points formed by intersecting lines is always invariant, regardless of any spatial transformation. In 1859 Cayley outlined a notion of distance in projective geometry (a projective metric), and he was one of the first to realize that Euclidean geometry is a special case of projective geometry—an insight that reversed current thinking. Ten years later, Cayley's projective metric provided a key for understanding the relationship between the various types of non-Euclidean geometries.

While Cayley was essentially a pure mathematician, he also pursued mechanics and astronomy. He was active in lunar studies and produced two widely praised reports on dynamics (1857, 1862). Cayley had an extraordinarily prolific career, producing almost a thousand mathematical papers. His habit was to embark on long studies punctuated by rapidly written "bulletins from the front." Cayley wrote French effortlessly and often published in Continental journals. As a young graduate at Cambridge, he was inspired by the work of the mathematician Karl Jacobi (1804–51), and in 1876 Cayley published his only book, *An Elementary Treatise on Elliptic Functions*, which drew out this widely studied subject from Jacobi's point of view.

Cayley was awarded numerous honours, including the Copley Medal in 1882 by the Royal Society. At various times he was president of the Cambridge Philosophical Society, the London Mathematical Society, the British Association for the Advancement of Science, and the Royal Astronomical Society.

ÉVARISTE GALOIS

(b. Oct. 25, 1811, Bourg-la-Reine, near Paris, France—d. May 31, 1832, Paris)

Évariste Galois, detail of an engraving, 1848, after a drawing by Alfred Galois. Bibliotheque Nationale, Paris, France/The Bridgeman Art Library/ Getty Images

French mathematician Évariste Galois is famous for his contributions to the part of higher algebra now known as group theory. His theory provided a solution to the long-standing question of determining when an algebraic equation can be solved by radicals (a solution containing square roots, cube roots, and so on, but no trigonometry functions or other nonalgebraic functions).

Galois was the son of Nicolas-Gabriel

Galois, an important citizen in the Paris suburb of Bourg-la-Reine. In 1815, during the Hundred Days regime that followed Napoleon's escape from Elba, his father was elected mayor. Galois was educated at home until 1823, when he entered the Collège Royal de Louis-le-Grand. There his education languished at the hands of mediocre and uninspiring teachers. But his mathematical ability blossomed when he began to study the works of his countrymen Adrien-Marie Legendre on geometry and Joseph-Louis Lagrange on algebra.

Under the guidance of Louis Richard, one of his teachers at Louis-le-Grand, Galois's further study of algebra led him to take up the question of the solution of algebraic equations. Mathematicians for a long time had used explicit formulas, involving only rational operations and extractions of roots, for the solution of equations up to degree four, but they had been defeated by equations of degree five and higher. In 1770 Lagrange took the novel but decisive step of treating the roots of an equation as objects in their own right and studying permutations (a change in an ordered arrangement) of them. In 1799 the Italian mathematician Paolo Ruffini attempted to prove the impossibility of solving the general quintic equation by radicals. Ruffini's effort was not wholly successful, but in 1824 the Norwegian mathematician Niels Abel gave a correct proof.

Galois, stimulated by Lagrange's ideas and initially unaware of Abel's work, began searching for the necessary and sufficient conditions under which an algebraic equation of any degree can be solved by radicals. His method was to analyze the "admissible" permutations of the roots of the equation. His key discovery, brilliant and highly imaginative, was that solvability by radicals is possible if and only if the group of automorphisms (functions that take elements of a set to other elements of the set while preserving algebraic operations) is solvable, which means essentially that the group can be broken down into simple "prime-order" constituents that always have an easily understood structure. The term *solvable* is used because of this connection with solvability by radicals. Thus, Galois perceived that solving equations of the quintic and beyond required a wholly different kind of treatment than that required for quadratic, cubic, and quartic equations. Although Galois used the concept of group and other associated concepts, such as coset and subgroup, he did not actually define these concepts, and he did not construct a rigorous formal theory.

While still at Louis-le-Grand, Galois published one minor paper, but his life was soon overtaken by disappointment and tragedy. A memoir on the solvability of algebraic equations that he had submitted in 1829 to the French Academy of Sciences was lost by Augustin-Louis Cauchy. He failed in two attempts (1827 and 1829) to gain admission to the École Polytechnique, the leading school of French mathematics — his second attempt marred by a disastrous encounter with an oral examiner. Also in 1829 his father, after bitter clashes with conservative elements in his hometown, committed suicide. The same year, Galois enrolled as a student teacher in the less prestigious École Normale Supérieure and turned to political activism. Meanwhile he continued his research, and in the spring of 1830, he had three short articles published. At the same time, he rewrote the paper that had been lost and presented it again to the Academy — but for a second time the manuscript went astray. Jean-Baptiste-Joseph Fourier took it home but died a few weeks later, and the manuscript was never found.

The July Revolution of 1830 sent the last Bourbon monarch, Charles X, into exile. But republicans were deeply disappointed when yet another king, Louis-Philippe, ascended the throne—even though he was the "Citizen King" and wore the tricoloured flag of the French Revolution. When Galois wrote a vigorous article expressing pro-republican views, he was promptly expelled from the École Normale Supérieure. Subsequently, he was arrested twice for republican activities. He was acquitted the first time but spent six months in prison on the second charge. In 1831 he presented his memoir on the theory of equations for the third time to the Academy. This time it was returned but with a negative report. The judges, who included Siméon-Denis Poisson, did not understand what Galois had written and (incorrectly) believed that it contained a significant error. They had been quite unable to accept Galois's original ideas and revolutionary mathematical methods.

The circumstances that led to Galois's death in a duel in Paris are not altogether clear, but recent scholarship suggests that it was at his own insistence that the duel was staged and fought to look like a police ambush. In any case, anticipating his death the night before the duel, Galois hastily wrote a scientific last testament addressed to his friend Auguste Chevalier in which he summarized his work and included some new theorems and conjectures.

Galois's manuscripts, with annotations by Joseph Liouville, were published in 1846 in the *Journal de Mathématiques Pures et Appliquées*. But it was not until 1870, with the publication of Camille Jordan's *Traité des Substitutions*, that group theory became a fully established part of mathematics.

CARL FRIEDRICH GAUSS

(b. April 30, 1777, Brunswick [Germany]—d. Feb. 23, 1855, Göttingen, Hanover)

German mathematician Carl Friedrich Gauss is generally regarded as one of the greatest mathematicians of all time for his contributions to number theory, geometry, probability theory, geodesy, planetary astronomy, the theory of functions, and potential theory (including electromagnetism).

Gauss was was born Johann Friedrich Carl Gauss, the only child of poor parents. He was rare among mathematicians in that he was a calculating prodigy, and he retained the ability to do elaborate calculations in his head most of his life. Impressed by this ability and by his gift for languages, his teachers and his devoted mother recommended him to the duke of Brunswick in 1791, who granted him financial assistance to continue his education locally and then to study mathematics at the University of Göttingen from 1795 to 1798. Gauss's pioneering work gradually established him as the era's preeminent mathematician, first in the German-speaking world and then farther afield, although he remained a remote and aloof figure.

Gauss's first significant discovery, in 1792, was that a regular polygon of 17 sides can be constructed by ruler and compass alone. Its significance lies not in the result but in the proof, which rested on a profound analysis of the factorization of polynomial equations and opened the door to later ideas of Galois theory. His doctoral thesis of 1797 gave a proof of the fundamental theorem of algebra: every polynomial equation with real or complex coefficients has as many roots (solutions) as its degree (the highest power of the variable). Gauss's proof, though not wholly convincing, was remarkable for its critique of earlier attempts. Gauss later gave three more proofs of this major result, the last on the 50th anniversary of the first, which shows the importance he attached to the topic.

Gauss's recognition as a truly remarkable talent, though, resulted from two major publications in 1801. Foremost was his publication of the first systematic textbook on algebraic number theory, *Disquisitiones*

Arithmeticae. This book begins with the first account of modular arithmetic, gives a thorough account of the solutions of quadratic polynomials in two variables in integers, and ends with the theory of factorization mentioned above. This choice of topics and its natural generalizations set the agenda in number theory for much of the 19th century, and Gauss's continuing interest in the subject spurred much research, especially in German universities.

The second publication was his rediscovery of the asteroid Ceres. Its original discovery, by the Italian astronomer Giuseppe Piazzi in 1800, had caused a sensation, but it vanished behind the Sun before enough observations could be taken to calculate its orbit with sufficient accuracy to know where it would reappear. Many astronomers competed for the honour of finding it again, but Gauss won. His success rested on a novel method for dealing with errors in observations, today called the method of least squares. Thereafter Gauss worked for many years as an astronomer and published a major work on the computation of orbits—the numerical side of such work was much less onerous for him than for most people. As an intensely loyal subject of the duke of Brunswick—and, after 1807 when he returned to Göttingen as an astronomer, of the duke of Hanover—Gauss felt that the work was socially valuable.

Similar motives led Gauss to accept the challenge of surveying the territory of Hanover, and he was often out in the field in charge of the observations. The project, which lasted from 1818 to 1832, encountered numerous difficulties, but it led to a number of advancements. One was Gauss's invention of the heliotrope (an instrument that reflects the Sun's rays in a focused beam that can be observed from several miles away), which improved the accuracy of the observations. Another was his discovery of a way of formulating the concept of the curvature of a surface. Gauss showed that there is an intrinsic measure of curvature that is not altered if the surface is bent without being stretched. For example, a circular cylinder and a flat sheet of paper have the same intrinsic curvature, which is why exact copies of figures on the cylinder can be made on the paper (as, for example, in printing). But a sphere and a plane have different curvatures, which is why no completely accurate flat map of the Earth can be made.

Gauss published works on number theory, the mathematical theory of map construction, and many other subjects. In the 1830s he became interested in terrestrial magnetism and participated in the first worldwide survey of the Earth's magnetic field (to measure it, he invented the magnetometer). With his Göttingen colleague, the physicist Wilhelm Weber, he made the first electric telegraph, but a certain parochialism prevented him from pursuing the invention energetically. Instead, he drew important mathematical consequences from this work for what is today called potential theory, an important branch of mathematical physics arising in the study of electromagnetism and gravitation.

Gauss also wrote on cartography, the theory of map projections. For his study of angle-preserving maps, he was awarded the prize of the Danish Academy of Sciences in 1823. This work came close to suggesting that complex functions of a complex variable are generally angle-preserving, but Gauss stopped short of making that fundamental insight explicit, leaving it for Bernhard Riemann, who had a deep appreciation of Gauss's work. Gauss also had other unpublished insights into the nature of complex functions and their integrals, some of which he divulged to friends.

In fact, Gauss often withheld publication of his discoveries. As a student at Göttingen, he began to doubt the a priori truth of Euclidean geometry and suspected that its truth might be empirical. For this to be the case, there must exist an alternative geometric description of space. Rather than publish such a description, Gauss confined himself to criticizing various a priori defenses of Euclidean geometry. It would seem that he was gradually convinced that there exists a logical alternative to Euclidean geometry. However, when the Hungarian János Bolyai and the Russian Nikolay Lobachevsky published their accounts of a new, non-Euclidean geometry about 1830, Gauss failed to give a coherent account of his own ideas. It is possible to draw these ideas together into an impressive whole, in which his concept of intrinsic curvature plays a central role, but Gauss never did this. Some have attributed this failure to his innate conservatism, others to his incessant inventiveness that always drew him on to the next new idea, still others to his failure to find a central idea that would govern geometry once Euclidean geometry was no longer unique. All these explanations have some merit, though none has enough to be the whole explanation.

Another topic on which Gauss largely concealed his ideas from his contemporaries was elliptic functions. He published an account in 1812 of an interesting infinite series, and he wrote but did not publish an account of the differential equation that the infinite series satisfies. He showed that the series, called the hypergeometric series, can be used to define many familiar and many new functions. But by then he knew how to use the differential equation to produce a very general theory of elliptic functions and to free the theory entirely from its origins in the theory of elliptic integrals. This was a major breakthrough, because, as Gauss had discovered in the 1790s, the theory of elliptic functions naturally treats them as complex-valued functions of a complex variable, but the contemporary theory of complex integrals was utterly inadequate for the task. When some of this theory was published by the Norwegian Niels Abel and the German Carl Jacobi about 1830, Gauss commented to a friend that Abel had come one-third of the way. This was accurate, but it is a sad measure of Gauss's personality in that he still withheld publication.

Gauss delivered less than he might have in a variety of other ways also. The University of Göttingen was small, and he did not seek to enlarge it or to bring in extra students. Toward the end of his life, mathematicians of the calibre of Richard Dedekind and Riemann passed through Göttingen, and he was helpful, but contemporaries compared his writing style to thin gruel: it is clear and sets high standards for rigour, but it lacks motivation and can be slow and wearing to follow. He corresponded with many, but not all, of the people rash enough to write to him, but he did little to support them in public. A rare exception was when Lobachevsky was attacked by other Russians for his ideas on non-Euclidean geometry. Gauss taught himself enough Russian to follow the controversy and proposed Lobachevsky for the Göttingen Academy of Sciences. In contrast, Gauss wrote a letter to Bolyai telling him that he had already discovered everything that Bolyai had just published.

After Gauss's death in 1855, the discovery of so many novel ideas among his unpublished papers extended his influence well into the remainder of the century. Acceptance of non-Euclidean geometry had not come with the original work of Bolyai and Lobachevsky, but it came instead with the almost simultaneous publication of Riemann's general ideas about geometry, the Italian Eugenio Beltrami's explicit and rigorous account of it, and Gauss's private notes and correspondence.

SIR WILLIAM ROWAN HAMILTON
(b. Aug. 3/4, 1805, Dublin, Ire.—d. Sept. 2, 1865, Dublin)

Sir William Rowan Hamilton was an Irish mathematician who contributed to the development of optics, dynamics, and algebra—in particular, discovering the algebra of quaternions. His work proved significant for the development of quantum mechanics.

Hamilton was the son of a solicitor. He was educated by his uncle, James Hamilton, an Anglican priest with whom he lived from before the age of three until he entered college. An aptitude for languages was soon apparent. At five he was already making progress with

William Hamilton. Hulton Archive/ Getty Images

Latin, Greek, and Hebrew, broadening his studies to include Arabic, Sanskrit, Persian, Syriac, French, and Italian before he was 12.

Hamilton was proficient in arithmetic at an early age. But a serious interest in mathematics was awakened on reading the *Analytic Geometry of Bartholomew Lloyd* at the age of 16. (Before that, his acquaintance with mathematics was limited to Euclid, sections of Isaac Newton's *Principia*, and introductory textbooks on algebra and optics.) Further reading included works of the French mathematicians Pierre-Simon Laplace and Joseph-Louis Lagrange.

Hamilton entered Trinity College, Dublin, in 1823. He excelled as an undergraduate, not only in mathematics and physics but also in classics, while he continued with his own mathematical investigations. A substantial paper of his on optics was accepted for publication by the Royal Irish Academy in 1827. In the same year, while still an undergraduate, Hamilton was appointed professor of astronomy at Trinity College and Royal Astronomer of Ireland. His home thereafter was at Dunsink Observatory, a few miles outside Dublin.

Hamilton was deeply interested in literature and metaphysics, and he wrote poetry throughout his life. While touring England in 1827, he visited William Wordsworth. A friendship was immediately established, and they corresponded often thereafter. Hamilton also admired the poetry and metaphysical writings of Samuel Taylor Coleridge, whom he visited in 1832. Hamilton and Coleridge were both heavily influenced by the philosophical writings of Immanuel Kant.

Hamilton's first published mathematical paper, "Theory of Systems of Rays," begins by proving that a system of light rays filling a region of space can be focused down to a single point by a suitably curved mirror if and only if those light rays are orthogonal to some series of surfaces. Moreover, the latter property is preserved under reflection in any number of mirrors. Hamilton's innovation was to associate with such a system of rays a characteristic function, constant on each of the surfaces to which the rays are orthogonal, which he employed in the mathematical investigation of the foci and caustics of reflected light.

The theory of the characteristic function of an optical system was further developed in three supplements. In the third of these, the characteristic function depends on the Cartesian coordinates of two points (initial and final) and measures the time taken for light to travel through the optical system from one to the other. If the form of this function is known, then basic properties of the optical system (such as the directions of the emergent rays) can easily be obtained. In applying his methods in 1832 to the study of the propagation of light in anisotropic media, in which the speed of light is dependent on the direction and polarization of the ray, Hamilton was led to a remarkable prediction: if a single ray of light is incident at certain angles on a face of a biaxial crystal (such as aragonite), then the refracted light will form a hollow cone.

Hamilton's colleague Humphrey Lloyd, professor of natural philosophy at Trinity College, sought to verify this prediction experimentally. Lloyd had difficulty obtaining a crystal of aragonite of sufficient size and purity, but eventually he was able to observe this phenomenon of conical refraction. This discovery excited considerable interest within the scientific community and established the reputations of both Hamilton and Lloyd.

From 1833 onward, Hamilton adapted his optical methods to the study of problems in dynamics. Out of laborious preparatory work emerged an elegant theory, associating a characteristic function with any system of attracting or repelling point particles. If the form of this function is known, then the solutions of the equations of motion of the system can easily be obtained. Hamilton's two major papers "On a General Method in Dynamics" were published in 1834 and 1835. In the second of these, the equations of motion of a dynamical system are expressed in a particularly elegant form (Hamilton's equations of motion). Hamilton's approach was further refined by the German mathematician Carl Jacobi, and its significance became apparent in the development of celestial mechanics and quantum mechanics. Hamiltonian mechanics underlies contemporary mathematical research in symplectic geometry (a field of research in algebraic geometry) and the theory of dynamical systems.

In 1835 Hamilton was knighted by the lord lieutenant of Ireland in the course of a meeting in Dublin of the

British Association for the Advancement of Science. Hamilton served as president of the Royal Irish Academy from 1837 to 1846.

Hamilton had a deep interest in the fundamental principles of algebra. His views on the nature of real numbers were set forth in a lengthy essay, "On Algebra as the Science of Pure Time." Complex numbers were then represented as "algebraic couples"—i.e., ordered pairs of real numbers, with appropriately defined algebraic operations. For many years Hamilton sought to construct a theory of triplets, analogous to the couplets of complex numbers, that would be applicable to the study of three-dimensional geometry. Then, on Oct. 16, 1843, while walking with his wife beside the Royal Canal on his way to Dublin, Hamilton suddenly realized that the solution lay not in triplets but in quadruplets, which could produce a noncommutative four-dimensional algebra, the algebra of quaternions. Thrilled by his inspiration, he stopped to carve the fundamental equations of this algebra on a stone of a bridge they were passing.

Hamilton devoted the last 22 years of his life to the development of the theory of quaternions and related systems. For him, quaternions were a natural tool for the investigation of problems in three-dimensional geometry. Many basic concepts and results in vector analysis have their origin in Hamilton's papers on quaternions. A substantial book, *Lectures on Quaternions*, was published in 1853, but it failed to achieve much influence among mathematicians and physicists. A longer treatment, *Elements of Quaternions*, remained unfinished at the time of his death.

In 1856 Hamilton investigated closed paths along the edges of a dodecahedron (one of the Platonic solids) that visit each vertex exactly once. In graph theory such paths are known today as Hamiltonian circuits.

CHARLES HERMITE

(b. Dec. 24, 1822, Dieuze, France — d. Jan. 14, 1901, Paris)

Charles Hermite was a French mathematician whose work in the theory of functions included the application of elliptic functions to provide the first solution to the general equation of the fifth degree, the quintic equation.

Although Hermite had proved himself a creative mathematician at the age of 20, his difficulty in passing his formal examinations forced him to devote five of his most productive years to preparing for his examination for the bachelor of science degree, which he obtained in 1848. He was given a minor teaching position at the École Polytechnique, Paris, before being appointed to the Collège de France, Paris, in the same year. It was not until 1869, with his appointment as professor at the École Normale, Paris, that he attained a position commensurate with his ability. In 1870 he became professor of higher algebra at the Sorbonne.

In 1873 Hermite published the first proof that e is a transcendental number; i.e., it is not the root of any algebraic equation with rational coefficients.

Hermite was a major figure in the development of the theory of algebraic forms, the arithmetical theory of quadratic forms, and the theories of elliptic and Abelian functions. He first studied the representation of integers in what are now called Hermitian forms. His famous solution of the general quintic equation appeared in *Sur la résolution de l'équation du cinquième degré* (1858; "On the Solution of the Equation of the Fifth Degree"). Many late 19th-century mathematicians first gained recognition for their work largely through the encouragement and publicity supplied by Hermite.

FELIX KLEIN

(b. April 25, 1849, Düsseldorf, Prussia [Ger.] — d. June 22, 1925, Göttingen, Ger.)

Christian Felix Klein was a German mathematician whose unified view of geometry as the study of the properties of a space that are invariant under a given group of transformations, known as the *Erlanger Programm*, profoundly influenced mathematical developments.

As a student at the University of Bonn (Ph.D., 1868), Klein worked closely with the physicist and geometer Julius Plücker (1801–68). After Plücker's death, he worked with the geometer Alfred Clebsch (1833–72), who headed the mathematics department at the University of Göttingen. On Clebsch's recommendation, Klein was appointed professor of mathematics at the University of Erlangen (1872–75), where he set forth the views contained in his *Erlanger Programm*. These ideas reflected his close collaboration with the Norwegian mathematician Sophus Lie, whom he met in Berlin in 1869. Before the outbreak of the Franco-German War in July 1870, they were together in Paris developing their early ideas on the role of transformation groups in geometry and on the theory of differential equations.

Klein later taught at the Institute of Technology in Munich (1875–80) and then at the Universities of Leipzig (1880–86) and Göttingen (1886–1913). From 1874 he was the editor of *Mathematische Annalen* ("Annals of Mathematics"), one of the world's leading mathematics journals, and from 1895 he supervised the great *Encyklopädie der mathematischen Wissenschaften mit Einschluss iher Anwendungen* ("Encyclopedia of Pure and Applied Mathematics"). His works on elementary mathematics, including *Elementarmathematik vom höheren Standpunkte aus* (1908; "Elementary Mathematics from an Advanced

Standpoint"), reached a wide public. His technical papers were collected in *Gesammelte Mathematische Abhandlungen*, 3 vol., (1921–23; "Collected Mathematical Treatises").

Beyond his own work, Klein made his greatest impact on mathematics as the principal architect of the modern community of mathematicians at Göttingen, which emerged as one of the world's leading research centres under Klein and David Hilbert (1862–1943) during the period from 1900 to 1914. After Klein's retirement, Richard Courant (1888–1972) gradually assumed Klein's role as the organizational leader of this still vibrant community.

LEOPOLD KRONECKER

(b. Dec. 7, 1823, Liegnitz, Prussia [now Legnica, Pol.] — d. Dec. 29, 1891, Berlin, Ger.)

Leopold Kronecker was a German mathematician whose primary contributions were in the theory of equations and higher algebra.

Kronecker acquired a passion for number theory from Ernst Kummer, his instructor in mathematics at the Liegnitz Gymnasium, and earned his doctor's degree at the University of Berlin with a dissertation (1845) on those special complex units that appear in certain algebraic number fields. He managed the family mercantile and land business until age 30, when he was financially able to retire. While in business he pursued mathematics as a recreation. From 1861 to 1883, Kronecker lectured at the University of Berlin, and in 1883 he succeeded Kummer as professor there.

Kronecker was primarily an arithmetician and algebraist. His major contributions were in elliptic functions, the theory of algebraic equations, and the theory of algebraic numbers. In the last field, he created an alternative to the theory of his fellow countryman Julius Dedekind. Kronecker's theory of algebraic magnitudes (1882) presents a part of this theory. His philosophy of mathematics, however, seems destined to outlast his more technical contributions. He was the first to doubt the significance of nonconstructive existence proofs (proofs that show something must exist, often by using a proof through contradiction, but that give no method of producing them), and for many years he carried on a polemic against the analytic school of the German mathematician Karl Weierstrass concerning these proofs and other points of classical analysis. Kronecker joined Weierstrass in approving the universal arithmetization of analysis, but he insisted that all mathematics should be reduced to the positive whole numbers.

ERNST EDUARD KUMMER

(b. Jan. 29, 1810, Sorau, Brandenburg, Prussia [Ger.] — d. May 14, 1893, Berlin)

Ernst Eduard Kummer was a German mathematician whose introduction of ideal numbers, which are defined as a special subgroup of a ring, extended the fundamental theorem of arithmetic (unique factorization of every integer into a product of primes) to complex number fields.

After teaching in *Gymnasium* 1 year at Sorau and 10 years at Liegnitz, Kummer became professor of mathematics at the University of Breslau (now Wrocław, Pol.) in 1842. In 1855 he succeeded Peter Gustav Lejeune Dirichlet as professor of mathematics at the University of Berlin, at the same time also becoming a professor at the Berlin War College.

In 1843 Kummer showed Dirichlet an attempted proof of Fermat's last theorem, which states that the formula $x^n + y^n = z^n$, where n is an integer greater than 2, has no solution for positive integral values of x, y, and z. Dirichlet found an error, and Kummer continued his search and developed the concept of ideal numbers. Using this concept, he proved the insolubility of the Fermat relation for all but a small group of primes, and he thus laid the foundation for an eventual complete proof of Fermat's last theorem. For his great advance, the French Academy of Sciences awarded him its Grand Prize in 1857. The ideal numbers have made possible new developments in the arithmetic of algebraic numbers.

Inspired by the work of Sir William Rowan Hamilton on systems of optical rays, Kummer developed the surface (residing in four-dimensional space) now named in his honour. Kummer also extended the work of Carl Friedrich Gauss on the hypergeometric series, adding developments that are useful in the theory of differential equations.

Sophus Lie

(b. Dec. 17, 1842, Nordfjordeid, Nor.—d. Feb. 18, 1899, Kristiania)

Norwegian mathematician Sophus Lie founded the theory of continuous groups and their applications to the theory of differential equations. His investigations led to one of the major branches of 20th-century mathematics, the theory of Lie groups and Lie algebras.

Lie attended a broad range of science and mathematics courses at the University of Kristiania (now Oslo) from 1859 to 1865 without deciding on a subject for graduate study. He supported himself for the following few years by giving private lessons while studying astronomy, mechanics, and mathematics on his own. His interest in geometry deepened in 1868 and resulted in his first mathematical paper being published in *Crelle's Journal* in 1869. Awarded a scholarship to travel abroad, Lie immediately went to the University of Berlin, where he soon began an intense collaboration with the German mathematician Felix Klein. They were working together in Paris on a unified view of geometry, among other topics, when the Franco-German War began in July 1870 and Klein returned to Berlin. (After Klein went to the University of Erlangen in 1872, the development of a unified theory of geometry became known as the *Erlanger Programm*.) When Lie decided to leave for Italy in August, after the French army suffered a major defeat, he was arrested near Fontainebleau and detained as a German spy—his mathematical notes were taken for coded dispatches. Freed one month later through the efforts of the French mathematician Jean-Gaston Darboux, he returned to Berlin by way of Italy.

In 1871 Lie became an assistant tutor at Kristiania and submitted his doctoral dissertation on the theory of contact transformations. Appointed extraordinary professor in 1872, he began to research continuous transformation groups in 1873. After working in virtual isolation for more than 10 years, Lie was joined by the German mathematician Friedrich Engel (1861–1941), who had just received his doctorate from the University of Leipzig in 1883. During a nine-year collaboration with Engel, Lie published *Theorie der Transformationsgruppen*, 3 vol. (1888–93; "Theory of Transformation Groups"), which contains his investigations of the general theory of continuous groups. In 1886 Lie succeeded Klein as professor of geometry at Leipzig, where Engel had moved in 1885. Over the next 12 years, Lie attracted a number of talented students. One of these, Georg Scheffers (1866–1945), wrote three introductory texts based on Lie's important Leipzig lecture courses, *Differentialgleichungen* (1891; "Differential Equations"), *Vorlesungen über continuierliche Gruppen* (1893; "Lectures on Continuous Groups"), and *Geometrie der Berührungstransformationen* (1896; "Geometry of Contact Transformations").

In 1898 Lie returned to Kristiania to accept a special post created for him, but his health was already failing and he died soon after his arrival. Besides his development of transformation groups, he made contributions to differential geometry. His primary aim, however, was the advancement of the theory of differential equations. Lie's mathematical papers are contained in *Gesammelte Abhandlungen*, 7 vol. (1922–60; "Collected Works").

JOSEPH LIOUVILLE

(b. March 24, 1809, Saint-Omer, France—d. Sept. 8, 1882, Paris)

French mathematician Joseph Liouville is known for his work in analysis, differential geometry, and number theory and for his discovery of transcendental numbers—i.e., numbers that are not the roots of algebraic equations having rational coefficients. He was also influential as a journal editor and teacher.

Liouville, the son of an army captain, was educated in Paris at the École Polytechnique from 1825 to 1827 and then at the École Nationale des Ponts et Chaussées ("National School of Bridges and Roads") until 1830. At the École Polytechnique, Liouville was taught by André-Marie Ampère, who recognized his talent and encouraged him to follow his course on mathematical physics at the Collège de France. In 1836 Liouville founded and became editor of the *Journal des Mathématiques Pures et Appliquées* ("Journal of Pure and Applied Mathematics"), sometimes known as the *Journal de Liouville*, which did much to raise and maintain the standard of French mathematics throughout the 19th century. The manuscripts of the French mathematician Évariste Galois were first published by Liouville in 1846, 14 years after Galois's death.

In 1833 Liouville was appointed professor at the École Centrale des Arts et Manufactures, and in 1838 he became professor of analysis and mechanics at the École Polytechnique—a position that he held until 1851, when he was elected a professor of mathematics at the Collège de France. In 1839 he was elected a member of the astronomy section of the French Academy of Sciences, and the following year, he was elected a member of the prestigious Bureau of Longitudes.

At the beginning of his career, Liouville worked on electrodynamics and the theory of heat. During the early 1830s, he created the first comprehensive theory of fractional calculus, the theory that generalizes the meaning of differential and integral operators. This was followed by his theory of integration in finite terms (1832–33), the main goals of which were to decide whether given algebraic functions have integrals that can be expressed in finite (or elementary) terms. He also worked in differential equations and boundary value problems, and, together with Charles-François Sturm—the two were devoted friends—he published a series of articles (1836–37) that created a completely new subject in mathematical analysis. Sturm-Liouville theory, which underwent substantial generalization and rigorization in the late 19th century, became of major importance in 20th-century mathematical physics as well as in the theory of integral equations. In 1844 Liouville was the first to prove the existence of transcendental numbers, and he constructed an infinite class of such numbers. Liouville's theorem, concerning the measure-preserving property of Hamiltonian dynamics (conservation of total energy), is now known to be basic to statistical mechanics and measure theory.

In analysis Liouville was the first to deduce the theory of doubly periodic functions (functions with two distinct periods whose ratio is not a real number) from general theorems (including his own) in the theory of analytic functions of a complex variable—also known as holomorphic functions or regular functions; a complex-valued function defined and differentiable over some subset of the complex number plane. In number theory he produced more than 200 publications, most of which are in the form of short notes. Although nearly all of this work was published without indication of the means by which he had obtained his results, proofs have since been provided. Altogether, Liouville's publications comprise about 400 memoirs, articles, and notes.

PAOLO RUFFINI

(b. Sept. 22, 1765, Valentano, Papal States—d. May 9, 1822, Modena, duchy of Modena)

Italian mathematician and physician Paolo Ruffini made studies of equations that anticipated the algebraic theory of groups. He is regarded as the first to make a significant attempt to show that there is no algebraic solution to the general quintic equation (an equation whose highest-degree term is raised to the fifth power).

When Ruffini was still a teenager, his family moved to Reggio, near Modena, Italy. He entered the University of Modena in 1783 and while still a student taught a course there in the foundations of analysis for the 1787–88 academic year. Ruffini received degrees in philosophy, medicine, and mathematics from Modena in 1788, and in the fall, obtained a permanent position there as a professor of mathematics. In 1791 he received a license to practice medicine from the Collegiate Medical Court of Modena.

Following the conquest of Modena by Napoleon Bonaparte in 1796, Ruffini found himself appointed as a representative to the Junior Council of the Cisalpine Republic (consisting of Bologna, Emilia, Lombardy, and

Modena). Although he returned to his academic life early in 1788, he soon refused, for religious reasons, to take a civil oath of allegiance to the new republic and was therefore barred from teaching and public office. Unperturbed, Ruffini practiced medicine and continued his mathematical research until the defeat of Napoleon in 1814, when he returned permanently to the University of Modena as rector, in addition to holding professorships in mathematics and medicine.

Ruffini's proof of the unsolvability of the general quintic equation, based on relations between the coefficients and permutations discovered earlier by the Italian-French mathematician Joseph-Louis Lagrange (1736–1813), was published in 1799. His first demonstration was regarded as insufficient, and he published a revised version in 1813 after discussions with several prominent mathematicians. This version also was regarded skeptically by some mathematicians, but it was approved by Augustin-Louis Cauchy, one of the leading French mathematicians of the time. In 1824 the Norwegian mathematician Niels Henrik Abel published a different proof that finally established the result with full rigour. Ruffini's contribution to the understanding of groups provided a foundation for more extensive work by Cauchy and by the French mathematician Évariste Galois (1811–32), leading eventually to a nearly complete understanding of the conditions for solving polynomial equations.

SEKI TAKAKAZU
(b. c. 1640, Fujioka, Japan—d. Oct. 24, 1708, Edo [now Tokyo])

Seki Takakazu (also called Seki Kowa) was the most important figure of the *wasan* ("Japanese calculation") tradition that flourished from the early 17th century until the opening of Japan to the West in the mid-19th century. Seki was instrumental in recovering neglected and forgotten mathematical knowledge from ancient Chinese sources and then extending and generalizing the main problems.

Little is known about Seki's life and intellectual formation. He was the second son of Nagaakira Uchiyama, a samurai. He was adopted at an early age by Seki Gorozaemon, a samurai official with the Bureau of Supply in Edo, to carry on the Seki family name. Seki Takakazu assumed various positions as an examiner of accounts for the lord of Kofu, Tokugawa Tsunashige (until 1678), and then his son, the future shogun Tokugawa Ienobu. The functions that he carried out were relatively modest, although some anecdotes mention special rewards conferred on him. Even though some of these accounts may be disputed, they do suggest that his scientific and technical skills were encouraged.

The exact source of Seki's early education is unknown, but, as a resident of Edo, the political and cultural centre of the times, he was well placed for access to the latest publications, and his first writings testify to an uncommon knowledge of contemporary mathematics. Zhu Shijie's *Suanxue qimeng* (1299; "Introduction to Mathematical Science"), Yang Hui's *Yang Hui suanfa* (13th century; "Yang Hui's Mathematical Methods"), and Cheng Dawei's *Suanfa tongzong* (1592; "Systematic Treatise on Arithmetic") were among the Chinese treatises that inspired him.

Seki's most productive research was in algebra, a field in which he created powerful new tools and provided many definitive solutions. A concern for generality can be observed throughout his work, especially in his way of reformulating and extending traditional problems. He substituted a tabular notational system for the cumbersome Chinese method of counting rods, thereby simplifying the handling of equations in more than one unknown. In his *Kaifukudai no ho* (1683; "Method for

Solving Concealed Problems"), he described some important properties related to such computations. Another topic of Seki's research was the extraction of roots (solutions) of higher-degree polynomial equations. In *Kaiindai no ho* (1685; "Method for Solving Hidden Problems"), he described an ancient Chinese method for obtaining a root and extended the method to get all the real roots of the equation.

Because of his disciples' zealous diffusion of his work, Seki had an immediate impact on his contemporaries. In particular, Takebe Katahiro and his brother Kataaki helped to deepen and consolidate Seki's work, making it difficult now to apportion credit properly. The publication of *Katsuyo sanpo* (1712; "Compendium of Mathematics"), containing Seki's research on the measure of circle and arc, is due to another disciple who used this work to open a Seki School of Mathematics—a prestigious centre that attracted the best mathematicians in the country until the 19th century.

JAMES JOSEPH SYLVESTER
(b. Sept. 3, 1814, London, Eng.—d. March 15, 1897, London)

British mathematician James Joseph Sylvester, along with Arthur Cayley, was a cofounder of invariant theory, the study of properties that are unchanged (invariant) under some transformation, such as rotating or translating the coordinate axes. He also made significant contributions to number theory and elliptic functions.

In 1837 Sylvester came second in the mathematical tripos at the University of Cambridge but, as a Jew, was prevented from taking his degree or securing an appointment there. In 1838 he became a professor of natural philosophy at University College, London (the only nonsectarian British university). In 1841 he accepted a professorship of mathematics at the University of Virginia, Charlottesville, U.S., but resigned after only three months following an altercation with a student for which the school's administration did not take his side. He returned to England in 1843. The following year he went to London, where he became an actuary for an insurance company, retaining his interest in mathematics only through tutoring (his students included Florence Nightingale). In 1846 he became a law student at the Inner Temple, and in 1850 he was admitted to the bar. While working as a lawyer, Sylvester began an enthusiastic and profitable collaboration with Cayley.

From 1855 to 1870, Sylvester was a professor of mathematics at the Royal Military Academy in Woolwich. He went to the United States once again in 1876 to become a professor of mathematics at Johns Hopkins University in Baltimore, Maryland. While there he founded (1878) and became the first editor of the *American Journal of Mathematics*, introduced graduate work in mathematics into American universities, and greatly stimulated the American mathematical scene. In 1883 he returned to England to become the Savilian Professor of Geometry at the University of Oxford.

Sylvester was primarily an algebraist. He did brilliant work in the theory of numbers, particularly in partitions (the possible ways a number can be expressed as a sum of positive integers) and Diophantine analysis (a means for finding whole-number solutions to certain algebraic equations). He worked by inspiration, and frequently it is difficult to detect a proof in what he confidently asserted. His work is characterized by powerful imagination and inventiveness. He was proud of his mathematical vocabulary and coined many new terms, although few have survived. He was elected a fellow of the Royal Society in 1839, and he was the second president of the London Mathematical Society (1866–68). His mathematical output includes several hundred papers and one book, *Treatise on Elliptic Functions* (1876). He also wrote poetry, although not to critical acclaim, and published *Laws of Verse* (1870).

FRANÇOIS VIÈTE

(b. 1540, Fontenay-le-Comte, France—d. Dec. 13, 1603, Paris)

François Viète (Latin: Franciscus Vieta) was a French mathematician who introduced the first systematic algebraic notation and contributed to the theory of equations.

Viète, a Huguenot sympathizer, solved a complex cipher of more than 500 characters used by King Philip II of Spain in his war to defend Roman Catholicism from the Huguenots. When Philip, assuming that the cipher could not be broken, discovered that the French were aware of his military plans, he complained to the pope that black magic was being employed against his country.

Viète's *Canon mathematicus seu ad triangula* (1579; "Mathematical Laws Applied to Triangles") is probably the first western European work dealing with a systematic development of methods—utilizing all six trigonometric functions—for computing plane and spherical triangles. Viète has been called "the father of modern algebraic notation," and his *In artem analyticem isagoge* (1591; "Introduction to the Analytical Arts") closely resembles a modern elementary algebra text. His contribution to the theory of equations is *De aequationum recognitione et emendatione* (1615; "Concerning the Recognition and Emendation of Equations"), in which he presented methods for solving equations of second, third, and fourth degree. He knew the connection between the positive roots of an equation (which, in his time, were thought of as the only roots) and the coefficients of the different powers of the unknown quantity.

ALGEBRAISTS OF THE STRUCTURAL PERIOD (20TH–21ST CENTURIES)

EMIL ARTIN

(b. March 3, 1898, Vienna, Austria—d. Dec. 20, 1962, Hamburg, W.Ger.)

Austro-German mathematician Emil Artin made fundamental contributions to class field theory, notably the general law of reciprocity.

After one year at the University of Göttingen, Artin joined the staff of the University of Hamburg in 1923. He emigrated to the United States in 1937, where he taught at Notre Dame University (1937–38), Indiana University, Bloomington (1938–46), and Princeton University (1946–58). In 1958 he returned to the University of Hamburg.

Artin's early work centred on the analytical and arithmetic theory of quadratic number fields. He made major advances in abstract algebra in 1926, and the following year, used the theory of formal-real fields to solve the Hilbert problem of definite functions. In 1927 he also made notable contributions in hypercomplex numbers, primarily the expansion of the theory of associative ring algebras. In 1944 he discovered rings with minimum conditions for right ideals, now known as Artin rings. He presented a new foundation for and extended the arithmetic of semisimple algebras over the rational number field.

His theory of braids, set forth in 1925, was a major contribution to the study of nodes in three-dimensional space. Artin's books include *Geometric Algebra* (1957) and, with John T. Tate, *Class Field Theory* (1961). Most of his technical papers are found in *The Collected Papers of Emil Artin* (1965).

Richard Ewen Borcherds
(b. Nov. 29, 1959, Cape Town, S.Af.)

Richard Ewen Borcherds was a British mathematician who won the Fields Medal in 1998 for his work in algebra.

Borcherds studied undergraduate mathematics at the University of Cambridge and went on to finish his doctorate there in 1983. Afterward he held teaching and research positions at Cambridge and at the University of California at Berkeley.

Borcherds received the Fields Medal at the International Congress of Mathematicians in Berlin in 1998 for his work on vertex algebras and Kac-Moody Lie algebras, which he used to prove the so-called Moonshine conjectures. The Moonshine conjectures asserted a mysterious connection between certain families of modular functions and the representation theory of the largest sporadic simple group (the "Monster"). Borcherds's work also drew on superstring theory and had profound implications for conformal field theory.

Nicolas Bourbaki

Nicolas Bourbaki was a pseudonym chosen by eight or nine young mathematicians in France in the mid 1930s to represent the essence of a "contemporary mathematician." The surname, selected in jest, was that of a French general who fought in the Franco-German War (1870–71). The mathematicians, who collectively wrote under the Bourbaki pseudonym at one time, studied at the École Normale Supérieure in Paris and were admirers of the German mathematician David Hilbert. The founders included the Frenchmen Claude Chevalley, André Weil, Henri Cartan, and Jean Dieudonné. After World War II, they were joined by the Polish American Samuel Eilenberg.

Members agreed to retire from the group at age 50, but the group's ranks were replenished with new recruits.

The group's purpose was originally to write a rigorous textbook in analysis, but it grew to include presentations of many branches of algebra and analysis, including topology, from an axiomatic point of view. The Bourbaki writings commenced in 1939 with the first volume of their *Éléments de mathématique* ("Elements of Mathematics"). The still-incomplete series of more than 30 monographs soon became a standard reference on the fundamental aspects of modern mathematics. The various historical notes included at the ends of chapters were published as a collection in 1960 in *Eléments d'histoire des mathématiques* ("History of the Elements of Mathematics").

RICHARD DAGOBERT BRAUER
(b. Feb. 10, 1901, Berlin, Ger.—d. April 17, 1977, Belmont, Mass., U.S.)

Richard Dagobert Brauer was a German-born American mathematician and educator, a pioneer in the development of modern algebra.

Brauer graduated from the University of Königsberg and received his Ph.D. in 1925 from the University of Berlin. He accepted a teaching position at Königsberg and remained there until 1933, when all Jews were dismissed from their academic posts in Germany. He immediately obtained a position in the United States at the University of Kentucky, and the following year, he left to work with Hermann Weyl at the Institute for Advanced Study, Princeton, New Jersey. Their work later had a bearing on Nobel laureate Paul Dirac's theory of the spinning electron. Brauer then became interested in the work of Georg Frobenius, who had introduced group characters in 1896. Brauer carried forward Frobenius's work and developed a theory of modular characters that gave new insights into the study of group characters and advanced the development of algebra.

In 1935 he accepted a position at the University of Toronto and was there until 1948, when he left to join the faculty at the University of Michigan. He became a professor in Harvard University's mathematics department in 1952 and remained there until his retirement in 1971. He was chairman of the department from 1959 to 1963. In the late 1950s, he began formulating a method for classifying finite simple groups, a task that absorbed his attention for the rest of his life. In 1971 Brauer was awarded the National Medal of Science.

His *Collected Papers* was published in 1980.

ÉLIE-JOSEPH CARTAN
(b. April 9, 1869, Dolomieu, France—d. May 6, 1951, Paris)

French mathematician Élie-Joseph Cartan greatly developed the theory of Lie groups and contributed to the theory of subalgebras.

In 1894 Cartan became a lecturer at the University of Montpellier, where he studied the structure of continuous groups introduced by the noted Norwegian mathematician Sophus Lie. He later examined theories of equivalence and their relation to the theory of integral invariants, mechanics, and the general theory of relativity. After he moved to the University of Lyon in 1896, he worked on linear associative algebra, developing general theorems based on the work of Benjamin Peirce of Harvard and exhibiting a subalgebra of the German mathematician Ferdinand Georg Frobenius. In 1912 Cartan became a professor at the Sorbonne. A year later he discovered the spinors, complex vectors that are used to transform three-dimensional rotations into two-dimensional representations.

Although a profound theorist, Cartan was also able to explain difficult concepts to the ordinary student. Recognition of his work did not come until late in his life. He was made a member of the Academy of Sciences in France in 1931 and a fellow of the Royal Society of London in 1947. His works include *La Géométrie des espaces de Riemann* (1925; "The Geometry of Riemann Spaces") and *La Théorie des groupes continus et des espaces généralisés* (1935; "The Theory of Continuous Groups and Generalized Spaces").

GEORGE DANTZIG

(b. Nov. 8, 1914, Portland, Ore., U.S.—d. May 13, 2005, Stanford, Calif.)

American mathematician George Dantzig devised the simplex method, an algorithm for solving problems that involve numerous conditions and variables, and in the process founded the field of linear programming.

Dantzig earned a bachelor's degree in mathematics and physics from the University of Maryland (1936) and a master's degree in mathematics from the University of Michigan (1937), before joining the U.S. Bureau of Labor Statistics as a statistician. In 1939 he entered the graduate mathematics program at the University of California, Berkeley. From 1941 to 1946, Dantzig was the civilian head of the Combat Analysis Branch of the U.S. Army Air Forces Office of Statistical Control. In 1946 he returned for one semester to Berkeley to receive a doctorate in mathematics, and then he went back to Washington, D.C., to work for the U.S. Department of Defense.

While working on allocation of resources (materials and personnel) for various projects and deployments of the U.S. Army Air Forces, Dantzig invented (1947) the simplex algorithm for optimization. At that time such scheduling was called programming, and it soon became apparent that the simplex algorithm was ideal for translating formerly intractable problems involving hundreds, or even thousands, of factors for solution by the recently invented computer. From 1952 to 1960, he was a research mathematician at the RAND Corporation, where he helped develop the field of operations research (essentially, the application of computers to optimization problems). From 1960 to 1966, he served as chairman of the Operations Research Center at Berkeley, and from 1966 until his retirement in 1997, he was a professor of operations research and computer science at Stanford University.

Among Dantzig's numerous awards were the John von Neumann Theory Prize in operations research (1975), the National Medal of Science (1975), and the National Academy of Sciences Award in applied mathematics and numerical analysis (1977).

LEONARD EUGENE DICKSON

(b. Jan. 22, 1874, Independence, Iowa, U.S.—d. Jan. 17, 1954, Harlingen, Texas)

American mathematician Leonard Eugene Dickson made important contributions to the theory of numbers and the theory of groups.

Appointed associate professor of mathematics at the University of Texas at Austin in 1899, Dickson joined the staff of the University of Chicago in 1900, where he remained until 1939. A prolific mathematician, Dickson published the first extensive work on the theory of finite fields and expanded the Wedderburn and Cartan theories of linear associative algebras. One of his most-engrossing studies concerned the relationships between the theory of invariants and number theory. Using the analytic results of the Russian mathematician Ivan M. Vinogradov, he proved the ideal Waring theorem in his investigations of additive number theory. Of his 18 published books, the most monumental is *History of the Theory of Numbers,* 3 vol. (1919–23).

JEAN DIEUDONNÉ

(b. July 1, 1906, Lille, France—d. Nov. 29, 1992, Paris)

Jean Dieudonné, a French mathematician and educator, was known for his writings on abstract algebra, functional analysis, topology, and his theory of Lie groups.

Jean-Alexandre-Eugène Dieudonné was educated in Paris, receiving both his bachelor's degree (1927) and his doctorate (1931) from the École Normale Supérieure. He was a founding member of the Nicolas Bourbaki group in the mid-1930s. After teaching at universities in Rennes and Nancy, France, and in São Paulo, Brazil, Dieudonné came to the United States in 1952 and taught mathematics at the University of Michigan and at Northwestern University. He returned to Paris to teach at the Institute of Advanced Scientific Studies (1959–64). He became professor of mathematics at the University of Nice in 1964, dean of the science faculty in 1965, and professor emeritus in 1970. In 1968 he was elected to the French Academy of Sciences.

Dieudonné's publications include *La Géométrie des groupes classiques* (1955), *Foundations of Modern Analysis* (1960), *Algèbre linéaire et géométrie élémentaire* (1964; "Linear Algebra and Elementary Geometry"), and *Éléments d'analyse,* 9 vol. (1968–82).

GEORG FROBENIUS

(b. Oct. 26, 1849, Berlin, Prussia [Germany]—d. Aug. 3, 1917, Berlin)

Ferdinand Georg Frobenius was a German mathematician who made major contributions to group theory.

Frobenius studied for one year at the University of Göttingen before returning home in 1868 to study at the

University of Berlin. After receiving a doctorate in 1870, he taught at various secondary schools before he became an assistant professor of mathematics at the University of Berlin in 1874. He was appointed a professor of mathematics at the Federal Polytechnic in Zürich, Switz., in 1875. Frobenius finally returned to the University of Berlin in 1892 to occupy the mathematics chair vacated by the death of Leopold Kronecker. The next year Frobenius was elected to the Prussian Academy of Sciences.

As the major mathematics figure at Berlin, Frobenius continued the university's antipathy to applied mathematics, which he thought belonged in technical schools. In some respects, this attitude contributed to the relative decline of Berlin in favour of Göttingen. On the other hand, he and his students made major contributions to the development of the modern concept of an abstract group—such emphasis on abstract mathematical structure became a central theme of mathematics during the 20th century. With Frobenius's disdain for applied mathematics, it is somewhat ironic that his fundamental work in the theory of finite groups was later found to have surprising and important applications in quantum mechanics and theoretical physics.

Frobenius's collected works, *Gesammelte Abhandlungen* (1968), in three volumes, were edited by Jean-Pierre Serre.

ALEKSANDR OSIPOVICH GELFOND

(b. Oct. 24, 1906, St. Petersburg, Russia—d. Nov. 7, 1968, Moscow, Russia, U.S.S.R.)

Russian mathematician Aleksandr Osipovich Gelfond originated basic techniques in the study of transcendental numbers (numbers that cannot be expressed as the root or solution of an algebraic equation with rational coefficients). He profoundly advanced transcendental number theory and the theory of interpolation and approximation of complex variable functions.

Gelfond taught mathematics at the Moscow Technological College (1929–30) and, from 1931, at Moscow State University, at various times holding chairs of analysis, number theory, and history of mathematics.

In 1934 Gelfond proved that a^b is transcendental if a is an algebraic number not equal to 0 or 1 and if b is an irrational algebraic number. This statement, now known as Gelfond's theorem, solved the seventh of 23 famous problems that had been posed by the German mathematician David Hilbert in 1900. Gelfond's methods were readily accepted by other mathematicians, and important new concepts in transcendental number theory were rapidly developed. Much of his work, including the construction of new classes of transcendental numbers, is found in his *Transtsendentnye i algebraicheskie chisla* (1952; *Transcendental and Algebraic Numbers*). In *Ischislenie konechnykh raznostey* (1952; "Calculus of Finite Differences"), he summarized his approximation and interpolation studies.

DAVID HILBERT

(b. Jan. 23, 1862, Königsberg, Prussia [now Kaliningrad, Russia]—d. Feb. 14, 1943, Göttingen, Ger.)

German mathematician David Hilbert reduced geometry to a series of axioms and contributed substantially to the establishment of the formalistic foundations of mathematics. His work in 1909 on integral equations led to 20th-century research in functional analysis.

The first steps of Hilbert's career occurred at the University of Königsberg, at which, in 1884, he finished his *Inaugurel-dissertation* (Ph.D.). He remained at Königsberg as a *Privatdozent* (lecturer, or assistant professor) in 1886–92, as an *Extraordinarius* (associate professor) in

1892–93, and as an *Ordinarius* in 1893–95. In 1892 he married Käthe Jerosch, and they had one child, Franz. In 1895 Hilbert accepted a professorship in mathematics at the University of Göttingen, at which he remained for the rest of his life.

The University of Göttingen had a flourishing tradition in mathematics, primarily as the result of the contributions of Carl Friedrich Gauss, Peter Gustav Lejeune Dirichlet, and Bernhard Riemann in the 19th century. During the first three decades of the 20th century, this mathematical tradition achieved even greater eminence, largely because of Hilbert. The Mathematical Institute at Göttingen drew students and visitors from all over the world.

Hilbert's intense interest in mathematical physics also contributed to the university's reputation in physics. His colleague and friend, the mathematician Hermann Minkowski, aided in the new application of mathematics to physics until his untimely death in 1909. Three winners of the Nobel Prize for Physics—Max von Laue in 1914, James Franck in 1925, and Werner Heisenberg in 1932—spent significant parts of their careers at the University of Göttingen during Hilbert's lifetime.

In a highly original way, Hilbert extensively modified the mathematics of invariants—the entities that are not altered during such geometric changes as rotation, dilation, and reflection. Hilbert proved the theorem of invariants—that all invariants can be expressed in terms of a finite number. In his *Zahlbericht* ("Commentary on Numbers"), a report on algebraic number theory published in 1897, he consolidated what was known in this subject and pointed the way to the developments that followed. In 1899 he published the *Grundlagen der Geometrie* (*The Foundations of Geometry*, 1902), which contained his definitive set of axioms for Euclidean geometry and a keen analysis of their significance. This popular book, which appeared in 10 editions, marked a turning point in the axiomatic treatment of geometry.

A substantial part of Hilbert's fame rests on a list of 23 research problems he enunciated in 1900 at the International Mathematical Congress in Paris. In his address, "The Problems of Mathematics," he surveyed nearly all the mathematics of his day and endeavoured to set forth the problems he thought would be significant for mathematicians in the 20th century. Many of the problems have since been solved, and each solution was a noted event. Of those that remain, however, one, in part, requires a solution to the Riemann hypothesis, which is usually considered to be the most important unsolved problem in mathematics.

In 1905 the first award of the Wolfgang Bolyai prize of the Hungarian Academy of Sciences went to Henri Poincaré, but it was accompanied by a special citation for Hilbert.

In 1905 (and again from 1918) Hilbert attempted to lay a firm foundation for mathematics by proving consistency—that is, that finite steps of reasoning in logic could not lead to a contradiction. But in 1931 the Austrian–U.S. mathematician Kurt Gödel showed this goal to be unattainable: propositions may be formulated that are undecidable; thus, it cannot be known with certainty that mathematical axioms do not lead to contradictions. Nevertheless, the development of logic after Hilbert was different, for he established the formalistic foundations of mathematics.

Hilbert's work in integral equations in about 1909 led directly to 20th-century research in functional analysis (the branch of mathematics in which functions are studied collectively). His work also established the basis for his work on infinite-dimensional space, later called Hilbert space, a concept that is useful in mathematical analysis and quantum mechanics. Making use of his results on integral equations, Hilbert contributed to the development of mathematical physics by his important memoirs on kinetic gas theory and the theory of radiations. In 1909 he proved the conjecture in number theory that for any n, all positive integers are sums of a certain fixed number of nth powers. For example, $5 = 2^2 + 1^2$, in which $n = 2$. In 1910 the second Bolyai award went to Hilbert alone and, appropriately, Poincaré wrote the glowing tribute.

The city of Königsberg in 1930, the year of his retirement from the University of Göttingen, made Hilbert an honorary citizen. For this occasion he prepared an address entitled "Naturerkennen und Logik" ("The Understanding of Nature and Logic"). The last six words of Hilbert's address sum up his enthusiasm for mathematics and the devoted life he spent raising it to a new level: "Wir müssen wissen, wir werden wissen" ("We must know, we shall know"). In 1939 the first Mittag-Leffler prize of the Swedish Academy went jointly to Hilbert and the French mathematician Émile Picard.

The last decade of Hilbert's life was darkened by the tragedy brought to himself and to so many of his students and colleagues by the Nazi regime.

SAUNDERS MAC LANE

(b. Aug. 4, 1909, Taftville, Conn., U.S.—d. April 14, 2005, San Francisco, Calif.)

American mathematician Saunders Mac Lane was a cocreator of category theory, an architect of homological algebra, and an advocate of categorical foundations for mathematics.

Mac Lane graduated from Yale University in 1930 and then began graduate work at the University of Chicago. He soon moved to Germany, where he, with a dissertation on mathematical logic, received a doctorate degree in 1933 from the University of Göttingen. While in Germany, he stayed in the homes of Hermann Weyl and Richard Courant, and he saw his dissertation adviser Paul Bernays barred from teaching by the Nazis. Mac Lane returned home and taught at various universities before settling permanently at the University of Chicago in 1947.

About 1940 Mac Lane made some purely algebraic calculations in group theory, and the Polish American mathematician Samuel Eilenberg noticed that they applied to the topology of infinitely coiled curves called solenoids. To understand and generalize this link between algebra and topology, the two men created category theory, the general cohomology of groups, and the basis for the Eilenberg-Steenrod axioms for homology of topological spaces. Mac Lane worked with categorical duality and defined categorical universal properties. He defined and named Abelian categories, further developed by Alexandre Grothendieck to become central to homological algebra.

From the 1960s, Mac Lane pursued aspects of category theory, including the work of the American mathematician F. William Lawvere on categorical foundations for mathematics. Mac Lane served as president of the Mathematical Association of America (1951–52), the American Philosophical Society (1968–71), and the American Mathematical Society (1973–74). He served as vice president of the National Academy of Sciences (1973–81). His works include *A Survey of Modern Algebra* (1941, with Garrett Birkhoff); *Homology* (1963); *Categories for the Working Mathematician* (1971); and *Sheaves in Geometry and Logic: A First Introduction to Topos Theory* (1992, with Ieke Moerdijk).

GREGORI ALEKSANDROVICH MARGULIS
(b. Feb. 24, 1946, Moscow, Russia, U.S.S.R.)

Russian mathematician Gregori Aleksandrovich Margulis was awarded the Fields Medal in 1978 for his contributions to the theory of Lie groups. Margulis attended Moscow State University (Ph.D., 1970).

In 1978 Margulis was awarded the Fields Medal at the International Congress of Mathematicians in Helsinki, Fin., but was not allowed by the Soviet government to travel to Finland to receive the award. In 1990 Margulis immigrated to the United States. After brief appointments at Harvard University, Cambridge, Mass., and the Institute for Advanced Study, Princeton, N.J., he was appointed to a position at Yale University, New Haven, Conn. Margulis's work was largely involved in solving a number of problems in the theory of Lie groups. In particular, Margulis proved a long-standing conjecture by Atle Selberg concerning discrete subgroups of semisimple Lie groups. The techniques he used in his work were drawn from combinatorics, ergodic theory, dynamical systems, and differential geometry.

Margulis' publications include *Discrete Subgroups of Semisimple Lie Groups* (1991).

EMMY NOETHER

(b. March 23, 1882, Erlangen, Ger. —d. April 14, 1935, Bryn Mawr, Penn., U.S.)

Emmy Noether was a German mathematician whose innovations in higher algebra gained her recognition as the most creative abstract algebraist of modern times.

Amalie Emmy Noether received a Ph.D. degree from the University of Erlangen in 1907, with a dissertation on algebraic invariants. From 1913 she lectured occasionally at Erlangen, substituting for her father, Max Noether (1844–1921). In 1915 she went to the University of Göttingen and was persuaded by the eminent mathematicians David Hilbert and Felix Klein to remain there over the objections of some faculty members. She won formal admission as an academic lecturer in 1919.

The appearance of *Moduln in nichtkommutativen Bereichen, insbesondere aus Differential- und Differenzen-Ausdrücken* (1920; *Concerning Moduli in Noncommutative Fields, Particularly in Differential and Difference Terms*), written in collaboration with a Göttingen colleague, Werner Schmeidler, and published in *Mathematische Zeitschrift*, marked the first notice of Noether as an extraordinary mathematician. For the next six years, her investigations centred on the general theory of ideals (special subsets of rings), for which her residual theorem is an important part. On an axiomatic basis, she developed a general theory of ideals for all cases. Her abstract theory helped draw together many important mathematical developments.

From 1927 Noether concentrated on noncommutative algebras (algebras in which the order in which numbers are multiplied affects the answer), their linear transformations, and their application to commutative number fields. She built up the theory of noncommutative algebras in a newly unified and purely conceptual way. In collaboration with Helmut Hasse and Richard Brauer, she investigated the structure of noncommutative algebras and their application to commutative fields by means of cross product (a form of multiplication

Emmy Noether. Pictorial Parade/Hulton Archive/Getty Images

used between two vectors). Important papers from this period are "Hyperkomplexe Grössen und Darstellungstheorie" (1929; "Hypercomplex Number Systems and Their Representation") and "Nichtkommutative Algebra" (1933; "Noncommutative Algebra").

In addition to research and teaching, Noether helped edit the *Mathematische Annalen*. From 1930 to 1933, she was the centre of the strongest mathematical activity at Göttingen. The extent and significance of her work cannot be accurately judged from her papers. Much of her work appeared in the publications of students and colleagues. Many times a suggestion or even a casual remark revealed her great insight and stimulated another to complete and perfect some idea.

When the Nazis came to power in Germany in 1933, Noether and many other Jewish professors at Göttingen were dismissed. In October she left for the United States to become visiting professor of mathematics at Bryn Mawr College and to lecture and conduct research at the Institute for Advanced Study in Princeton, New Jersey.

DANIEL GRAY QUILLEN
(b. June 27, 1940, Orange, N.J., U.S.)

American mathematician Daniel Gray Quillen was awarded the Fields Medal in 1978 for his contributions to algebraic K-theory.

Quillen attended Harvard University, Cambridge, Mass. (Ph.D., 1969), and held appointments at the Massachusetts Institute of Technology (1973–88) and the Mathematical Institute of Oxford (Eng.) University (1988–).

Quillen was awarded the Fields Medal at the International Congress of Mathematicians in Helsinki,

Fin., in 1978. In addition to Quillen's application of geometric and topological techniques to the study of algebraic K-theory, he made contributions in topology to the cobordism theory of René Thom. In 1976 he solved a well-known problem that had been posed 20 years earlier by Jean-Pierre Serre concerning the structure of certain abstract mathematical spaces. He showed that many of the highly generalized spaces that have been developed so extensively in 20th-century mathematics can be developed from elementary components, dimension by dimension.

Quillen's publications include *Homotopical Algebra* (1967) and, edited with Graeme B. Segal and Sheung Tsun Tsou, *The Interface of Mathematics and Particle Physics* (1990).

ALFRED TARSKI

(b. Jan. 14, 1902, Warsaw, Pol., Russian Empire—d. Oct. 26, 1983, Berkeley, Calif., U.S.)

Polish-born American mathematician and logician Alfred Tarski made important studies of general algebra, measure theory, mathematical logic, set theory, and metamathematics.

Tarski completed his education at the University of Warsaw (Ph.D., 1923). He taught in Warsaw until 1939, when he moved to the United States (becoming a naturalized citizen in 1945). He joined the staff of the University of California at Berkeley in 1942, was appointed professor of mathematics (1949), and was research professor of the Miller Institute of Basic Research in Science there (1958–60). In succeeding years he was responsible for influencing the careers of many mathematics students. He became emeritus in 1968. He wrote a number of works on algebra, geometry, and logic.

HERMANN WEYL

(b. Nov. 9, 1885, Elmshorn, near Hamburg, Ger.—d. Dec. 8, 1955, Zürich, Switz.)

Hermann Weyl was a German-American mathematician who, through his widely varied contributions in mathematics, served as a link between pure mathematics and theoretical physics—in particular adding enormously to quantum mechanics and the theory of relativity.

As a student at the University of Göttingen (graduated 1908), Weyl came under the influence of David Hilbert. In 1913 he became professor of mathematics at the Technische Hochschule, Zürich, where he was a colleague of Albert Einstein. The outstanding characteristic of Weyl's work was his ability to unite previously unrelated subjects. In *Die Idee der Riemannschen Fläche* (1913; *The Concept of a Riemann Surface*), he created a new branch of mathematics by uniting function theory and geometry and thereby opening up the modern synoptic view of analysis, geometry, and topology.

The outgrowth of a course of lectures on relativity, Weyl's *Raum, Zeit, Materie* (1918; "Space, Time, Matter") reveals his keen interest in philosophy and embodies the bulk of his findings on relativity. He produced the first unified field theory for which Maxwell's equations of electromagnetic fields and the gravitational field appear as geometric properties of space-time. The influence of these studies on differential geometry is exemplified best by his treatment of the Italian mathematician Tullio Levi-Civita's concept of parallel displacement of a vector. Weyl freed the concept from dependence on a Riemann metric and thus set the stage for the rapid development of projective differential geometry by Oswald Veblen of the United States and by others.

From 1923 to 1938, Weyl evolved a general theory of continuous groups, using matrix representation. He found that most of the regularities of quantum phenomena on the atomic level can be most simply understood by using group theory. With the findings published in *Gruppentheorie und Quantenmechanik* (1928; "Group Theory and Quantum Mechanics"), Weyl helped mold modern quantum theory.

Weyl was appointed professor of mathematics at the University of Göttingen in 1930. The Nazi dismissal of many of his colleagues prompted him to leave Germany in 1933 and accept a position at the Institute for Advanced Study, Princeton, New Jersey. He became a U.S. citizen in 1939. After his retirement in 1955, Weyl remained professor emeritus of the institute and divided his time between Princeton and Zürich.

EFIM ISAAKOVICH ZELMANOV
(b. Sept. 7, 1955, Khabarovsk, Russia, U.S.S.R.)

Russian mathematician Efim Isaakovich Zelmanov was awarded the Fields Medal in 1994 for his work in group theory.

Zelmanov was educated at Novosibirsk State University (Ph.D., 1980) and Leningrad (now St. Petersburg) State University (D.Sc., 1985). He worked at the Institute of Mathematics of the Academy of Sciences of the U.S.S.R. in Novosibirsk until 1987. He then left the Soviet Union, eventually settling at the University of Wisconsin, Madison (U.S.), in 1990. He moved to the University of Chicago in 1994 and on to Yale University, New Haven, Conn., in 1995.

Zelmanov was awarded the Fields Medal at the International Congress of Mathematicians in Zürich in 1994. Zelmanov's prizewinning work was not directly related to his main field of research, nonassociative algebras. However, he made spectacular advances in group theory by solving the century-old restricted Burnside problem, using the theory of Lie algebras. Zelmanov's broad interests were critically important in this work, as a proof of his major result probably could not have been carried out by a traditional group theorist or Lie theorist. Zelmanov also made important contributions to the study of Jordan algebras, which are of interest in the study of quantum mechanics.

Zelmanov's publications include *Nil Rings and Periodic Groups* (1992).

CHAPTER 3
ALGEBRAIC TERMS AND CONCEPTS

An alphabetic compendium of terms and concepts commonly encountered in algebra is provided in this chapter.

ALGEBRAIC EQUATION

An algebraic equation is a statement of the equality of two expressions formulated by applying to a set of variables the algebraic operations, namely, addition, subtraction, multiplication, division, raising to a power, and extraction of a root. Examples are $x^3 + 1$ and $(y^4x^2 + 2xy - y)/(x - 1) = 12$. One important special case of such equations is that of polynomial equations, expressions of the form $ax^n + bx^{n-1} + \ldots + gx + h = k$. They have as many solutions as their degree (n), and the search for their solutions stimulated much of the development of classical and modern algebra. Equations like $x \sin(x) = c$ that involve nonalgebraic operations, such as logarithms or trigonometric functions, are said to be transcendental.

The solution of an algebraic equation is the process of finding a number or set of numbers that, if substituted for the variables in the equation, reduce it to an identity. Such a number is called a root of the equation.

ALGEBRAIC NUMBER

An algebraic number is any real number for which there exists a polynomial equation with integer coefficients such that the given real number is a solution. Algebraic numbers include all of the natural numbers, all rational numbers, some irrational numbers, and complex numbers of the form $pi + q$, where p and q are rational, and i is the square root of -1. For example, i is a root of the polynomial $x^2 + 1 = 0$. Numbers, such as that symbolized by the Greek letter π, that are not algebraic are called transcendental numbers. The mathematician Georg Cantor proved that, in a sense that can be made precise, there are many more transcendental numbers than there are algebraic numbers, even though there are infinitely many of these latter.

ASSOCIATIVE LAW

The associative law is either of two laws relating to number operations of addition and multiplication, stated symbolically: $a + (b + c) = (a + b) + c$, and $a(bc) = (ab)c$. That is, the terms or factors may be associated in any way desired. While associativity holds for ordinary arithmetic with real or imaginary numbers, there are certain applications — such as nonassociative algebras — in which it does not hold.

AUTOMORPHISM

An automorphism is a correspondence that associates to every element in a set a unique element of the set (perhaps itself) and for which there is a companion correspondence, known as its inverse, such that one followed by the other produces the identity correspondence (i); i.e., the correspondence that associates every element with itself. In symbols, if f is the original correspondence and g is its inverse, then $g(f(a)) = i(a) = a = i(a) = f(g(a))$ for every a in the set. Furthermore, operations such as addition and multiplication must be preserved. For example, $f(a + b) = f(a) + f(b)$ and $f(a \cdot b) = f(a) \cdot f(b)$ for every a and b in the set.

The collection of all possible automorphisms for a given set A, denoted Aut(A), forms a group, which can be examined to determine various symmetries in the structure of the set A.

BINOMIAL THEOREM

The binomial theorem is a statement that, for any positive integer n, the nth power of the sum of two numbers a and b may be expressed as the sum of $n + 1$ terms of the form

$$\binom{n}{r} a^{n-r} b^r;$$

in the sequence of terms, the index r takes on the successive values 0, 1, 2, . . ., n. The coefficients, called the binomial coefficients, are defined by the formula

$$\binom{n}{r} = n! / (n - r)! r!,$$

in which $n!$ (called n factorial) is the product of the first n natural numbers 1, 2, 3,..., n (and where 0! is defined as equal to 1). The coefficients may also be found in the array often called Pascal's triangle

$$
\begin{array}{ccccccccc}
 & & & & 1 & & & & \\
 & & & 1 & & 1 & & & \\
 & & 1 & & 2 & & 1 & & \\
 & 1 & & 3 & & 3 & & 1 & \\
1 & & 4 & & 6 & & 4 & & 1 \\
\end{array}
$$

by finding the rth entry of the nth row (counting begins with a zero in both directions). Each entry in the interior of Pascal's triangle is the sum of the two entries above it.

The theorem is useful in algebra as well as for determining permutations, combinations, and probabilities. For positive integer exponents, n, the theorem was known to Islamic and Chinese mathematicians of the late medieval period. Isaac Newton stated in 1676, without proof, the general form of the theorem (for any real number n), and a proof by Jakob Bernoulli was published in 1713, after Bernoulli's death. The theorem can be generalized to include complex exponents, n, and this was first proved by Niels Henrik Abel in the early 19th century.

BOOLEAN ALGEBRA

Boolean algebra is a symbolic system of mathematical logic that represents relationships between entities — either ideas or objects. The basic rules of this system were formulated in 1847 by George Boole of England and were subsequently refined by other mathematicians and applied to set theory. Today, Boolean algebra is of significance to the theory of probability, geometry of sets, and information theory. Furthermore, it constitutes the basis for the design of circuits used in electronic digital computers.

In a Boolean algebra a set of elements is closed under two commutative binary operations that can be described by any of various systems of postulates, all of which can be deduced from the basic postulates that an identity element exists for each operation, that each operation is distributive over the other, and that for every element in the set there is another element that combines with the first under either of the operations to yield the identity element of the other.

The ordinary algebra (in which the elements are the real numbers and the commutative binary operations are addition and multiplication) does not satisfy all the requirements of a Boolean algebra. The set of real numbers is closed under the two operations (that is, the sum or the product of two real numbers also is a real number). Identity elements exist—0 for addition and 1 for multiplication (that is, $a + 0 = a$ and $a \times 1 = a$ for any real number a). Also, multiplication is distributive over addition (that is, $a \times [b + c] = [a \times b] + [a \times c]$), but addition is not distributive over multiplication (that is, $a + [b \times c]$ does not, in general, equal $[a + b] \times [a + c]$).

George Boole, whose work on logic led him to develop what is now known as Boolean algebra. Keystone/Hulton Archive/Getty Images

The advantage of Boolean algebra is that it is valid when truth-values—i.e., the truth or falsity of a given proposition or logical statement—are used as variables instead of the numeric quantities employed by ordinary algebra. It lends itself to manipulating propositions that are either true (with truth-value 1) or false (with truth-value 0). Two such propositions can be combined to form a compound proposition by use of the logical connectives, or operators, AND or OR. (The standard symbols for these connectives are $\land$ and $\lor$, respectively.) The truth-value of the resulting proposition is dependent on the truth-values of the components and the connective employed. For example, the propositions a and b may be true or false, independently of one another. The connective AND produces a proposition, $a \wedge b$, that is true when both a and b are true, and false otherwise.

COMMUTATIVE LAW

The commutative law is either of two laws relating to number operations of addition and multiplication, stated symbolically: $a + b = b + a$ and $ab = ba$. From these laws it follows that any finite sum or product is unaltered by reordering its terms or factors. While commutativity holds for many systems, such as the real or complex numbers, there are other systems, such as the system of $n \times n$ matrices or the system of quaternions, in which commutativity of multiplication is invalid. Scalar multiplication of two vectors (to give the so-called dot product) is commutative (i.e., $a \cdot b = b \cdot a$), but vector multiplication (to give the cross product) is not (i.e., $a \times b = -b \times a$). The commutative law does not necessarily hold for multiplication of conditionally convergent series.

COMPLEX NUMBER

A complex number is any number of the form $x + yi$ in which x and y are real numbers and i is the imaginary unit such that $i^2 = -1$.

CRAMER'S RULE

Cramer's rule is a procedure in linear and multilinear algebra for solving systems of simultaneous linear equations by means of determinants. Although Cramer's rule is not an effective method for solving systems of linear equations in more than three variables, it is of use in studying how the solutions to a system $AX = B$ depend on the vector B. If

$$a_{11}x_1 + \ldots + a_{1n}x_n = b_1$$
$$a_{n1}x_1 + \ldots + a_{nn}x_n = b_n$$

is a system of n simultaneous linear equations in n unknowns, then a solution of this system is

$$x_i = \det B_i / \det A; \quad i = 1, 2, \ldots, n$$

in which $\det A$ is the determinant of the matrix A (in which the elements of each row are the coefficients a_{ij} of one of the equations) and the matrix B_i is formed by replacing the ith column of A by the column of constants $b_1, \ldots, b_n$.

If $\det A$ equals zero, the system has no unique solution. That is, there is no set $x_1, \ldots, x_n$ that satisfies all of the equations.

DEGREE OF FREEDOM

A degree of freedom is any of the number of independent quantities necessary to express the values of all the variable properties of a system. A system composed of a point moving without constraints in space, for example, has three degrees of freedom because three coordinates are needed to determine the position of the point.

The number of degrees of freedom is reduced by constraints such as the requirement that a point move along a particular path. Thus, a simple pendulum has only one degree of freedom because its angle of inclination is specified by a single number. In a chemical system, the condition of equilibrium imposes constraints: properties such as temperature and composition of coexisting phases cannot all vary independently.

If, in a statistical sample distribution, there are n variables and m constraints on the distribution, there are $n - m$ degrees of freedom.

DETERMINANT

In linear and multilinear algebra, a determinant is a value, denoted $\det A$, associated with a square matrix A of n rows and n columns. Designating any element of the matrix by the symbol arc (the subscript r identifies the row and c the column), the determinant is evaluated by finding the sum of $n!$ terms, each of which is the product of the coefficient $(-1)^{r+c}$ and n elements, no two from the same row or column. Determinants are of use in ascertaining whether a system of n equations in n unknowns has a solution. If B is an $n \times 1$ vector and the determinant of A is nonzero, the system of equations $AX = B$ always has a solution.

For the trivial case of $n = 1$, the value of the determinant is the value of the single element a_{11}. For $n = 2$, the matrix is

$$\begin{bmatrix} a_{11} & a_{12} \\ a_{21} & a_{22} \end{bmatrix}$$

and the determinant is $a_{11}a_{22} - a_{12}a_{21}$.

Larger determinants ordinarily are evaluated by a step-wise process, expanding them into sums of terms, each the product of a coefficient and a smaller determinant. Any row or column of the matrix is selected, each of its elements arc is multiplied by the factor $(-1)^{r+c}$ and by the smaller determinant Mrc formed by deleting the rth row and cth column from the original array. Each of these products is expanded in the same way until the small determinants can be evaluated by inspection. At each stage, the process is facilitated by choosing the row or column containing the most zeros.

For example, the determinant of the matrix

$$A = \begin{bmatrix} 2 & 0 & 3 \\ 4 & 1 & -1 \\ 1 & 0 & 7 \end{bmatrix}$$

is most easily evaluated with respect to the second column:

$$\det A = 0 \cdot (-1)^3 M_{12} + 1 \cdot (-1)^4 M_{22} +$$

$$0 \cdot (-1)^5 M_{32} = M_{22} = (2 \cdot 7 - 3 \cdot 1) = 11.$$

DISCRIMINANT

A discriminant is a parameter of an object or system calculated as an aid to its classification or solution. In the case of a quadratic equation $ax^2 + bx + c = 0$, the discriminant is $b^2 - 4ac$. For a cubic equation $x^3 + ax^2 + bx + c = 0$, the discriminant is $a^2b^2 + 18abc - 4b^3 - 4a^3c - 27c^2$. The roots of a quadratic or cubic equation with real coefficients are real and distinct if the discriminant is positive, are real with at least two equal if the discriminant is zero, and include a conjugate pair of complex roots if the discriminant is negative. A discriminant can be found for the general quadratic, or conic, equation $ax^2 + bxy + cy^2 + dx + ey + f = 0$. It indicates whether the conic represented is an ellipse, a hyperbola, or a parabola.

Discriminants also are defined for elliptic curves, finite field extensions, quadratic forms, and other mathematical entities. The discriminants of differential equations are algebraic equations that reveal information about the families of solutions of the original equations.

DISTRIBUTIVE LAW

The distributive law is the law relating the operations of multiplication and addition, stated symbolically, $a(b + c) = ab + ac$. That is, the monomial factor a is distributed, or separately applied, to each term of the binomial factor $b + c$, resulting in the product $ab + ac$. From this law it is easy to show that the result of first adding several numbers and then multiplying the sum by some number is the same as first multiplying each separately by the number and then adding the products.

EIGENVALUE

An eigenvalue is one of a set of discrete values of a parameter, k, in an equation of the form $P\psi = k\psi$, in which P is a linear operator (that is, a symbol denoting a linear operation to be performed), for which there are solutions satisfying given boundary conditions. The symbol ψ (psi) represents an eigenfunction (proper or characteristic function) belonging to that eigenvalue. The totality of eigenvalues is a set. In quantum mechanics P is frequently a Hamiltonian, or energy, operator and the eigenvalues are energy values, but operators corresponding to other dynamical variables such as total angular momentum are also used. Experimental measurements of the proper dynamical variable will yield eigenvalues.

EQUATION

A mathematical equation is a statement of equality between two expressions consisting of variables and/or numbers. In essence, equations are questions, and the development of mathematics has been driven by attempts to find answers to those questions in a systematic way. Equations vary in complexity from simple algebraic equations (involving only addition or multiplication) to differential equations, exponential equations (involving exponential expressions), and integral equations. They are used to express many of the laws of physics.

FACTOR

A factor is a number or algebraic expression that divides another number or expression evenly—i.e., with no remainder. For example, 3 and 6 are factors of 12 because $12 \div 3 = 4$ exactly and $12 \div 6 = 2$ exactly. The other factors of 12 are 1, 2, 4, and 12. A positive integer greater than 1, or an algebraic expression, that has only two factors (i.e., itself and 1) is termed prime. A positive integer or an algebraic expression that has more than two factors is termed composite. The prime factors of a number or an algebraic expression are those factors which are prime. By the fundamental theorem of arithmetic, except for the order in which the prime factors are written, every whole number larger than 1 can be uniquely expressed as the product of its prime factors. For example, 60 can be written as the product $2 \cdot 2 \cdot 3 \cdot 5$.

Methods for factoring large whole numbers are of great importance in public-key cryptography, and on such methods rests the security (or lack thereof) of data transmitted over the Internet. Factoring is also a particularly important step in the solution of many algebraic problems. For example, the polynomial equation $x^2 - x - 2 = 0$ can be factored as $(x - 2)(x + 1) = 0$. Since in an integral domain $a \cdot b = 0$ implies that either $a = 0$ or $b = 0$, the simpler equations $x - 2 = 0$ and $x + 1 = 0$ can be solved to yield the two solutions $x = 2$ and $x = -1$ of the original equation.

FUNDAMENTAL THEOREM OF ALGEBRA

The fundamental theorem of algebra is the theorem of equations proved by Carl Friedrich Gauss in 1799. It

Carl Friedrich Gauss, whose many contributions to the field of mathematics include the development of the fundamental theorem of algebra. Hulton Archive/Getty Images

states that every polynomial equation of degree n with complex number coefficients has n roots, or solutions, in the complex numbers

GAUSS ELIMINATION

The Gauss elimination is a process employed in linear and multilinear algebra for finding the solutions of a system of simultaneous linear equations by first solving one of the equations for one variable (in terms of all the others) and then substituting this expression into the remaining equations. The result is a new system in which the number of equations and variables is one less than in the original system. The same procedure is applied to another variable and the process of reduction continued until there remains one equation, in which the only unknown quantity is the last variable. Solving this equation makes it possible to "back substitute" this value in an earlier equation that contains this variable and one other unknown in order to solve for another variable. This process is continued until all the original variables have been evaluated. The whole process is greatly simplified using matrix operations, which can be performed by computers.

GROUP

A mathematical group is a set that has a multiplication that is associative [$a(bc) = (ab)c$ for any a, b, c] and that has an identity element and inverses for all elements of the set. Systems obeying the group laws first appeared in 1770 in Joseph-Louis Lagrange's studies of permutations of roots of equations in his work *Reflections sur la Theorie Algebrigres des Equations*. However, the word *group* was first attached to a system of permutations by Évariste Galois in 1831. It was Heinrich Weber, in 1882, who first gave a purely axiomatic description of a group independently of the nature of its elements. Today, groups are fundamental entities in abstract algebra and are of considerable importance in geometry, physics, and chemistry.

GROUP THEORY

In modern algebra, group theory is a system consisting of a set of elements and an operation for combining the elements, which together satisfy certain axioms. These require that the group be closed under the operation (the combination of any two elements produces another element of the group); that it obey the associative law; that it contain an identity element (which, combined with any other element, leaves the latter unchanged); and that each element have an inverse (which combines with an element to produce the identity element). If the group also satisfies the commutative law, it is called a commutative, or Abelian, group. The set of integers under addition, where the identity element is o and the inverse is the negative of a positive number or vice versa, is an Abelian group.

HODGE CONJECTURE

In algebraic geometry, the Hodge conjecture is an assertion that for certain "nice" spaces (projective algebraic varieties), their complicated shapes can be covered (approximated) by a collection of simpler geometric pieces called algebraic cycles. The conjecture was first formulated by British mathematician William Hodge in 1941, though it received little attention before he presented it in an address during the 1950 International Congress of Mathematicians, held in Cambridge, Mass., U.S. In 2000 it was designated one of the Millennium Problems, seven mathematical problems selected by the Clay Mathematics Institute of Cambridge, Mass., for a special award. The solution for each Millennium Problem is worth $1 million. In 2008 the U.S. Defense Advanced Research Projects Agency (DARPA) listed it as one of the 23 DARPA Mathematical Challenges, mathematical problems for which it was soliciting research proposals for funding— "Mathematical Challenge Twenty-one: Settle the Hodge Conjecture. This conjecture in algebraic geometry is a metaphor for transforming transcendental computations into algebraic ones."

HOMOMORPHISM

A homomorphism (from Greek *homoios morphe*, "similar form") is a special correspondence between the members (elements) of two algebraic systems, such as two groups, two rings, or two fields. Two homomorphic systems have the same basic structure, and, while their elements and operations may appear entirely different, results on one system often apply as well to the other system. Thus, if a new system can be shown to be homomorphic to a known system, certain known features of one can be applied to the other, thereby simplifying the analysis of the new system.

In a homomorphism, corresponding elements of two systems behave very similarly in combination with other corresponding elements. For example, let G and H be groups. The elements of G are denoted $g, g',\ldots$, and they are subject to some operation $\oplus$. (Although the symbol may be thought of as some operation like multiplication, it can just as well indicate rotation or some other non-arithmetic operation.) Similarly, the elements of H are denoted by $h, h',\ldots$, and they are subject to some operation $\otimes$. A homomorphism from G to H is a correspondence $g \to h$ between all elements of G and some elements of H that has the following property: if $g \to h$ and $g' \to h'$, then $g \oplus g' \to h \otimes h'$. In other words, the element of H corresponding to a product of elements in G is the product, in the same order, of the elements of H corresponding to the two elements in G. Expressed more compactly, the "image" of the product is the product of the images, or the correspondence preserves the operation.

A correspondence between members of two algebraic systems may be written as a function f from G to H, and one speaks of f as "mapping" G to H. The condition that f be a homomorphism of the group G to the group H may be expressed as the requirement that $f(g \oplus g') = f(g) \otimes f(g')$.

Homomorphisms impose conditions on a mapping f: if e is the identity of G, then $g \oplus e = g$, so $f(g \oplus e) = f(g)$. Furthermore, since f is a homomorphism, $f(g \oplus e) = f(g) \otimes f(e)$, so $f(g) = f(g) \otimes f(e)$. By the cancellation laws for groups, this implies that $f(e)$ is equal to the identity in H. Thus, homomorphisms map the unique identity element of one group to the unique identity element of the other group. Similarly, homomorphisms map the inverse of an element g in one group to the inverse of the element $f(g)$. This is why homomorphisms are called structure-preserving maps.

Special types of homomorphisms have their own names. A one-to-one homomorphism from G to H is called a monomorphism, and a homomorphism that is "onto," or covers every element of H, is called an epimorphism. An especially important homomorphism is an isomorphism, in which the homomorphism from G to H is both one-to-one and onto. In this last case, G and H are essentially the same system and differ only in the names of their elements. Thus, homomorphisms are useful in classifying and enumerating algebraic systems since they allow one to identify how closely different systems are related.

IDEAL

In modern algebra, an ideal is a subring of a mathematical ring with certain absorption properties. The concept of an ideal was first defined and developed by German mathematician Richard Dedekind in 1871. In particular, he used ideals to translate ordinary properties of arithmetic into properties of sets.

A ring is a set having two binary operations, typically addition and multiplication. Addition (or another operation) must be commutative ($a + b = b + a$ for any a, b) and associative [$a + (b + c) = (a + b) + c$ for any a, b, c], and multiplication (or another operation) must be associative [$a(bc) = (ab)c$ for any a, b, c]. There must also be a zero (which functions as an identity element for addition), negatives of all elements (so that adding a number and its negative produces the ring's zero element), and two distributive laws relating addition and multiplication [$a(b + c) = ab + ac$ and $(a + b)c = ac + bc$ for any a, b, c]. A subset of a ring that forms a ring with respect to the operations of the ring is known as a subring.

For a subring I of a ring R to be an ideal, ax and xa must be in I for all a in R and x in I. In other words, multiplying (on the left or right) any element of the ring by an element of the ideal produces another element of the ideal. Note that ax may not equal xa, as multiplication does not have to be commutative.

Furthermore, each element a of R forms a coset $(a + I)$, where every element from I is substituted into the expression to produce the full coset. For an ideal I, the set of all cosets forms a ring, with addition and multiplication, respectively, defined by: $(a + I) + (b + I) = (a + b) + I$ and $(a + I)(b + I) = ab + I$. The ring of cosets is called a quotient ring R/I, and the ideal I is its zero element. For example, the set of integers ($\mathbf{Z}$) forms a ring with ordinary addition and multiplication. The set $3\mathbf{Z}$ formed by multiplying each integer by 3 forms an ideal, and the quotient ring $\mathbf{Z}/3\mathbf{Z}$ has only three elements:

1. $0 + 3\mathbf{Z} = 3\mathbf{Z} = \{0, \pm3, \pm6, \pm9,\ldots\}$
2. $1 + 3\mathbf{Z} = \{\ldots, -8, -5, -2, 1, 4, 7,\ldots\}$
3. $2 + 3\mathbf{Z} = \{\ldots, -7, -4, -1, 2, 5, 8,\ldots\}$

IMAGINARY NUMBER

An imaginary number is any product of the form ai, in which a is a real number and i is the imaginary unit defined as -1.

INJECTION

An injection is a mapping (or function) between two sets such that the domain (input) of the mapping consists of all the elements of the first set, the range (output) consists of some subset of the second set, and each element of the first set is mapped to a different element of the second set (one-to-one). The sets need not be different. For example, the function that multiplies each integer by two is an injection from the set of integers to the set of even integers, which is a subset of the integers. If the range of a mapping consists of all the elements of the second set, it is known as a surjection, or onto. A mapping that is both an injection and a surjection is known as a bijection.

IRRATIONAL NUMBER

An irrational number is any real number that cannot be expressed as the quotient of two integers. For example, there is no number among integers and fractions that equals the square root of 2. A counterpart problem in measurement would be to find the length of the diagonal of a square whose side is one unit long. There is no subdivision of the unit length that will divide evenly into the length of the diagonal. It thus became necessary, early in the history of mathematics, to extend the concept of number to include irrational numbers. Each irrational number can be expressed as an infinite decimal expansion with no regularly repeating digit or group of digits. Together with the rational numbers, they form the real numbers.

LINEAR EQUATION

A linear equation is a statement that a first-degree polynomial—that is, the sum of a set of terms, each of which is the product of a constant and the first power of a variable—is equal to a constant. Specifically, a linear equation in n variables is of the form $a_0 + a_1 x_1 + \ldots + a_n x_n = c$, in which $x_1, \ldots, x_n$ are variables, the coefficients $a_0, \ldots, a_n$ are constants, and c is a constant. If there is more than one variable, the equation may be linear in some variables and not in the others. Thus, the equation $x + y = 3$ is linear in both x and y, whereas $x + y^2 = 0$ is linear in x but not in y. Any equation of two variables, linear in each, represents a straight line in Cartesian coordinates. If the constant term $c = 0$, the line passes through the origin.

A set of equations that has a common solution is called a system of simultaneous equations. For example, in the system

$$2x - y = 1$$
$$x + 2y = 8$$

both equations are satisfied by the solution $x = 2, y = 3$. The point $(2, 3)$ is the intersection of the straight lines represented by the two equations.

A linear differential equation is of first degree with respect to the dependent variable (or variables) and its (or their) derivatives. As a simple example, note $dy/dx + Py = \mathcal{Q}$, in which P and $\mathcal{Q}$ can be constants or may be functions of the independent variable, x, but do not involve the dependent variable, y. In the special case that P is a constant and $\mathcal{Q} = 0$, this represents the very important equation for exponential growth or decay (such as radioactive decay) whose solution is $y = ke^{-Px}$, where e is the base of the natural logarithm.

LIOUVILLE NUMBER

A Liouville number is any irrational number α such that for each positive integer n there exists a rational number

p/q for which $p/q < |a - (p/q)| < 1/q^n$. All Liouville numbers are transcendental numbers—that is, numbers that cannot be expressed as the solution (root) of a polynomial equation with integer coefficients. Such numbers are named for the French mathematician Joseph Liouville, who first proved the existence of transcendental numbers in 1844 and constructed the first proven transcendental number, known as Liouville's constant, in 1850.

MATRIX

A matrix is a set of numbers arranged in rows and columns so as to form a rectangular array. The numbers are called the elements, or entries, of the matrix. Matrices have wide applications in engineering, physics, economics, and statistics as well as in various branches of mathematics. Historically, it was not the matrix but a certain number associated with a square array of numbers called the determinant that was first recognized. Only gradually did the idea of the matrix as an algebraic entity emerge. The term *matrix* was introduced by the 19th-century English mathematician James Sylvester, but it was his friend the mathematician Arthur Cayley who

Arthur Cayley, who helped advance understanding of matrices by making a connection between matrices and algebra. SSPL/Getty Images

ALGEBRAIC TERMS AND CONCEPTS

developed the algebraic aspect of matrices in two papers in the 1850s. Cayley first applied them to the study of systems of linear equations, where they are still very useful. They are also important because, as Cayley recognized, certain sets of matrices form algebraic systems in which many of the ordinary laws of arithmetic (e.g., the associative and distributive laws) are valid but in which other laws (e.g., the commutative law) are not valid. Matrices have also come to have important applications in computer graphics, where they have been used to represent rotations and other transformations of images.

If there are m rows and n columns, the matrix is said to be an "m by n" matrix, written "$m \times n$." For example,

$$\begin{bmatrix} 1 & 3 & 8 \\ 2 & -4 & 5 \end{bmatrix}$$

is a 2×3 matrix. A matrix with n rows and n columns is called a square matrix of order n. An ordinary number can be regarded as a 1×1 matrix. Thus, 3 can be thought of as the matrix [3].

In a common notation, a capital letter denotes a matrix, and the corresponding small letter with a double subscript describes an element of the matrix. Thus, a_{ij} is the element in the ith row and jth column of the matrix A. If A is the 2×3 matrix shown above, then $a_{11} = 1$, $a_{12} = 3$, $a_{13} = 8$, $a_{21} = 2$, $a_{22} = -4$, and $a_{23} = 5$. Under certain conditions, matrices can be added and multiplied as individual entities, giving rise to important mathematical systems known as matrix algebras.

Matrices occur naturally in systems of simultaneous equations. In the following system for the unknowns x and y,

$$2x + 3y = 7$$
$$3x + 4y = 10,$$

the array of numbers

$$\begin{bmatrix} 2 & 3 \\ 3 & 4 \end{bmatrix}$$

is a matrix whose elements are the coefficients of the unknowns. The solution of the equations depends entirely on these numbers and on their particular arrangement. If 3 and 4 were interchanged, the solution would not be the same.

Two matrices A and B are equal to one another if they possess the same number of rows and the same number of columns and if $a_{ij} = b_{ij}$ for each i and each j. If A and B are two $m \times n$ matrices, their sum $S = A + B$ is the $m \times n$ matrix whose elements $s_{ij} = a_{ij} + b_{ij}$. That is, each element of S is equal to the sum of the elements in the corresponding positions of A and B.

A matrix A can be multiplied by an ordinary number c, which is called a scalar. The product is denoted by cA or Ac and is the matrix whose elements are ca_{ij}.

The multiplication of a matrix A by a matrix B to yield a matrix C is defined only when the number of columns of the first matrix A equals the number of rows of the second matrix B. To determine the element c_{ij}, which is in the ith row and jth column of the product, the first element in the ith row of A is multiplied by the first element in the jth column of B, the second element in the row by the second element in the column, and so on until the last element in the row is multiplied by the last element of the column. The sum of all these products gives the element c_{ij}. In symbols, for the case where A has m columns and B has m rows,

$$c_{ij} = a_{i1}b_{1j}b_{2j} + \dots + a_{im}b_{mj}.$$

The matrix C has as many rows as A and as many columns as B.

Unlike the multiplication of ordinary numbers a and b, in which ab always equals ba, the multiplication of matrices A and B is not commutative. It is, however, associative and distributive over addition. That is, when the operations are possible, the following equations always hold true: $A(BC) = (AB)C$, $A(B + C) = AB + AC$, and $(B + C)A = BA + CA$. If the 2×2 matrix A whose rows are $(2, 3)$ and $(4, 5)$ is multiplied by itself, then the product, usually written A^2, has rows $(16, 21)$ and $(28, 37)$.

A matrix O with all its elements 0 is called a zero matrix. A square matrix A with 1s on the main diagonal (upper left to lower right) and 0s everywhere else is called a unit matrix. It is denoted by I or I_n to show that its order is n. If B is any square matrix and I and O are the unit and zero matrices of the same order, it is always true that $B + O = O + B = B$ and $BI = IB = B$. Hence O and I behave like the 0 and 1 of ordinary arithmetic. In fact, ordinary arithmetic is the special case of matrix arithmetic in which all matrices are 1×1.

Associated with each square matrix A is a number that is known as the determinant of A, denoted det A. For example, for the 2×2 matrix

$$A = \begin{bmatrix} a & b \\ c & d \end{bmatrix},$$

det $A = ad - bc$. A square matrix B is called nonsingular if det $B \neq 0$. If B is nonsingular, there is a matrix called the inverse of B, denoted B^{-1}, such that $BB^{-1} = B^{-1}B = I$. The equation $AX = B$, in which A and B are known matrices and X is an unknown matrix, can be solved uniquely if A is a nonsingular matrix, for then A^{-1} exists and both sides of the equation can be multiplied on the left by it:

$A^{-1}(AX) = A^{-1}B$. Now $A^{-1}(AX) = (A^{-1}A)X = IX = X$. Hence, the solution is $X = A^{-1}B$. A system of m linear equations in n unknowns can always be expressed as a matrix equation $AX = B$ in which A is the $m \times n$ matrix of the coefficients of the unknowns, X is the $n \times 1$ matrix of the unknowns, and B is the $n \times 1$ matrix containing the numbers on the right-hand side of the equation.

A problem of great significance in many branches of science is the following: given a square matrix A of order n, find the $n \times 1$ matrix X, called an n-dimensional vector, such that $AX = cX$. Here c is a number called an eigenvalue, and X is called an eigenvector. The existence of an eigenvector X with eigenvalue c means that a certain transformation of space associated with the matrix A stretches space in the direction of the vector X by the factor c.

MULTINOMIAL THEOREM

The multinomial theorem is a generalization of the binomial theorem to more than two variables. In statistics, the corresponding multinomial series appears in the multinomial distribution, which is a generalization of the binomial distribution.

The multinomial theorem provides a formula for expanding an expression such as $(x_1 + x_2 + \cdots + x_k)^n$ for integer values of n. In particular, the expansion is given by

$$\left(x_1 + x_2 + \ldots + x_k \right)^n = \sum_{n_1, n_2, \ldots, n_k \geq 0} \frac{n!}{n_1! n_2! \ldots n_k!} x_1^{n_1} x_2^{n_2} \ldots x_k^{n_k},$$

where $n_1 + n_2 + \cdots + n_k = n$ and $n!$ is the factorial notation for $1 \times 2 \times 3 \times \cdots \times n$.

For example, the expansion of $(x_1 + x_2 + x_3)^3$ is $x_1^3 + 3x_1^2 x_2 + 3x_1^2 x_3 + 3x_1 x_2^2 + 3x_1 x_3^2 + 6x_1 x_2 x_3 + x_2^3 + 3x_2^2 x_3 + 3x_2 x_3^2 + x_3^3$.

PARAMETER

A parameter is any variable for which the range of possible values identifies a collection of distinct cases in a problem. Any equation expressed in terms of parameters is a parametric equation. The general equation of a straight line in slope-intercept form, $y = mx + b$, in which m and b are parameters, is an example of a parametric equation. When values are assigned to the parameters, such as the slope $m = 2$ and the y-intercept $b = 3$, and substitution is made, the resulting equation, $y = 2x + 3$, is that of a specific straight line and is no longer parametric.

In the set of equations $x = 2t + 1$ and $y = t^2 + 2$, t is called the parameter. As the parameter varies over a given domain of values, the set of solutions, or points (x, y), describes a curve in the plane. The use of parameters often enables descriptions of very simple curves for which it is difficult to write down a single equation in x and y.

In statistics, the parameter in a function is a variable whose value is sought by means of evidence from samples. The resulting assigned value is the estimate, or statistic.

PASCAL'S TRIANGLE

In algebra, Pascal's triangle is a triangular arrangement of numbers that gives the coefficients in the expansion of any binomial expression, such as $(x + y)^n$. It is named for the 17th-century French mathematician Blaise Pascal, but it is far older. Chinese mathematician Jia Xian devised a triangular representation for the coefficients in the 11th century. His triangle was further studied and popularized by Chinese mathematician Yang Hui in the 13th century, for which reason in China it is often called the Yanghui triangle. It was included as an illustration in Chinese mathematician Zhu Shijie's *Siyuan yujian* (1303; "Precious

Chinese mathematician Jia Xian devised a triangular representation for the coefficients in an expansion of binomial expressions in the 11th century. His triangle was further studied and popularized by Chinese mathematician Yang Hui in the 13th century, for which reason in China it is often called the Yanghui triangle. It was reinvented in 1665 by French mathematician Blaise Pascal in the West, where it is known as Pascal's triangle. By permission of the Syndics of Cambridge University Library

Mirror of Four Elements"), where it was already called the "Old Method." The remarkable pattern of coefficients was also studied in the 11th century by Persian poet and astronomer Omar Khayyam.

The triangle can be constructed by first placing a 1 (Chinese "一") along the left and right edges. Then the triangle can be filled out from the top by adding together the two numbers just above to the left and right of each position in the triangle. Thus, the third row, in Hindu-Arabic numerals, is 1 2 1, the fourth row is 1 4 6 4 1, the fifth row is 1 5 10 10 5 1, and so forth. The first row, or just 1, gives the coefficient for the expansion of $(x + y)^0 = 1$; the second row, or 1 1, gives the coefficients for $(x + y)^1 = x + y$;

Polish mathematician Wacław Sierpiński described the fractal that bears his name in 1915, although the design as an art motif dates at least to 13th-century Italy. Begin with a solid equilateral triangle, and remove the triangle formed by connecting the midpoints of each side. The midpoints of the sides of the resulting three internal triangles can be connected to form three new triangles that can be removed to form nine smaller internal triangles. The process of cutting away triangular pieces continues indefinitely, producing a region with a Hausdorff dimension of a bit more than 1.5 (indicating that it is more than a one-dimensional figure but less than a two-dimensional figure). Encyclopædia Britannica, Inc.

the third row, or 1 2 1, gives the coefficients for $(x + y)^2 = x^2 + 2xy + y^2$; and so forth.

The triangle displays many interesting patterns. For example, drawing parallel "shallow diagonals" and adding the numbers on each line together produces the Fibonacci numbers (1, 1, 2, 3, 5, 8, 13, 21,. . .,), which were first noted by the medieval Italian mathematician Leonardo Pisano ("Fibonacci") in his *Liber abaci* (1202; "Book of the Abacus").

Another interesting property of the triangle is that if all the positions containing odd numbers are shaded black and all the positions containing even numbers are shaded white, a fractal known as the Sierpinski gadget, after 20th-century Polish mathematician Wacław Sierpiński, will be formed.

POLYNOMIAL

A polynomial is an expression consisting of numbers and variables grouped according to certain patterns. Specifically, polynomials are sums of monomials of the form ax^n, where a (the coefficient) can be any real number and n (the degree) must be a whole number. A polynomial's degree is that of its monomial of highest degree. Like whole numbers, polynomials may be prime or factorable into products of primes. They may contain any number of variables, provided that the power of each variable is a nonnegative integer. They are the basis of algebraic equation solving. Setting a polynomial equal to zero results in a polynomial equation. Equating it to a variable results in a polynomial function, a particularly useful tool in modeling physical situations. Polynomial equations and functions can be analyzed completely by methods of algebra and calculus.

QUADRATIC EQUATION

A quadratic equation is an algebraic equation of the second degree (having one or more variables raised to the second power). Old Babylonian cuneiform texts, dating from the time of Hammurabi, show a knowledge of how to solve quadratic equations, but it appears that ancient Egyptian mathematicians did not know how to solve them. Since the time of Galileo, they have been important in the physics of accelerated motion, such as free fall in a vacuum. The general quadratic equation in one variable is $ax^2 + bx + c = 0$, in which a, b, and c are arbitrary constants (or parameters) and a is not equal to 0. Such an equation has two roots (not necessarily distinct), as given by the quadratic formula

$$x = \frac{-b \pm \sqrt{b^2 - 4ac}}{2a}.$$

The discriminant $b^2 - 4ac$ gives information concerning the nature of the roots. If, instead of equating the above to zero, the curve $ax^2 + bx + c = y$ is plotted, it is seen that the real roots are the x coordinates of the points at which the curve crosses the x-axis. The shape of this curve in Euclidean two-dimensional space is a parabola. In Euclidean three-dimensional space, it is a parabolic cylindrical surface, or paraboloid.

In two variables, the general quadratic equation is $ax^2 + bxy + cy^2 + dx + ey + f = 0$, in which a, b, c, d, e, and f are arbitrary constants and a, $c \neq 0$. The discriminant (symbolized by the Greek letter delta, Δ) and the invariant ($b^2 - 4ac$) together provide information as to the shape of the curve. The locus in Euclidean two-dimensional space of every general quadratic in two variables is a conic section or its degenerate.

More general quadratic equations, in the variables $x, y,$ and z, lead to generation (in Euclidean three-dimensional space) of surfaces known as the quadrics, or quadric surfaces.

QUATERNION

A quaternion is a generalization of two-dimensional complex numbers to three dimensions. Quaternions and rules for operations on them were invented by Irish mathematician Sir William Rowan Hamilton in 1843. He devised them as a way of describing three-dimensional problems in mechanics. Following a long struggle to devise mathematical operations that would retain the normal properties of algebra, Hamilton hit upon the idea of adding a fourth dimension. This allowed him to retain the normal rules of algebra except for the commutative law for multiplication (in general, $ab \neq ba$), so that the quaternions only form an associative group—in particular, a non-Abelian group. The quaternions are the most widely known and used hypercomplex numbers, though they have been mostly replaced in practice by operations with matrices and vectors. Still, the quaternions can be regarded as a four-dimensional vector space formed by combining a real number with a three-dimensional vector, with a basis (set of generating vectors) given by the unit vectors $1, i, j,$ and k such that

$$i^2 = j^2 = k^2 = ijk = -1.$$

RATIONAL NUMBER

Rational numbers are numbers that can be represented as the quotient p/q of two integers such that $q \neq 0$. In addition to all the fractions, the set of rational numbers includes all the integers, each of which can be written as a quotient with the integer as the numerator and 1 as the denominator. In decimal form, rational numbers are either terminating or repeating decimals. For example, $\frac{1}{7} = 0.\overline{142857}$, where the bar over 142857 indicates a pattern that repeats forever.

A real number that cannot be expressed as a quotient of two integers is known as an irrational number.

RING

A mathematical ring is a set having an addition that must be commutative ($a + b = b + a$ for any a, b) and associative [$a + (b + c) = (a + b) + c$ for any a, b, c], and a multiplication that must be associative [$a(bc) = (ab)c$ for any a, b, c]. There must also be a zero (which functions as an identity element for addition), negatives of all elements (so that adding a number and its negative produces the ring's zero element), and two distributive laws relating addition and multiplication [$a(b + c) = ab + ac$ and $(a + b)c = ac + bc$ for any a, b, c]. A commutative ring is a ring in which multiplication is commutative—that is, in which $ab = ba$ for any a, b.

The simplest example of a ring is the collection of integers (. . ., -3, -2, -1, 0, 1, 2, 3, . . .) together with the ordinary operations of addition and multiplication.

ROOT

A root is a solution to an equation, usually expressed as a number or an algebraic formula.

In the 9th century, Arab writers usually called one of the equal factors of a number *jadhr* ("root"), and their medieval European translators used the Latin word *radix* (from which derives the adjective *radical*). If a is a positive real number and n a positive integer, there exists a unique positive real number x such that $x^n = a$. This number—the (principal) nth root of a—is written $\sqrt[n]{a}$ or $a^{1/n}$. The integer n is called the index of the root. For $n = 2$, the root is called the square root and is written $\sqrt{a}$. The root $\sqrt[3]{a}$ is called the cube root of a. If a is negative and n is odd, the unique negative nth root of a is termed principal. For example, the principal cube root of -27 is -3.

If a whole number (positive integer) has a rational nth root—i.e., one that can be written as a common fraction— then this root must be an integer. Thus, 5 has no rational square root because 2^2 is less than 5 and 3^2 is greater than 5. Exactly n complex numbers satisfy the equation $x^n = 1$, and they are called the complex nth roots of unity. If a regular polygon of n sides is inscribed in a unit circle centred at the origin so that one vertex lies on the positive half of the x-axis, the radii to the vertices are the vectors representing the n complex nth roots of unity. If the root whose vector makes the smallest positive angle with the positive direction of the x-axis is denoted by the Greek letter omega, ω, then ω, ω^2, ω^3, . . ., $\omega^n = 1$ constitute all the nth roots of unity. For example, $\omega = -1/2 + -3/2$, $\omega^2 = -1/2 - \sqrt{-3}/2$, and $\omega^3 = 1$ are all the cube roots of unity. Any root, symbolized by the Greek letter epsilon, ε, that has the property that ε, ε^2, . . ., $\varepsilon^n = 1$ give all the nth roots of unity is called primitive. Evidently the problem of finding the nth roots of unity is equivalent to the problem of inscribing a regular polygon of n sides in a circle. For every integer n, the nth roots of unity can be determined in terms of the rational numbers by means of rational operations and radicals. But they can be constructed by ruler and compasses (i.e., determined in terms of the ordinary operations of arithmetic and square roots) only if n is a product of distinct prime numbers of the form $2^b + 1$, or 2^k times such a product, or is of the form 2^k. If a is a complex number not 0, the equation $x^n = a$ has exactly n roots, and all the nth roots of a are the products of any one of these roots by the nth roots of unity.

The term *root* has been carried over from the equation $x^n = a$ to all polynomial equations. Thus, a solution of the equation $f(x) = a_0 x^n + a_1 x^{n-1} + \ldots + a_{n-1} x + a_n = 0$, with $a_0 \neq 0$, is called a root of the equation. If the coefficients lie in the complex field, an equation of the nth degree has exactly n (not necessarily distinct) complex roots. If the coefficients are real and n is odd, there is a real root. But an equation does not always have a root in its coefficient field. Thus, $x^2 - 5 = 0$ has no rational root, although its coefficients (1 and -5) are rational numbers.

More generally, the term *root* may be applied to any number that satisfies any given equation, whether a polynomial equation or not. Thus π is a root of the equation $x \sin (x) = 0$.

SQUARE ROOT

A square root is any factor of a number that, when multiplied by itself, gives the original number. For example, both 3 and -3 are square roots of 9. As early as the 2nd millennium BCE, the Babylonians possessed effective methods for approximating square roots.

SURJECTION

A surjection is a mapping (or function) between two sets such that the range (output) of the mapping consists of every element of the second set. A mapping that is both an injection (a one-to-one correspondence for all elements from the first set to elements in the second set) and a surjection is known as a bijection.

SYNTHETIC DIVISION

Synthetic division is a short method of dividing a polynomial of degree n of the form $a_0x^n + a_1x^{n-1} + a_2x^{n-2} + \ldots + a_n$, in which $a_0 \neq 0$, by another of the same form but of lesser degree (usually of the form $x - a$). Based on the remainder theorem, it is sometimes called the method of detached coefficients.

To divide $2x^3 - 7x^2 + 11$ by $x - 3$, the coefficients of the dividend are written in order of diminishing powers of x, zeros being inserted for each missing power. The variable and its exponents are omitted throughout. The coefficient of the highest power of x (2 in this example) is brought down as is, multiplied by the constant term of the divisor (-3) with its sign changed, and added to the coefficient following, giving -1. The sum -1 is likewise multiplied and added to the next coefficient, giving -3, and so on.

$$\begin{array}{rrrr|r}
2 & -7 & 0 & 11 & \\
 & 6 & -3 & -9 & 3 \\
\hline
2 & -1 & -3 & 2 &
\end{array}$$

The result, $2x^2 - x - 3$ with a remainder of 2, can be readily checked by long division:

$$\begin{array}{r}
+2x^2 - x - 3 + \dfrac{2}{x-3} \\[2pt]
x-3\overline{)2x^3 - 7x^2 + 0x + 11} \\
\underline{2x^3 - 6x^2} \\
-x^2 + 0x \\
\underline{-x^2 + 3x} \\
-3x + 11 \\
\underline{-3x + 9} \\
2\,(= \text{remainder}).
\end{array}$$

SYSTEM OF EQUATIONS

A system of equations (or simultaneous equations,) are two or more equations to be solved together (i.e., the solution must satisfy all the equations in the system). For a system to have a unique solution, the number of equations must equal the number of unknowns. Even then a solution is not guaranteed. If a solution exists, the system is consistent. If not, it is inconsistent. A system of linear equations can be represented by a matrix whose elements are the coefficients of the equations. Though simple systems of two equations in two unknowns can be solved by substitution, larger systems are best handled with matrix techniques.

VARIABLE

A variable is a symbol (usually a letter) standing in for an unknown numerical value in an equation. Commonly used variables include x and y (real-number unknowns), z (complex-number unknowns), t (time), r (radius), and s (arc length). Variables should be distinguished from coefficients, fixed values that multiply powers of variables in polynomials and algebraic equations. In the quadratic equation $ax^2 + bx + c = 0$, x is the variable, and a, b, and c are coefficients whose values must be specified to solve the equation. In translating word problems into algebraic equations, quantities to be determined can be represented by variables.

VECTOR

A vector is a quantity that has both magnitude and direction but not position. Examples of such quantities are velocity and acceleration. In their modern form, vectors appeared late in the 19th century when Josiah Willard Gibbs and Oliver Heaviside (of the United States and Britain, respectively) independently developed vector analysis to express the new laws of electromagnetism discovered by the Scottish physicist James Clerk Maxwell. Since that time, vectors have become essential in physics, mechanics, electrical engineering, and other sciences to describe forces mathematically.

Vectors may be visualized as directed line segments whose lengths are their magnitudes. Since only the magnitude and direction of a vector matter, any directed segment may be replaced by one of the same length and direction but beginning at another point, such as the origin of a coordinate system. Vectors are usually indicated by a bold-face letter, such as v. A vector's magnitude, or length, is indicated by $|v|$, or v, which represents a one-dimensional quantity (such as an ordinary number) known as a scalar. Multiplying a vector by a scalar changes the vector's length but not its direction, except that multiplying by a negative number will reverse the direction of the vector's arrow. For example, multiplying a vector by 1/2 will result in a vector half as long in the same direction, while multiplying a vector by -2 will result in a vector twice as long but pointed in the opposite direction.

Two vectors can be added or subtracted. For example, to add or subtract vectors v and w graphically (*see* the diagram on page 79), move each to the origin and complete the parallelogram formed by the two vectors; $v + w$ is then one diagonal vector of the parallelogram, and $v - w$ is the other diagonal vector.

There are two different ways of multiplying two vectors together. The cross, or vector, product results in another vector that is denoted by $v \times w$. The cross product magnitude is given by $|v \times w| = vw \sin \theta$, where θ is the smaller

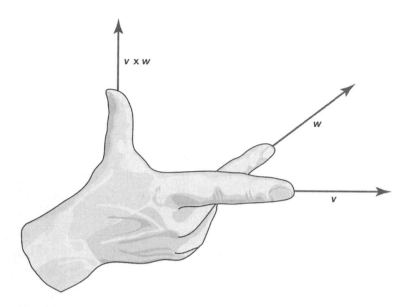

The ordinary, or dot, product of two vectors is simply a one-dimensional number, or scalar. In contrast, the cross product of two vectors results in another vector whose direction is orthogonal to both of the original vectors, as illustrated by the right hand rule. The magnitude, or length, of the cross product vector is given by vw sin θ, where θ is the angle between the original vectors v and w. Encyclopædia Britannica, Inc.Encyclopædia Britannica, Inc.

angle between the vectors (with their "tails" placed together). The direction of $v \times w$ is perpendicular to both v and w, and its direction can be visualized with the right-hand rule, as shown in the figure above.

The cross product is frequently used to obtain a "normal" (a line perpendicular) to a surface at some point, and it occurs in the calculation of torque and the magnetic force on a moving charged particle.

The other way of multiplying two vectors together is called a dot product, or sometimes a scalar product because it results in a scalar. The dot product is given by $v \cdot w = vw \cos \theta$, where θ is the smaller angle between the vectors. The dot product is used to find the angle between two vectors. (Note that the dot product is zero when the vectors are perpendicular.) A typical physical application is to find the work W performed by a constant force F acting on a moving object d. The work is given by $W = Fd \cos \theta$.

VECTOR OPERATIONS

Vector operations are an extension of the laws of elementary algebra to vectors. They include addition, subtraction, and three types of multiplication. The sum of two vectors is a third vector, represented as the diagonal of the parallelogram constructed with the two original vectors as sides. When a vector is multiplied by a positive scalar (i.e., number), its magnitude is multiplied by the scalar and its direction remains unchanged (if the scalar is negative, the direction is reversed). The multiplication of a vector a by another vector b leads to the dot product, written $a \cdot b$, and the cross product, written $a \times b$. The dot product, also called the scalar product, is a scalar real number equal to the product of the lengths of vectors a ($|a|$) and b ($|b|$) and the cosine of the angle (θ) between them: $a \cdot b = |a| \, |b| \cos \theta$. This equals zero if the two vectors are perpendicular (*see* orthogonality). The cross product, also called the vector product, is a third vector (c), perpendicular to the plane of the original vectors. The magnitude of c is equal to the product of the lengths of vectors a and b and the sine of the angle (θ) between them: $|c| = |a| \, |b| \sin \theta$. The associative law and commutative law hold for vector addition and the dot product. The cross product is associative but not commutative.

VECTOR SPACE

A vector space is a set of multidimensional quantities, known as vectors, together with a set of one-dimensional quantities, known as scalars, such that vectors can be added together and vectors can be multiplied by scalars while preserving the ordinary arithmetic properties (associativity, commutativity, distributivity, and so forth). Vector spaces are fundamental to linear algebra and appear throughout mathematics and physics.

The idea of a vector space developed from the notion of ordinary two- and three-dimensional spaces as collections of vectors $\{u, v, w, \ldots\}$ with an associated field of real numbers $\{a, b, c, \ldots\}$. Vector spaces as abstract algebraic entities were first defined by the Italian mathematician Giuseppe Peano in 1888. Peano called his vector spaces "linear systems" because he correctly saw that one can obtain any vector in the space from a linear combination of finitely many vectors and scalars—$av + bw + \ldots + cz$. A set of vectors that can generate every vector in the space through such linear combinations is known as a spanning set. The dimension of a vector space is the number of vectors in the smallest spanning set. (For example, the unit vector in the x-direction together with the unit vector in the y-direction suffice to generate any vector in the two-dimensional Euclidean plane when combined with the real numbers.)

The linearity of vector spaces has made these abstract objects important in diverse areas such as statistics, physics, and economics, where the vectors may indicate probabilities, forces, or investment strategies and where the vector space includes all allowable states.

CHAPTER 4
TRIGONOMETRY

Trigonometry is the branch of mathematics concerned with specific functions of angles and their application to calculations. There are six functions of an angle commonly used in trigonometry. Their names and abbreviations are sine (sin), cosine (cos), tangent (tan), cotangent (cot), secant (sec), and cosecant (csc).

Trigonometry developed from a need to compute angles and distances in such fields as astronomy, map making, surveying, and artillery range finding. Problems involving angles and distances in one plane are covered in plane trigonometry. Applications to similar problems in more than one plane of three-dimensional space are considered in spherical trigonometry.

HISTORY OF TRIGONOMETRY

CLASSICAL TRIGONOMETRY

The word "trigonometry" comes from the Greek words *trigonon* ("triangle") and *metron* ("to measure"). Until about the 16th century, trigonometry was chiefly concerned with computing the numerical values of the missing parts of a triangle (or any shape that can be dissected into triangles) when the values of other parts were given. For example, if the lengths of two sides of a triangle and the measure of the enclosed angle are known, the third side and the two remaining angles can be calculated. Such calculations distinguish trigonometry from geometry, which mainly investigates qualitative relations. Of course, this distinction is not always absolute: the Pythagorean theorem, for example, is a statement about the lengths of the three sides in a right triangle and is thus quantitative in nature. Still, in its original form, trigonometry was by and large an offspring of geometry. It was not until the 16th century that the two became separate branches of mathematics.

ANCIENT EGYPT AND THE MEDITERRANEAN WORLD

Several ancient civilizations—in particular, the Egyptian, Babylonian, Hindu, and Chinese—possessed a considerable knowledge of practical geometry, including some concepts that were a prelude to trigonometry. The Rhind papyrus, an Egyptian collection of 84 problems in arithmetic, algebra, and geometry dating from about 1800 BCE, contains five problems dealing with the *seked*. A close analysis of the text, with its accompanying figures, reveals that this word means the slope of an incline—essential knowledge for huge construction projects such as the pyramids. For example, problem 56 asks: "If a pyramid is 250 cubits high and the side of its base is 360 cubits long, what is its *seked*?" The solution is given as 5 1/25 palms per cubit. And since one cubit equals 7 palms, this fraction is equivalent to the pure ratio 18/25. This is actually the "run-to-rise" ratio of the pyramid in question—in effect, the cotangent of the angle between the base and face. It shows that the Egyptians had at least some knowledge of the numerical relations in a triangle, a kind of "proto-trigonometry."

Trigonometry in the modern sense began with the Greeks. Hipparchus (*c.* 190–120 BCE) was the first to construct a table of values for a trigonometric function. He considered every triangle—planar or spherical—as being inscribed in a circle, so that each side becomes a chord (that is, a straight line that connects two points on a curve or surface, as shown by the inscribed triangle *ABC* in the figure on page 204.

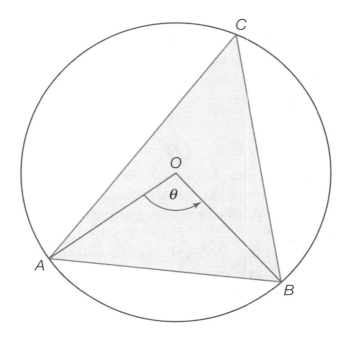

This figure illustrates the relationship between a central angle θ (an angle formed by two radii in a circle) and its chord AB *(equal to one side of an inscribed triangle).* Encyclopædia Britannica, Inc.

To compute the various parts of the triangle, one has to find the length of each chord as a function of the central angle that subtends it—or, equivalently, the length of a chord as a function of the corresponding arc width. This became the chief task of trigonometry for the next several centuries. As an astronomer, Hipparchus was mainly interested in spherical triangles, such as the imaginary triangle formed by three stars on the celestial sphere, but he was also familiar with the basic formulas of plane trigonometry. In Hipparchus's time these formulas were expressed in purely geometric terms as relations between the various chords and the angles (or arcs) that subtend them. The modern symbols for the trigonometric functions were not introduced until the 17th century.

The first major ancient work on trigonometry to reach Europe intact after the Dark Ages was the *Almagest* by Ptolemy (*c.* 100–170 CE). He lived in Alexandria, the intellectual centre of the Hellenistic world, but little else is known about him. Although Ptolemy wrote works on mathematics, geography, and optics, he is chiefly known for the *Almagest*, a 13-book compendium on astronomy that became the basis for mankind's world picture until the heliocentric system of Nicolaus Copernicus (1473–1543) began to supplant Ptolemy's geocentric system in the mid-16th century. In order to develop this world picture — the essence of which was a stationary Earth around which the Sun, Moon, and the five known planets move

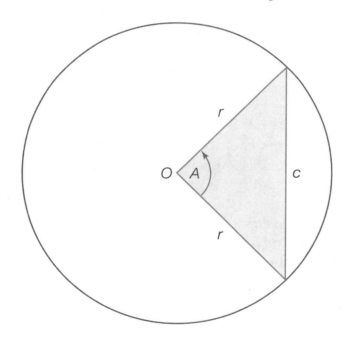

By labeling the central angle A, the radii r, and the chord c in the figure, it can be shown that c = 2r sin (A/2). *Hence, a table of values for chords in a circle of fixed radius is also a table of values for the sine of angles (by doubling the arc).* Encyclopædia Britannica, Inc.

in circular orbits—Ptolemy had to use some elementary trigonometry. Chapters 10 and 11 of the first book of the *Almagest* deal with the construction of a table of chords, in which the length of a chord in a circle is given as a function of the central angle that subtends it, for angles ranging from 0° to 180° at intervals of one-half degree. This is essentially a table of sines, which can be seen by denoting the radius r, the arc A, and the length of the subtended chord c (*see* the figure on page 205), to obtain $c = 2r \sin A/2$. Because Ptolemy used the Babylonian sexagesimal numerals and numeral systems (base 60), he did his computations with a standard circle of radius $r = 60$ units, so that $c = 120 \sin A/2$. Thus, apart from the proportionality factor 120, his was a table of values of $\sin A/2$ and therefore (by doubling the arc) of $\sin A$. With the help of his table, Ptolemy improved on existing geodetic measures of the world and refined Hipparchus's model of the motions of the heavenly bodies.

INDIA AND THE ISLAMIC WORLD

The next major contribution to trigonometry came from India. In the sexagesimal system, multiplication or division by 120 (twice 60) is analogous to multiplication or division by 20 (twice 10) in the decimal system. Thus, rewriting Ptolemy's formula as $c/120 = \sin B$, where $B = A/2$, the relation expresses the half-chord as a function of the arc B that subtends it—precisely the modern sine function. The first table of sines is found in the *Aryabhatiya*. Its author, Aryabhata I (*c.* 475–550), used the word *ardha-jya* for half-chord, which he sometimes turned around to *jya-ardha* ("chord-half"). In due time he shortened it to *jya* or *jiva*. Later, when Muslim scholars translated this work into Arabic, they retained the word *jiva* without translating its meaning. In Semitic languages words consist mostly of consonants, the pronunciation of the missing vowels being understood by common usage. Thus *jiva* could also be pronounced as *jiba* or *jaib*, and this last word in Arabic means "fold" or "bay." When the Arab translation was later translated into Latin, *jaib* became *sinus*, the Latin word for bay. The word *sinus* first appeared in the writings of Gherardo of Cremona (*c.* 1114–87), who translated many of the Greek texts, including the *Almagest*, into Latin. Other writers followed, and soon the word *sinus*, or *sine*, was used in the mathematical literature throughout Europe. The abbreviated symbol *sin* was first used in 1624 by Edmund Gunter, an English minister and instrument maker. The notations for the five remaining trigonometric functions were introduced shortly thereafter.

During the Middle Ages, while Europe was plunged into darkness, the torch of learning was kept alive by Arab and Jewish scholars living in Spain, Mesopotamia, and Persia. The first table of tangents and cotangents was constructed around 860 by Habash al-Hasib ("the Calculator"), who wrote on astronomy and astronomical instruments. Another Arab astronomer, al-Battānī (*c.* 858–929), gave a rule for finding the elevation θ of the Sun above the horizon in terms of the length s of the shadow cast by a vertical gnomon of height h. Al-Battānī's rule, $s = h \sin (90° - \theta)/\sin \theta$, is equivalent to the formula $s = h \cot \theta$. Based on this rule, he constructed a "table of shadows"—essentially a table of cotangents—for each degree from 1° to 90°. It was through al-Battānī's work that the Hindu half-chord function—equivalent to the modern sine—became known in Europe.

PASSAGE TO EUROPE

Until the 16th century, it was chiefly spherical trigonometry that interested scholars—a consequence of the predominance of astronomy among the natural sciences. The first definition of a spherical triangle is contained in Book 1 of the *Sphaerica*, a three-book treatise by Menelaus of

Alexandria (*c.* 100 CE) in which Menelaus developed the spherical equivalents of Euclid's propositions for planar triangles. A spherical triangle was understood to mean a figure formed on the surface of a sphere by three arcs of great circles, that is, circles whose centres coincide with the centre of the sphere. There are several fundamental differences between planar and spherical triangles. For example, two spherical triangles whose angles are equal in pairs are congruent (identical in size as well as in shape), whereas they are only similar (identical in shape) for the planar case. Also, the sum of the angles of a spherical triangle is always greater than 180°, in contrast to the planar case where the angles always sum to exactly 180°.

Several Arab scholars, notably Naṣīr al-Dīn al-Ṭūsī (1201–74) and al-Battānī, continued to develop spherical trigonometry and brought it to its present form. Al-Ṭūsī was the first (*c.* 1250) to write a work on trigonometry independently of astronomy. But the first modern book devoted entirely to trigonometry appeared in the Bavarian city of Nürnberg in 1533 under the title *On Triangles of Every Kind*. Its author was the astronomer Regiomontanus (1436–76). *On Triangles* contains all the theorems needed to solve triangles, planar or spherical—although these theorems are expressed in verbal form, as symbolic algebra had yet to be invented. In particular, the law of sines is stated in essentially the modern way. *On Triangles* was greatly admired by future generations of scientists. The astronomer Nicolaus Copernicus studied it thoroughly, and his annotated copy survives.

The final major development in classical trigonometry was the invention of logarithms by the Scottish mathematician John Napier in 1614. His tables of logarithms greatly facilitated the art of numerical computation—including the compilation of trigonometry tables—and were hailed as one of the greatest contributions to science.

MODERN TRIGONOMETRY

FROM GEOMETRIC TO ANALYTIC TRIGONOMETRY

In the 16th century, trigonometry began to change its character from a purely geometric discipline to an algebraic-analytic subject. Two developments spurred this transformation: the rise of symbolic algebra, pioneered by the French mathematician François Viète (1540–1603), and the invention of analytic geometry by two other Frenchmen, Pierre de Fermat and René Descartes. Viète showed that the solution of many algebraic equations could be expressed by the use of trigonometric expressions. For example, the equation $x^3 = 1$ has the three solutions:

- $x = 1$,
- $\cos 120° + i \sin 120° = {}^{-1+}i\sqrt{3}/2$, and
- $\cos 240° + i \sin 240° = {}^{-1-}i\sqrt{3}/2$.

(Here i is the symbol for $\sqrt{-1}$, the "imaginary unit.") That trigonometric expressions may appear in the solution of a purely algebraic equation was a novelty in Viète's time. He used it to advantage in a famous encounter between King Henry IV of France and Netherlands' ambassador to France. The latter spoke disdainfully of the poor quality of French mathematicians and challenged the king with a problem posed by Adriaen van Roomen, professor of mathematics and medicine at the University of Louvain (Belgium), to solve a certain algebraic equation of degree 45. The king summoned Viète, who immediately found one solution and on the following day came up with 22 more.

Viète was also the first to legitimize the use of infinite processes in mathematics. In 1593 he discovered the infinite product,

$$^2/_\Pi = \sqrt{2}/_2 \cdot \sqrt{(2 + \sqrt{2})}/_2 \cdot \sqrt{(2 + \sqrt{(2 + \sqrt{2})})}/_2 \cdots,$$

which is regarded as one of the most beautiful formulas in mathematics for its recursive pattern. By computing more and more terms, one can use this formula to approximate the value of π to any desired accuracy. In 1671 James Gregory (1638–75) found the power series for the inverse tangent function (arc tan, or tan^{-1}), from which he got, by letting $x = 1$, the formula

$$^\Pi/_4 = 1 - {}^1/_3 + {}^1/_5 - {}^1/_7 + \cdots,$$

which demonstrated a remarkable connection between Π and the integers. Although the series converged too slowly for a practical computation of Π (it would require 628 terms to obtain just two accurate decimal places). This was soon followed by Isaac Newton's (1642–1727) discovery of the power series for sine and cosine. Recent research, however, has brought to light that some of these formulas were already known, in verbal form, by the Indian astronomer Madhava (c. 1340–1425).

The gradual unification of trigonometry and algebra — and in particular the use of complex numbers (numbers of the form $x + iy$, where x and y are real numbers and $i = -1$) in trigonometric expressions — was completed in the 18th century. In 1722 Abraham de Moivre (1667–1754) derived, in implicit form, the famous formula

$$(\cos \varnothing + i \sin \varnothing)\, n = \cos n\varnothing + i \sin n\varnothing,$$

which allows one to find the nth root of any complex number. It was the Swiss mathematician Leonhard Euler (1707–83), though, who fully incorporated complex numbers into trigonometry. Euler's formula $e^{i\varnothing} = \cos \varnothing + i \sin \varnothing$, where $e \cong 2.71828$

is the base of natural logarithms, appeared in 1748 in his great work *Introductio in analysin infinitorum* — although Roger Cotes already knew the formula in its inverse form $\emptyset i = \log(\cos \emptyset + i \sin \emptyset)$ in 1714. Substituting into this formula the value $\emptyset = \pi$, one obtains $e^{i\pi} = \cos \pi + i \sin \pi = -1 + 0i = -1$ or equivalently, $e^{i\pi} + 1 = 0$. This most intriguing of all mathematical formulas contains the additive and multiplicative identities (0 and 1, respectively), the two

Leonhard Euler, whose work formed much of the basis of modern analytic trigonometry. Kean Collection/Hulton Archive/Getty Images

irrational numbers that occur most frequently in the physical world (π and e), and the imaginary unit (i), and it also employs the basic operations of addition and exponentiation — hence its great aesthetic appeal. Finally, by combining his formula with its companion formula

$$e^{-i\emptyset} = \cos(-\emptyset) + i \sin(-\emptyset) = \cos \emptyset - i \sin \emptyset,$$

Euler obtained the expressions

$$\cos \emptyset = \frac{e^{i\emptyset} + e^{-i\emptyset}}{2} \text{ and}$$
$$\sin \emptyset = \frac{e^{i\emptyset} - e^{-i\emptyset}}{2i},$$

which are the basis of modern analytic trigonometry.

Application to Science

While these developments shifted trigonometry away from its original connection to triangles, the practical aspects of the subject were not neglected. The 17th and 18th centuries saw the invention of numerous mechanical devices—from accurate clocks and navigational tools to musical instruments of superior quality and greater tonal range—all of which required at least some knowledge of trigonometry. A notable application was the science of artillery—and in the 18th century it was a science. Galileo Galilei (1564–1642) discovered that any motion—such as that of a projectile under the force of gravity—can be resolved into two components, one horizontal and the other vertical, and that these components can be treated independently of one another. This discovery led scientists to the formula for the range of a cannonball when its muzzle velocity v_0 (the speed at which it leaves the cannon) and the angle of elevation A of the cannon are given. The theoretical range, in the absence of air resistance, is given by

$$R = v_0{}^2 \sin^{2A}/g,$$

where g is the acceleration due to gravity (about 9.81 metres/second^2). This formula shows that, for a given muzzle velocity, the range depends solely on A. It reaches its maximum value when $A = 45°$ and falls off symmetrically on either side of $45°$. These facts, of course, had been known empirically for many years, but their theoretical explanation was a novelty in Galileo's time.

Another practical aspect of trigonometry that received a great deal of attention during this time period was surveying. The method of triangulation was first suggested in 1533 by the Dutch mathematician Gemma Frisius

(1508–55): one chooses a base line of known length, and from its endpoints the angles of sight to a remote object are measured. The distance to the object from either endpoint can then be calculated by using elementary trigonometry. The process is then repeated with the new distances as base lines, until the entire area to be surveyed is covered by a network of triangles. The method was first carried out on a large scale by another Dutchman, Willebrord van Roijen Snell (1581–1626), who surveyed a stretch of 130 km (80 miles) in Holland, using 33 triangles. The French government, under the leadership of the astronomer Jean Picard (1620–82), undertook to triangulate the entire country, a task that was to take over a century and involve four generations of the Cassini family (Gian, Jacques, César-François, and Dominique) of astronomers. The British undertook an even more ambitious task—the survey of the entire subcontinent of India. Known as the Great Trigonometric Survey, it lasted from 1800 to 1913 and culminated with the discovery of the tallest mountain on Earth—Peak XV, or Mount Everest.

Concurrent with these developments, 18th-century scientists also turned their attention to aspects of the trigonometric functions that arose from their periodicity. If the cosine and sine functions are defined as the projections on the x- and y-axes, respectively, of a point moving on a unit circle (a circle with its centre at the origin and a radius of 1), then these functions will repeat their values every 360°, or 2π radians. Hence, the importance of the sine and cosine functions in describing periodic phenomena—the vibrations of a violin string, the oscillations of a clock pendulum, or the propagation of electromagnetic waves. These investigations reached a climax when Joseph Fourier (1768–1830) discovered that almost any periodic function can be expressed as an infinite sum of sine and cosine functions, whose periods are integral divisors of the period of the original function. For example, the "sawtooth" function can be written as

$$2(\sin x - {}^{\sin 2x}/_2 + {}^{\sin 3x}/_3 - \cdots);$$

as successive terms in the series are added, an ever-better approximation to the sawtooth function results. These trigonometric or Fourier series have found numerous applications in almost every branch of science, from optics and acoustics to radio transmission and earthquake analysis. Their extension to nonperiodic functions played a key role in the development of quantum mechanics in the early years of the 20th century. Trigonometry, by and large, matured with Fourier's theorem. Further developments (e.g., generalization of Fourier series to other orthogonal, but nonperiodic, functions) are well beyond the scope of this book.

PRINCIPLES OF TRIGONOMETRY

TRIGONOMETRIC FUNCTIONS

A somewhat more general concept of angle is required for trigonometry than for geometry. An angle A with vertex at V, the initial side of which is VP and the terminal side of which is VQ, is indicated in the figure on page 215 by the solid circular arc. This angle is generated by the continuous counterclockwise rotation of a line segment about the point V from the position VP to the position VQ. A second angle A' with the same initial and terminal sides, indicated in the figure by the broken circular arc, is generated by the clockwise rotation of the line segment from the position VP to the position VQ. Angles are considered positive when generated

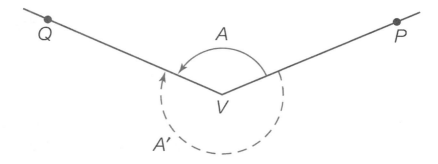

This figure shows a positive general angle A, *as well as a negative general angle* A'. Encyclopædia Britannica, Inc.

by counterclockwise rotations, negative when generated by clockwise rotations. The positive angle A and the negative angle A' in the figure are generated by less than one complete rotation of the line segment about the point V. All other positive and negative angles with the same initial and terminal sides are obtained by rotating the line segment one or more complete turns before coming to rest at VQ.

Numerical values can be assigned to angles by selecting a unit of measure. The most common units are the degree and the radian. There are 360° in a complete revolution, with each degree further divided into 60' (minutes) and each minute divided into 60" (seconds). In theoretical work, the radian is the most convenient unit. It is the angle at the centre of a circle that intercepts an arc equal in length to the radius. Simply put, there are 2π radians in one complete revolution. From these definitions, it follows that $1° = \pi/180$ radians.

Equal angles are angles with the same measure; i.e., they have the same sign and the same number of degrees. Any angle $-A$ has the same number of degrees as A but is of opposite sign. Its measure, therefore, is the negative of the measure of A. If two angles, A and B, have the initial

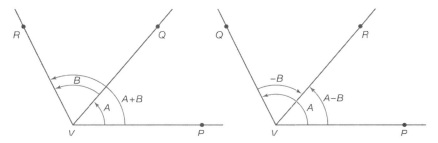

The figure indicates how to add a positive or negative angle (B) to a positive angle (A). Encyclopædia Britannica, Inc.

sides VP and VQ and the terminal sides VQ and VR, respectively, then the angle $A + B$ has the initial and terminal sides VP and VR (*see* the figure above.)

The angle $A + B$ is called the sum of the angles A and B, and its relation to A and B when A is positive and B is positive or negative is illustrated in the figure. The sum $A + B$ is the angle the measure of which is the algebraic sum of the measures of A and B. The difference $A - B$ is the sum of A and $-B$. Thus, all angles coterminal with angle A (i.e., with the same initial and terminal sides as angle A) are given by $A \pm 360n$, in which $360n$ is an angle of n complete revolutions. The angles $(180 - A)$ and $(90 - A)$ are the supplement and complement of angle A, respectively.

TRIGONOMETRIC FUNCTIONS OF AN ANGLE

To define trigonometric functions for any angle A, the angle is placed in position (*see* the figure on the top of page 217) on a rectangular coordinate system with the vertex of A at the origin and the initial side of A along the positive x-axis; r (positive) is the distance from V to any point Q on the terminal side of A, and (x, y) are the rectangular coordinates of Q. The six functions of A are then defined by six ratios exactly as in the earlier case for the triangle given in the introduction (*see* the figure on the bottom of page 217.)

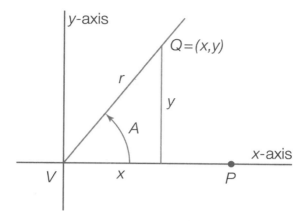

The figure shows an angle A *in standard position, that is, with initial side on the* x-*axis.* Encyclopædia Britannica, Inc.

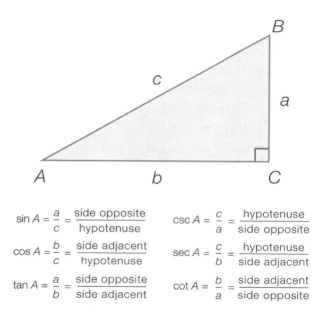

$$\sin A = \frac{a}{c} = \frac{\text{side opposite}}{\text{hypotenuse}} \qquad \csc A = \frac{c}{a} = \frac{\text{hypotenuse}}{\text{side opposite}}$$

$$\cos A = \frac{b}{c} = \frac{\text{side adjacent}}{\text{hypotenuse}} \qquad \sec A = \frac{c}{b} = \frac{\text{hypotenuse}}{\text{side adjacent}}$$

$$\tan A = \frac{a}{b} = \frac{\text{side opposite}}{\text{side adjacent}} \qquad \cot A = \frac{b}{a} = \frac{\text{side adjacent}}{\text{side opposite}}$$

Based on the definitions, various simple relationships exist among the functions. For example, csc A = 1/*sin* A, *sec* A = 1/*cos* A, *cot* A = 1/*tan* A, *and tan* A = *sin* A/*cos* A. Encyclopædia Britannica, Inc.

Because division by zero is not allowed, the tangent and secant are not defined for angles the terminal side of which falls on the y-axis, and the cotangent and cosecant are undefined for angles the terminal side of which falls on the x-axis. When the Pythagorean equality $x^2 + y^2 = r^2$ is divided in turn by r^2, x^2, and y^2, the three squared relations relating cosine and sine, tangent and secant, cotangent and cosecant are obtained.

If the point Q on the terminal side of angle A in standard position has coordinates (x, y), this point will have coordinates $(x, -y)$ when on the terminal side of $-A$ in standard position. From this fact and the definitions are obtained further identities for negative angles. These relations may also be stated briefly by saying that cosine and secant are even functions (symmetrical about the y-axis), while the other four are odd functions (symmetrical about the origin).

It is evident that a trigonometric function has the same value for all coterminal angles. When n is an integer, therefore, $\sin(A \pm 360n) = \sin A$; there are similar relations for the other five functions. These results may be expressed by saying that the trigonometric functions are periodic and have a period of $360°$ or $180°$.

When Q on the terminal side of A in standard position has coordinates (x, y), it has coordinates $(-y, x)$ and $(y, -x)$ on the terminal side of $A + 90$ and $A - 90$ in standard position, respectively. Consequently, six formulas follow which display that a function of the complement of A is equal to the corresponding cofunction of A.

Of fundamental importance for the study of trigonometry are the addition formulas, functions of the sum or difference of two angles. From the addition formulas are derived the double-angle and half-angle formulas. Numerous identities of lesser importance can be derived from the above basic identities.

TABLES OF NATURAL FUNCTIONS

To be of practical use, the values of the trigonometric functions must be readily available for any given angle. Various trigonometric identities show that the values of the functions for all angles can readily be found from the values for angles from 0° to 45°. For this reason, it is sufficient to list in a table the values of sine, cosine, and tangent for all angles from 0° to 45° that are integral multiples of some convenient unit (commonly 1'). Before computers rendered them obsolete in the late 20th century, such trigonometry tables were helpful to astronomers, surveyors, and engineers.

For angles that are not integral multiples of the unit, the values of the functions may be interpolated. Because the values of the functions are in general irrational numbers, they are entered in the table as decimals, rounded off at some convenient place. For most purposes, four or five decimal places are sufficient, and tables of this accuracy are common. Simple geometrical facts alone, however, suffice to determine the values of the trigonometric functions for the angles 0°, 30°, 45°, 60°, and 90°.

PLANE TRIGONOMETRY

In many applications of trigonometry, the essential problem is the solution of triangles. If enough sides and angles are known, the remaining sides and angles as well as the area can be calculated, and the triangle is then said to be solved. Triangles can be solved by the law of sines and the law of cosines. To secure symmetry in the writing of these laws, the angles of the triangle are lettered A, B, and C and the lengths of the sides opposite the angles are lettered a, b, and c, respectively. An example of this standardization is shown in the figure on the top of page 216.

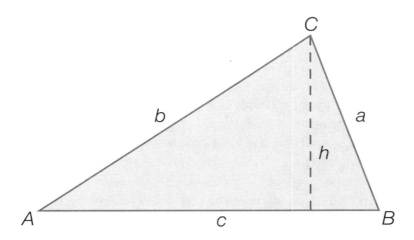

In addition to the angles (A, B, C) and sides (a, b, c), one of the three heights of the triangle (h) is included by drawing the line segment from one of the triangle's vertices (in this case C) that is perpendicular to the opposite side of the triangle. Encyclopædia Britannica, Inc.

The law of sines is expressed as an equality involving three sine functions while the law of cosines is an identification of the cosine with an algebraic expression formed from the lengths of sides opposite the corresponding angles. To solve a triangle, all the known values are substituted into equations expressing the laws of sines and cosines, and the equations are solved for the unknown quantities. For example, the law of sines is employed when two angles and a side are known or when two sides and an angle opposite one are known. Similarly, the law of cosines is appropriate when two sides and an included angle are known or three sides are known.

Texts on trigonometry derive other formulas for solving triangles and for checking the solution. Older textbooks frequently included formulas especially suited to logarithmic calculation. Newer textbooks, however, frequently include simple computer instructions for use with a symbolic mathematical program such as Mathematica™ or Maple™.

SPHERICAL TRIGONOMETRY

Spherical trigonometry involves the study of spherical triangles, which are formed by the intersection of three great circle arcs on the surface of a sphere. Spherical triangles were subject to intense study from antiquity because of their usefulness in navigation, cartography, and astronomy.

The angles of a spherical triangle are defined by the angle of intersection of the corresponding tangent lines to each vertex. The sum of the angles of a spherical triangle is always greater than the sum of the angles in a planar triangle (π radians, equivalent to two right angles). The amount by which each spherical triangle exceeds two right angles (in radians) is known as its spherical excess. The area of a spherical triangle is given by the product of its spherical excess E and the square of the radius r of the sphere it resides on—in symbols, Er^2.

By connecting the vertices of a spherical triangle with the centre O of the sphere that it resides on, a special "angle" known as a trihedral angle is formed. The central angles (also known as dihedral angles) between each pair of line segments OA, OB, and OC are labeled α, β, and γ to correspond to the sides (arcs) of the spherical triangle labeled a, b, and c, respectively. Because a trigonometric function of a central angle and its corresponding arc have the same value, spherical trigonometry formulas are given in terms of the spherical angles A, B, and C and, interchangeably, in terms of the arcs a, b, and c and the dihedral angles α, β, and γ. Furthermore, most formulas from plane trigonometry have an analogous representation in spherical trigonometry. For example, there is a spherical law of sines and a spherical law of cosines.

As was described for a plane triangle, the known values involving a spherical triangle are substituted in the analogous spherical trigonometry formulas, such as the laws of sines and cosines, and the resulting equations are then solved for the unknown quantities.

Many other relations exist between the sides and angles of a spherical triangle. Worth mentioning are Napier's analogies (derivable from the spherical trigonometry half-angle or half-side formulas), which are particularly well suited for use with logarithmic tables.

ANALYTIC TRIGONOMETRY

Analytic trigonometry combines the use of a coordinate system, such as the Cartesian coordinate system used in analytic geometry, with algebraic manipulation of the various trigonometry functions to obtain formulas useful for scientific and engineering applications.

Trigonometric functions of a real variable x are defined by means of the trigonometric functions of an angle. For example, sin x in which x is a real number is defined to have the value of the sine of the angle containing x radians. Similar definitions are made for the other five trigonometric functions of the real variable x. These functions satisfy the previously noted trigonometric relations with A, B, 90°, and 360° replaced by x, y, $\pi/2$ radians, and 2π radians, respectively. The minimum period of tan x and cot x is π, and of the other four functions it is 2π.

In the calculus it is shown that sin x and cos x are sums of power series. These series may be used to compute the sine and cosine of any angle. For example, to compute the sine of 10°, it is necessary to find the value of sin $\pi/18$ because 10° is the angle containing $\pi/18$ radians. When $\pi/18$ is substituted in the series for sin x, it is found that the first two terms give 0.17365, which is correct to five decimal places for the sine of 10°. By taking enough terms of

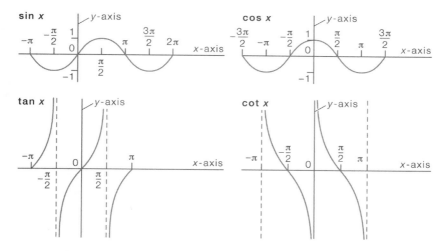

Note that each of these functions is periodic. Thus, the sine and cosine functions repeat every 2π, and the tangent and cotangent functions repeat every π.
Encyclopædia Britannica, Inc.

the series, any number of decimal places can be correctly obtained. Tables of the functions may be used to sketch the graphs of the functions, as shown in the figure above.

Each trigonometric function has an inverse function, that is, a function that "undoes" the original function. For example, the inverse function for the sine function is written arc sin or $\sin^{-1}$, thus $\sin^{-1}(\sin x) = \sin(\sin^{-1} x) = x$. The other trigonometric inverse functions are defined similarly.

COORDINATES AND TRANSFORMATION OF COORDINATES

POLAR COORDINATES

For problems involving directions from a fixed origin (or pole) O, it is often convenient to specify a point P by its polar coordinates (r, θ), in which r is the distance OP

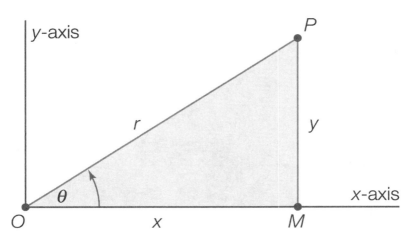

The point labeled P in the figure resides in the plane. Therefore, it requires two dimensions to fix its location, either in Cartesian coordinates (x, y) or in polar coordinates (r, θ). Encyclopædia Britannica, Inc.

and θ is the angle that the direction of r makes with a given initial line. The initial line may be identified with the x-axis of rectangular Cartesian coordinates, as shown in the figure above.

The point (r, θ) is the same as $(r, \theta + 2n\pi)$ for any integer n. It is sometimes desirable to allow r to be negative, so that (r, θ) is the same as $(-r, \theta + \pi)$.

Given the Cartesian equation for a curve, the polar equation for the same curve can be obtained in terms of the radius r and the angle θ by substituting $r \cos \theta$ and $r \sin \theta$ for x and y, respectively. For example, the circle $x^2 + y^2 = a^2$ has the polar equation $(r \cos \theta)^2 + (r \sin \theta)^2 = a^2$, which reduces to $r = a$. (The positive value of r is sufficient, if θ takes all values from $-\pi$ to π or from 0 to 2π). Thus, the polar equation of a circle simply expresses the fact that the curve is independent of θ and has constant radius. In a similar manner, the line $y = x \tan \phi$ has the polar equation $\sin \theta = \cos \theta \tan \phi$, which reduces to $\theta = \phi$. (The other solution, $\theta = \phi + \pi$, can be discarded if r is allowed to take negative values.)

TRANSFORMATION OF COORDINATES

A transformation of coordinates in a plane is a change from one coordinate system to another. Thus, a point in the plane will have two sets of coordinates giving its position with respect to the two coordinate systems used, and a transformation will express the relationship between the coordinate systems. For example, the transformation between polar and Cartesian coordinates discussed in the preceding section is given by $x = r \cos \theta$ and $y = r \sin \theta$. Similarly, it is possible to accomplish transformations between rectangular and oblique coordinates.

In a translation of Cartesian coordinate axes, a transformation is made between two sets of axes that are parallel to each other but have their origins at different positions. If a point P has coordinates (x, y) in one system, its coordinates in the second system are given by $(x - h, y - k)$ where (h, k) is the origin of the second system in terms of the first coordinate system. Thus, the transformation of P between the first system (x, y) and the second system (x', y') is given by the equations $x = x' + h$ and $y = y' + k$. The common use of translations of axes is to simplify the equations of curves. For example, the equation $2x^2 + y^2 - 12x - 2y + 17 = 0$ can be simplified with the translations $x' = x - 3$ and $y' = y - 1$ to an equation involving only squares of the variables and a constant term: $(x')^2 + (y')^2 2 = 1$. In other words, the curve represents an ellipse with its centre at the point $(3, 1)$ in the original coordinate system.

A rotation of coordinate axes is one in which a pair of axes giving the coordinates of a point (x, y) rotate through an angle ϕ to give a new pair of axes in which the point has coordinates (x', y'), as shown in the figure on page 226.

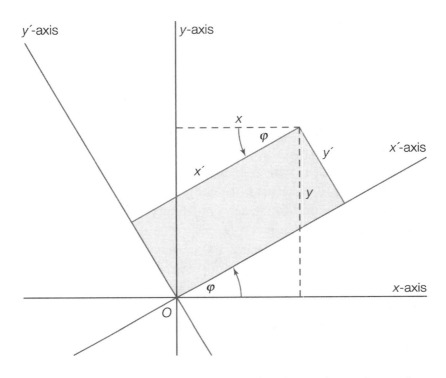

Rotating the coordinate axes through an angle φ changes the coordinates of a point from (x, y) to (x', y'). Encyclopædia Britannica, Inc.

The transformation equations for such a rotation are given by $x = x' \cos \phi - y' \sin \phi$ and $y = x' \sin \phi + y' \cos \phi$. The application of these formulas with $\phi = 45°$ to the difference of squares, $x^2 - y^2 = a^2$, leads to the equation $x'y' = c$ (where c is a constant that depends on the value of a). This equation gives the form of the rectangular hyperbola when its asymptotes (the lines that a curve approaches without ever quite meeting) are used as the coordinate axes.

CHAPTER 5
GREAT TRIGONOMETRICIANS

B orn in the ancient world as an offspring of geometry, trigonometry began in the 16th century to change its character from a purely geometric discipline to an algebraic-analytic subject. Great personalities who contributed to this development are presented in this chapter.

ARYABHATA I

(b. 476, possibly Ashmaka or Kusumapura, India)

Aryabhata I was an astronomer and the earliest Indian mathematician whose work and history are available to modern scholars. Known as Aryabhata I—or Aryabhata the Elder to distinguish him from a 10th-century Indian mathematician of the same name—he flourished in Kusumapura, near Patalipurta (Patna), then the capital of the Gupta dynasty. There he composed at least two works, *Aryabhatiya* (*c.* 499) and the now lost *Aryabhatasiddhanta*. *Aryabhatasiddhanta* circulated mainly in the northwest of India and, through the Sāsānian dynasty (224–651) of Iran, had a profound influence on the development of Islamic astronomy. Its contents are preserved to some extent in the works of Varahamihira (fl. *c.* 550), Bhaskara I (fl. *c.* 629), Brahmagupta (598–*c.* 665), and others. It is one of the earliest astronomical works to assign the start of each day to midnight.

Aryabhatiya was particularly popular in South India, where numerous mathematicians over the ensuing millennium wrote commentaries. Written in verse couplets, this work deals with mathematics and astronomy. Following an introduction that contains astronomical tables and Aryabhata's system of phonemic number notation, the work is characteristically divided into three sections: *Ganita* ("Mathematics"), *Kala-kriya* ("Time Calculations"), and *Gola* ("Sphere").

In *Ganita* Aryabhata names the first 10 decimal places and gives algorithms for obtaining square and cubic roots, utilizing the decimal number system. Then, he treats geometric measurements—employing 62,832/20,000 (= 3.1416) for π—and develops properties of similar right-angled triangles and of two intersecting circles. Utilizing the Pythagorean theorem, he obtained one of the two methods for constructing his table of sines. He also realized that second-order sine difference is proportional to sine. Mathematical series, quadratic equations, compound interest (involving a quadratic equation), proportions (ratios), and the solution of various linear equations are among the arithmetic and algebraic topics included. Aryabhata's general solution for linear indeterminate equations, which Bhaskara I called *kuttakara* ("pulverizer"), consisted of breaking the problem down into new problems with successively smaller coefficients—essentially the Euclidean algorithm and related to the method of continued fractions.

With *Kala-kriya* Aryabhata turned to astronomy—in particular, treating planetary motion along the ecliptic. The topics include definitions of various units of time, eccentric and epicyclic models of planetary motion, planetary longitude corrections for different terrestrial locations, and a theory of "lords of the hours and days" (an astrological concept used for determining propitious times for action).

Aryabhatiya ends with spherical astronomy in *Gola*, where he applied plane trigonometry to spherical geometry by projecting points and lines on the surface of a sphere onto appropriate planes. Topics include prediction of solar and lunar eclipses and an explicit statement that the apparent westward motion of the stars is due to the spherical Earth's rotation about its axis. Aryabhata also correctly ascribed the luminosity of the Moon and planets to reflected sunlight.

The Indian government named its first satellite Aryabhata (launched 1975) in his honour.

AL-BATTĀNĪ

(b. *c.* 858, in or near Haran, near Urfa, Syria—d. 929, near Sāmarrā', Iraq)

Abū 'abd Allāh Muḥammad ibn Jābir ibn Sinān al-Battānī al-Ḥarrani al-Ṣābi' was an Arab astronomer and mathematician who refined existing values for the length of the year and of the seasons, for the annual precession of the equinoxes, and for the inclination of the ecliptic. He showed that the position of the Sun's apogee, or farthest point from the Earth, is variable and that annular (central but incomplete) eclipses of the Sun are possible. He improved Ptolemy's astronomical calculations by replacing geometrical methods with trigonometry. From 877 he carried out many years of remarkably accurate observations at Al-Raqqah in Syria.

Al-Battānī was the best known of Arab astronomers in Europe during the Middle Ages (frequently under the Latin names Albatenius, Albategnus, or Albategni). His principal written work, a compendium of astronomical tables, was translated into Latin in about 1116 and into Spanish in the 13th century. A printed edition, under the title *De motu stellarum* ("On Stellar Motion"), was published in 1537.

ABRAHAM DE MOIVRE

(b. May 26, 1667, Vitry, France—d. Nov. 27, 1754, London, Eng.)

French mathematician Abraham de Moivre was a pioneer in the development of analytic trigonometry and in the theory of probability.

A French Huguenot, de Moivre was jailed as a Protestant upon the revocation of the Edict of Nantes in 1685. When he was released shortly thereafter, he fled to England. In London he became a close friend of Sir Isaac Newton and the astronomer Edmond Halley. De Moivre was elected to the Royal Society of London in 1697 and later to the Berlin and Paris academies. Despite his distinction as a mathematician, he never succeeded in securing a permanent position but eked out a precarious living by working as a tutor and a consultant on gambling and insurance.

De Moivre expanded his paper "De mensura sortis" (written in 1711), which appeared in *Philosophical Transactions,* into *The Doctrine of Chances* (1718). Although the modern theory of probability had begun with the unpublished correspondence (1654) between Blaise Pascal and Pierre de Fermat and the treatise *De Ratiociniis in Ludo Aleae* (1657; "On Ratiocination in Dice Games") by Christiaan Huygens of Holland, de Moivre's book greatly advanced probability study. The definition of statistical independence—namely, that the probability of a compound event composed of the intersection of statistically independent events is the product of the probabilities of its components—was first stated in de Moivre's *Doctrine.* Many problems in dice and other games were included, some of which appeared in the Swiss mathematician Jakob (Jacques) Bernoulli's *Ars conjectandi* (1713; "The Conjectural Arts"), which was published before de Moivre's *Doctrine* but after his "De mensura." He derived the principles of probability from the mathematical expectation of events, just the reverse of present-day practice.

De Moivre's second important work on probability was *Miscellanea Analytica* (1730; "Analytical Miscellany"). He was the first to use the probability integral in which the integrand is the exponential of a negative quadratic,

$$\int_0^\infty e^{-x^2}\,dx = \frac{\sqrt{\pi}}{2}.$$

He originated Stirling's formula, incorrectly attributed to James Stirling (1692–1770) of England, which states that for a large number n, $n!$ equals approximately $(2\pi n)1/2e^{-nnn}$; that is, n factorial (a product of integers with values descending from n to 1) approximates the square root of $2\pi n$, times the exponential of $-n$, times n to the nth power. In 1733 he used Stirling's formula to derive the normal frequency curve as an approximation of the binomial law.

De Moivre was one of the first mathematicians to use complex numbers in trigonometry. The formula known by his name, $(\cos x + i \sin x)^n = \cos nx + i \sin nx$, was instrumental in bringing trigonometry out of the realm of geometry and into that of analysis.

LEONHARD EULER

(b. April 15, 1707, Basel, Switz. — d. Sept. 18, 1783, St. Petersburg, Russia)

Swiss mathematician and physicist Leonhard Euler was one of the founders of pure mathematics. He not only made decisive and formative contributions to the subjects of geometry, calculus, mechanics, and number theory but also developed methods for solving problems in observational astronomy and demonstrated useful applications of mathematics in technology and public affairs.

Euler's mathematical ability earned him the esteem of Johann Bernoulli, one of the first mathematicians in Europe at that time, and of his sons Daniel and Nicolas. In 1727 he moved to St. Petersburg, where he became an associate of the St. Petersburg Academy of Sciences and in 1733 succeeded Daniel Bernoulli to the chair of mathematics.

By means of his numerous books and memoirs that he submitted to the academy, Euler carried integral calculus to a higher degree of perfection, developed the theory of trigonometric and logarithmic functions, reduced analytical operations to a greater simplicity, and threw new light on nearly all parts of pure mathematics. Overtaxing himself, Euler in 1735 lost the sight of one eye. Then, invited by Frederick the Great in 1741, he became a member of the Berlin Academy, where for 25 years he produced a steady stream of publications, many of which he contributed to the St. Petersburg Academy, which granted him a pension. In 1748, in his *Introductio in analysin infinitorum,* he developed the concept of function in mathematical analysis, through which variables are related to each other and in which he advanced the use of infinitesimals and infinite quantities. He did for modern analytic geometry and trigonometry what the *Elements* of Euclid had done for ancient geometry, and the resulting tendency to render mathematics and physics in arithmetical terms has continued ever since. He is known for familiar results in elementary geometry. For example, the Euler line through the orthocentre (the intersection of the altitudes in a triangle), the circumcentre (the centre of the circumscribed circle of a triangle), and the barycentre (the "centre of gravity," or centroid) of a triangle. He was responsible for treating trigonometric functions—i.e., the relationship of an angle to two sides of a triangle—as numerical ratios rather than as lengths of geometric lines and for relating them, through the so-called Euler identity ($e^{i\theta} = \cos\theta + i\sin\theta$), with complex numbers (e.g., $3 + 2\sqrt{-1}$). He discovered the imaginary logarithms of negative numbers and showed that each complex number has an infinite number of logarithms.

Euler's textbooks in calculus, *Institutiones calculi differentialis* in 1755 and *Institutiones calculi integralis* in 1768–70, have served as prototypes to the present because they contain formulas of differentiation and numerous methods of indefinite integration, many of which he invented himself, for determining the work done by a force and for solving geometric problems. He also made advances in the theory of linear differential equations, which are useful in solving problems in physics. Thus, he enriched mathematics with substantial new concepts and techniques. He introduced many current notations, such as Σ for the sum; $\int n$ for the sum of divisors of n; the symbol e for the base of natural logarithms; a, b, and c for the sides of a triangle and A, B, and C for the opposite angles; the letter f and parentheses for a function; the use of the symbol π for the ratio of circumference to diameter in a circle; and i for $\sqrt{-1}$.

After Frederick the Great became less cordial toward him, Euler in 1766 accepted the invitation of Catherine II to return to Russia. Soon after his arrival at St. Petersburg, a cataract formed in his remaining good eye, and he spent the last years of his life in total blindness. Despite this tragedy, his productivity continued undiminished, sustained by an uncommon memory and a remarkable facility in mental computations. His interests were broad, and his *Lettres à une princesse d'Allemagne* in 1768–72 were an admirably clear exposition of the basic principles of mechanics, optics, acoustics, and physical astronomy. Not a classroom teacher, Euler nevertheless had a more pervasive pedagogical influence than any modern mathematician. He had few disciples, but he helped to establish mathematical education in Russia.

Euler devoted considerable attention to developing a more perfect theory of lunar motion, which was particularly troublesome, since it involved the so-called three-body problem—the interactions of Sun, Moon, and Earth. (The problem is still unsolved.) His partial solution, published in 1753, assisted the British Admiralty in calculating lunar tables, of importance then in attempting to determine longitude at sea. One of the feats of his blind years was to perform all the elaborate calculations in his head for his second theory of lunar motion in 1772. Throughout his life Euler was much absorbed by problems dealing with the theory of numbers, which treats of the properties and relationships of integers, or whole numbers (0, ±1, ±2, etc.). In this, his greatest discovery, in 1783, was the law of quadratic reciprocity, which has become an essential part of modern number theory.

In his effort to replace synthetic methods by analytic ones, Euler was succeeded by Joseph-Louis Lagrange. But, where Euler had delighted in special concrete cases, Lagrange sought for abstract generality. And, while Euler incautiously manipulated divergent series, Lagrange attempted to establish infinite processes upon a sound basis. Thus, it is that Euler and Lagrange together are regarded as the greatest mathematicians of the 18th century. But Euler has never been excelled either in productivity or in the skillful and imaginative use of algorithmic devices (i.e., computational procedures) for solving problems.

JAMES GREGORY

(b. November 1638, Drumoak [near Aberdeen], Scot.—d. October 1675, Edinburgh)

Scottish mathematician and astronomer James Gregory (or James Gregorie) discovered infinite series representations

James Gregory. © Photos.com/Jupiterimages

for a number of trigonometry functions, although he is mostly remembered for his description of the first practical reflecting telescope, now known as the Gregorian telescope.

The son of an Anglican priest, Gregory received his early education from his mother. After his father's death in 1650, he was sent to Aberdeen, first to grammar school and then to Marischal College, graduating from the latter in 1657. (This Protestant college was combined with the Roman Catholic King's College in 1860 to form the University of Aberdeen.)

Following graduation, Gregory traveled to London where he published *Optica Promota* (1663; "The Advance of Optics"). This work analyzed the refractive and reflective properties of lens and mirrors based on various conic sections and substantially developed Johannes Kepler's (1571–1630) theory of the telescope. In the epilogue, Gregory proposed a new telescope design with a secondary mirror in the shape of a concave ellipsoid that would collect the reflection from a primary parabolic mirror and refocus the image back through a small hole in the centre of the primary mirror to an eyepiece, as shown in the figure below.

In this work Gregory also introduced estimation of stellar distances by photometric methods.

In 1663 Gregory visited The Hague and Paris before settling in Padua, Italy, to study geometry, mechanics, and

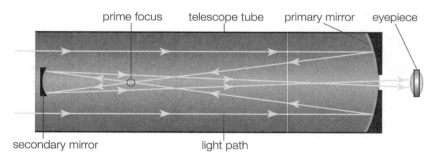

James Gregory's telescope design (1663) uses two concave mirrors—a primary parabolic-shaped mirror and a secondary elliptic-shaped mirror—to focus images in a short telescope tube. As indicated by the rays in the figure: (1) light enters the open end of the telescope; (2) light rays travel to the primary mirror, where they are reflected and concentrated at the prime focus; (3) a secondary mirror slightly beyond the prime focus reflects and concentrates the rays near a small aperture in the primary mirror; and (4) the image is viewed through an eyepiece. Encyclopædia Britannica, Inc.

astronomy. While in Italy he wrote *Vera Circuli et Hyperbolae Quadratura* (1667; "The True Squaring of the Circle and of the Hyperbola") and *Geometriae Pars Universalis* (1668; "The Universal Part of Geometry"). In the former work he used a modification of the method of exhaustion of Archimedes (*c.* 285–212/211 BCE) to find the areas of the circle and sections of the hyperbola. In his construction of an infinite sequence of inscribed and circumscribed geometric figures, Gregory was one of the first to distinguish between convergent and divergent infinite series. In the latter work Gregory collected the main results then known about transforming a very general class of curves into sections of known curves (hence the designation "universal"), finding the areas bounded by such curves, and calculating the volumes of their solids of revolution.

On the strength of his Italian treatises, Gregory was elected to the Royal Society on his return to London in 1668 and appointed to the University of St. Andrews, Scotland. In 1669, shortly after his return to Scotland, he married a young widow and started his own family. He visited London only once again, in 1673, to purchase supplies for what would have been Britain's first public astronomical observatory. In 1674, however, he became dissatisfied with the University of St. Andrews and left for the University of Edinburgh.

Although Gregory did not publish any more mathematical papers after his return to Scotland, his mathematical research continued. In 1670 and 1671 he communicated to the English mathematician John Collins a number of important results on infinite series expansions of various trigonometry functions, including what is now known as Gregory's series for the arctangent function:

$$\arctan x = x - \frac{x^3}{3} + \frac{x^5}{5} - \frac{x^7}{7} + \ldots$$

Knowing that the arctangent of 1 is equal to π/4 led to the immediate substitution of 1 for *x* in this equation to produce the first infinite series expansion for π. Unfortunately, this series converges too slowly to π for the practical generation of digits in its decimal expansion. Nevertheless, it encouraged the discovery of other, more rapidly convergent infinite series for π.

The extent of Gregory's work has only been known and appreciated since the publication of *James Gregory: Tercentenary Memorial Volume* (ed. by H.W. Turnbull; 1939), which contains most of his letters and posthumous manuscripts.

HIPPARCHUS

(b. Nicaea, Bithynia [now Iznik, Turkey]—d. after 127 BCE, Rhodes?)

Hipparchus (or Hipparchos), a Greek astronomer and mathematician, made fundamental contributions to the advancement of astronomy as a mathematical science and to the foundations of trigonometry. Although he is commonly ranked among the greatest scientists of antiquity, very little is known about his life, and only one of his many writings is still in existence. Knowledge of the rest of his work relies on second-hand reports, especially in the great astronomical compendium the *Almagest*, written by Ptolemy in the 2nd century CE.

LOVER OF TRUTH

As a young man in Bithynia, Hipparchus compiled records of local weather patterns throughout the year. Such weather calendars (*parapegmata*), which synchronized the onset of winds, rains, and storms with the astronomical seasons and the risings and settings of the constellations,

Hipparchus, depicted above, indulged interests in both astronomy and mathematics. His contributions in both fields are still relevant today, though much of his work lives on only through secondary accounts. Archive Photos/ Getty Images

were produced by many Greek astronomers from at least as early as the 4th century BCE.

Most of Hipparchus's adult life, however, seems to have been spent carrying out a program of astronomical observation and research on the island of Rhodes. Ptolemy cites more than 20 observations made there by Hipparchus on specific dates from 147 to 127, as well as three earlier observations from 162 to 158 that may be attributed to him. These must have been only a tiny fraction of Hipparchus's recorded observations. In fact, his astronomical writings were numerous enough that he published an annotated list of them.

Hipparchus also wrote critical commentaries on some of his predecessors and contemporaries. In *Ton Aratou kai Eudoxou Phainomenon exegeseos biblia tria* ("Commentary on the Phaenomena of Aratus and Eudoxus"), his only surviving book, he ruthlessly exposed errors in *Phaenomena*, a popular poem written by Aratus and based on a now-lost treatise of Eudoxus of Cnidus that named and described the constellations. Apparently his commentary *Against the Geography of Eratosthenes* was similarly unforgiving of loose and inconsistent reasoning. Ptolemy characterized him as a "lover of truth" (*philalethes*)—a trait that was more amiably manifested in Hipparchus's readiness to revise his own beliefs in the light of new evidence. He communicated with observers at Alexandria in Egypt, who provided him with some times of equinoxes, and probably also with astronomers at Babylon.

SOLAR AND LUNAR THEORY

Hipparchus's most important astronomical work concerned the orbits of the Sun and Moon, a determination of their sizes and distances from the Earth, and the study of eclipses. Like most of his predecessors—Aristarchus of Samos was an exception—Hipparchus assumed a spherical, stationary Earth at the centre of the universe (the geocentric cosmology). From this perspective, the Sun, Moon, Mercury, Venus, Mars, Jupiter, and Saturn (all of the solar system bodies visible to the naked eye), as well as the stars (whose realm was known as the celestial sphere), revolved around the Earth each day.

Every year the Sun traces out a circular path in a west-to-east direction relative to the stars (this is in addition to the apparent daily east-to-west rotation of the celestial sphere around the Earth). Hipparchus had good reasons for believing that the Sun's path, known as the ecliptic, is a great circle, i.e., that the plane of the ecliptic passes through the Earth's centre. The two points at which the ecliptic and the equatorial plane intersect, known as the vernal and autumnal equinoxes, and the two points of the ecliptic farthest north and south from the equatorial plane, known as the summer and winter solstices, divide the ecliptic into four equal parts. However, the Sun's passage through each section of the ecliptic, or season, is not symmetrical. Hipparchus attempted to explain how the Sun could travel with uniform speed along a regular circular path and yet produce seasons of unequal length.

Hipparchus knew of two possible explanations for the Sun's apparent motion, the eccenter and the epicyclic models. These models, which assumed that the apparent irregular motion was produced by compounding two or more uniform circular motions, were probably familiar to Greek astronomers well before Hipparchus. His contribution was to discover a method of using the observed dates of two equinoxes and a solstice to calculate the size and direction of the displacement of the Sun's orbit. With Hipparchus's mathematical model one could calculate not only the Sun's orbital location on any date, but also its position as seen from the Earth. The history of celestial mechanics until Johannes Kepler (1571–1630) was mostly an elaboration of Hipparchus's model.

Hipparchus also tried to measure as precisely as possible the length of the tropical year—the period for the Sun to complete one passage through the ecliptic. He made observations of consecutive equinoxes and solstices, but the results were inconclusive: he could not distinguish between possible observational errors and variations in the tropical year. However, by comparing his own observations of solstices with observations made in the 5th and 3rd centuries BCE, Hipparchus succeeded in obtaining an estimate of the tropical year that was only 6 minutes too long.

He was then in a position to calculate equinox and solstice dates for any year. Applying this information to recorded observations from about 150 years before his time, Hipparchus made the unexpected discovery that certain stars near the ecliptic had moved about 2° relative to the equinoxes. He contemplated various explanations—for example, that these stars were actually very slowly moving planets—before he settled on the essentially correct theory that all the stars made a gradual eastward revolution relative to the equinoxes. Since Nicolaus Copernicus (1473–1543) established his heliocentric model of the universe, the stars have provided a fixed frame of reference, relative to which the plane of the equator slowly shifts—a phenomenon referred to as the precession of the equinoxes.

Hipparchus also analyzed the more complicated motion of the Moon in order to construct a theory of eclipses. In addition to varying in apparent speed, the Moon diverges north and south of the ecliptic, and the periodicities of these phenomena are different. Hipparchus adopted values for the Moon's periodicities that were known to contemporary Babylonian astronomers, and he confirmed their accuracy by comparing recorded observations of lunar eclipses separated by intervals of several centuries. It remained, however, for Ptolemy (*c.* 100–170 CE) to finish fashioning a fully predictive lunar model.

In *On Sizes and Distances* (now lost), Hipparchus reportedly measured the Moon's orbit in relation to the size of the Earth. He had two methods of doing this. One method used an observation of a solar eclipse that had been total near the Hellespont (now called the Dardanelles) but only partial at Alexandria. Hipparchus assumed that the difference could be attributed entirely to the Moon's observable parallax against the stars, which amounts to supposing that the Sun, like the stars, is indefinitely far away. (Parallax is the apparent displacement of an object when viewed from different vantage points). Hipparchus thus calculated that the mean distance of the Moon from the Earth is 77 times the Earth's radius. In the second method he hypothesized that the distance from the centre of the Earth to the Sun is 490 times the Earth's radius — perhaps chosen because that is the shortest distance consistent with a parallax that is too small for detection by the unaided eye. Using the visually identical sizes of the solar and lunar discs, and observations of the Earth's shadow during lunar eclipses, Hipparchus found a relationship between the lunar and solar distances that enabled him to calculate that the Moon's mean distance from the Earth is approximately 63 times the Earth's radius. (The true value is about 60 times.)

OTHER SCIENTIFIC WORK

The eccenter and epicyclic models sufficed to describe the motion of a body that has a single periodic variation in apparent speed, which so far as Hipparchus knew was the case with the Sun and Moon. According to Ptolemy, Hipparchus was aware that the movements of the planets were too complex to be accounted for by the same simple models, but he did not attempt to devise a satisfactory planetary theory.

According to Pliny the Elder (23–79 CE), Hipparchus created a star catalog that assigned names to each star along with his measurements of their positions. However, the direct evidence for this catalog is very poor and does not reveal either the number of stars that it contained or how the positions were expressed—whether in terms of a coordinate system or by location within various constellations. In the *Almagest*, Ptolemy presents a catalog of 1,022 stars grouped by constellations, with apparent magnitudes (measure of brightness) and coordinates in degrees measured along the ecliptic and perpendicular to it. Although Ptolemy stated that his catalog was based on personal observations, some historians argue that it was derived in large part from Hipparchus's catalog, with a simple adjustment for the intervening precessional motion. This remains one of the most controversial topics in the study of ancient astronomy.

Hipparchus lived just before the rise of Greco-Roman astrology, but he surely knew about the Near Eastern traditions of astral divination that were already spreading in the classical world. In later astrological texts, he is occasionally cited as an authority, most credibly as a source for astrological correspondences between constellations and geographical regions.

Hipparchus's principal interest in geography, as quoted from *Against the Geography of Eratosthenes* by the Greek geographer Strabo (c. 64 BCE–23 CE), was the accurate determination of terrestrial locations. Ancient authors preserved only a few tantalizing allusions to Hipparchus's other scientific work. For instance, *On Bodies Carried Down by Their Weight* speculated on the principles of weight and motion, and a work on optics adhered to Euclid's theory from the *Optics* that vision is produced by an emanation of rays from the eyes. Hipparchus's calculation of the exact number (103,049) of possible logical statements constructible from 10 basic assertions according to certain rules of Stoic logic is a rare surviving instance of Greek interest in combinatoric mathematics. Hipparchus's most significant contribution to mathematics may have been to develop—if not actually invent—a trigonometry based on a table of the lengths of chords in a circle of unit radius tabulated as a function of the angle subtended at the centre. Such a table would, for the first time, allow a systematic solution of general trigonometric problems, and clearly Hipparchus used it extensively for his astronomical calculations. Like so much of Hipparchus's work, his chord table has not survived.

MENELAUS OF ALEXANDRIA

(fl. 1st century CE, Alexandria and Rome)

Greek mathematician and astronomer Menelaus of Alexandria first conceived and defined a spherical triangle (a triangle formed by three arcs of great circles on the surface of a sphere).

Menelaus's most important work is *Sphaerica*, on the geometry of the sphere, extant only in an Arabic translation. In Book I he established the basis for a mathematical treatment of spherical triangles analogous to Euclid's treatment of plane triangles. Furthermore, he originated the use of arcs of great circles instead of arcs of parallel circles on the sphere, a major turning point in the development of spherical trigonometry. Book II established theorems whose principal interest is their (unstated) application to problems in spherical astronomy. Book III, the last, concentrates on spherical trigonometry and introduces Menelaus's theorem. The form of this theorem for plane triangles, well known to his contemporaries, was expressed as follows: if the three sides of a triangle are crossed by a straight line (one of the sides is extended beyond its vertices), then the product of three of the nonadjacent line segments thus formed is equal to the product of three other line segments.

Although Book III contains the first-known extension of Menelaus's theorem for spherical triangles, it is quite possible that the theorem was already known and Menelaus simply transmitted it to later generations. In the form stated in Book III, the theorem became of fundamental importance in spherical trigonometry and astronomy, and the theorem has since been known by his name. Other works are attributed to him, including one on setting times of the signs of the zodiac, one (in six books) on chords in a circle, and one (in three books) on elements of geometry, but his only extant work is *Sphaerica*. Menelaus was not just a theoretical astronomer, as attested by the *Almagest* where Ptolemy (*c.* 100–170 CE) reports Menelaus's observations of lunar occultations of stars.

PTOLEMY

(b. *c.* 100 CE – d. *c.* 170)

(Latin: Claudius Ptolemaeus) was an Egyptian astronomer, mathematician, and geographer of Greek descent who flourished in Alexandria during the 2nd century CE. In several fields his writings represent the culminating achievement of Greco-Roman science, particularly his

CL·PTOLEMAEO·ALEX·

Ptolemy was notable for a number of reasons, including his application of mathematics to problems he encountered during his work in astronomy. Hulton Archive/Getty Images

geocentric (Earth-centred) model of the universe now known as the Ptolemaic system.

Virtually nothing is known about Ptolemy's life except what can be inferred from his writings. His first major astronomical work, the *Almagest*, was completed about

150 CE and contains reports of astronomical observations that Ptolemy had made over the preceding quarter of a century. The size and content of his subsequent literary production suggests that he lived until about 170 CE.

ASTRONOMER

The book that is now generally known as the *Almagest* (from a hybrid of Arabic and Greek, "the greatest") was called by Ptolemy *He mathematike syntaxis* ("The Mathematical Collection") because he believed that its subject, the motions of the heavenly bodies, could be explained in mathematical terms. The opening chapters present empirical arguments for the basic cosmological framework within which Ptolemy worked. The Earth, he argued, is a stationary sphere at the centre of a vastly larger celestial sphere that revolves at a perfectly uniform rate around the Earth, carrying with it the stars, planets, Sun, and Moon—thereby causing their daily risings and settings. Through the course of a year, the Sun slowly traces out a great circle, known as the ecliptic, against the rotation of the celestial sphere. (The Moon and planets similarly travel backward—hence, the planets were also known as "wandering stars"—against the "fixed stars" found in the ecliptic.) The fundamental assumption of the *Almagest* is that the apparently irregular movements of the heavenly bodies are in reality combinations of regular, uniform, circular motions.

How much of the *Almagest* is original is difficult to determine because almost all of the preceding technical astronomical literature is now lost. Ptolemy credited Hipparchus (mid-2nd century BCE) with essential elements of his solar theory, as well as parts of his lunar theory, while denying that Hipparchus constructed planetary models. Ptolemy made only a few vague and disparaging remarks regarding theoretical work over the intervening three centuries. Yet the study of the planets undoubtedly made great strides during that interval. Moreover, Ptolemy's veracity, especially as an observer, has been controversial since the time of the astronomer Tycho Brahe (1546–1601). Brahe pointed out that solar observations Ptolemy claimed to have made in 141 are definitely not genuine, and there are strong arguments for doubting that Ptolemy independently observed the more than 1,000 stars listed in his star catalog. What is not disputed, however, is the mastery of mathematical analysis that Ptolemy exhibited.

Ptolemy was preeminently responsible for the geocentric cosmology that prevailed in the Islamic world and in medieval Europe. This was not due to the *Almagest* so much as a later treatise, *Hypotheseis ton planomenon* (*Planetary Hypotheses*). In this work he proposed what is now called the Ptolemaic system—a unified system in which each heavenly body is attached to its own sphere and the set of spheres nested so that it extends without gaps from the Earth to the celestial sphere. The numerical tables in the *Almagest* (which enabled planetary positions and other celestial phenomena to be calculated for arbitrary dates) had a profound influence on medieval astronomy, in part through a separate, revised version of the tables that Ptolemy published as *Procheiroi kanones* ("Handy Tables"). Ptolemy taught later astronomers how to use dated, quantitative observations to revise cosmological models.

Ptolemy also attempted to place astrology on a sound basis in *Apotelesmatika* ("Astrological Influences"), later known as the *Tetrabiblos* for its four volumes. He believed that astrology is a legitimate, though inexact, science that describes the physical effects of the heavens on terrestrial life. Ptolemy accepted the basic validity of the traditional astrological doctrines, but he revised the details to reconcile the practice with an Aristotelian conception of nature, matter, and change. Of Ptolemy's writings, the *Tetrabiblos* is the most foreign to modern readers, who do not accept astral prognostication and a cosmology driven by the interplay of basic qualities such as hot, cold, wet, and dry.

MATHEMATICIAN

Ptolemy has a prominent place in the history of mathematics primarily because of the mathematical methods he applied to astronomical problems. His contributions to trigonometry are especially important. For instance, Ptolemy's table of the lengths of chords in a circle is the earliest surviving table of a trigonometric function. He also applied fundamental theorems in spherical trigonometry (apparently discovered half a century earlier by Menelaus of Alexandria) to the solution of many basic astronomical problems.

Among Ptolemy's earliest treatises, the *Harmonics* investigated musical theory while steering a middle course between an extreme empiricism and the mystical arithmetical speculations associated with Pythagoreanism. Ptolemy's discussion of the roles of reason and the senses in acquiring scientific knowledge have bearing beyond music theory.

Probably near the end of his life, Ptolemy turned to the study of visual perception in *Optica* ("Optics"), a work that only survives in a mutilated medieval Latin translation of an Arabic translation. The extent to which Ptolemy subjected visual perception to empirical analysis is remarkable when contrasted with other Greek writers on optics.

For example, Hero of Alexandria (mid-1st century CE) asserted, purely for philosophical reasons, that an object and its mirror image must make equal angles to a mirror. In contrast, Ptolemy established this principle by measuring angles of incidence and reflection for planar and curved mirrors set upon a disk graduated in degrees. Ptolemy also measured how lines of sight are refracted at the boundary between materials of different density, such as air, water, and glass, although he failed to discover the exact law relating the angles of incidence and refraction.

GEOGRAPHER

Ptolemy's fame as a geographer is hardly less than his fame as an astronomer. *Geographike hyphegesis* (*Guide to Geography*) provided all the information and techniques required to draw maps of the portion of the world known by Ptolemy's contemporaries. By his own admission, Ptolemy did not attempt to collect and sift all the geographical data on which his maps were based. Instead, he based them on the maps and writings of Marinus of Tyre (*c.* 100 CE), only selectively introducing more current information, chiefly concerning the Asian and African coasts of the Indian Ocean. Nothing would be known about Marinus if Ptolemy had not preserved the substance of his cartographical work.

Ptolemy's most important geographical innovation was to record longitudes and latitudes in degrees for roughly 8,000 locations on his world map, making it possible to make an exact duplicate of his map. Hence, we possess a clear and detailed image of the inhabited world as it was known to a resident of the Roman Empire at its height—a world that extended from the Shetland Islands in the north to the sources of the Nile in the south, from the Canary Islands in the west to China and Southeast Asia in the east. Ptolemy's map is seriously distorted in size and orientation compared to modern maps, a reflection of the incomplete and inaccurate descriptions of road systems and trade routes at his disposal.

Ptolemy also devised two ways of drawing a grid of lines on a flat map to represent the circles of latitude and longitude on the globe. His grid gives a visual impression of the Earth's spherical surface and also, to a limited extent, preserves the proportionality of distances. The more sophisticated of these map projections, using circular arcs to represent both parallels and meridians, anticipated later area-preserving projections. Ptolemy's geographical work was almost unknown in Europe until about 1300, when Byzantine scholars began producing many manuscript copies, several of them illustrated with expert reconstructions of Ptolemy's maps. The Italian Jacopo d'Angelo translated the work into Latin in 1406. The numerous Latin manuscripts and early print editions of Ptolemy's *Guide to Geography*, most of them accompanied by maps, attest to the profound impression this work made upon its rediscovery by Renaissance humanists.

REGIOMONTANUS

(b. June 6, 1436, Königsberg, archbishopric of Mainz [Ger.] — d. July 6, 1476, Rome, Papal States [Italy])

Johannes Müller von Königsberg, known by his Latin name, Regiomontanus, was the foremost mathematician and astronomer of 15th-century Europe, a sought-after astrologer, and one of the first printers.

Königsberg means "King's Mountain," which is what the Latinized version of his name, Joannes de Regio monte or Regiomontanus, also means. A miller's son, he entered

Cœli mediationum
LatitudoMeridiana.   41

♄ gr.	0 gr. m	1 gr. m	2 gr. m	3 gr. m	4 gr. m	5 gr. m	6 gr. m	7 gr. m	8 gr. m
0	270 0	270 0	270 0	270 0	270 0	270 0	270 0	270 0	270 0
1	271 6	271 6	271 7	271 7	271 8	271 8	271 9	271 9	271 10
2	272 12	272 12	272 14	272 14	272 16	272 16	272 18	272 18	272 20
3	273 17	273 19	273 20	273 21	273 23	273 24	273 26	273 27	273 29
4	274 22	274 24	274 27	274 28	274 31	274 32	274 35	274 36	274 39
5	275 27	275 30	275 33	275 35	275 38	275 40	275 43	275 45	275 49
6	276 33	276 36	276 39	276 42	276 45	276 48	276 51	276 54	276 58
7	277 38	277 42	277 45	277 49	277 52	277 56	278 0	278 3	278 8
8	278 45	278 47	278 51	278 55	278 59	279 4	279 8	279 12	279 17
9	279 48	279 52	279 57	280 1	280 6	280 11	280 16	280 21	280 26
10	280 53	280 58	281 3	281 8	281 13	281 19	281 24	281 30	281 35
11	281 58	282 4	282 9	282 15	282 20	282 26	282 32	282 38	282 44
12	283 3	283 9	283 15	283 22	283 27	283 33	283 40	283 46	283 53
13	284 8	284 14	284 21	284 27	284 34	284 41	284 48	284 55	285 2
14	285 13	285 19	285 27	285 33	285 41	285 48	285 56	286 3	286 11
15	286 17	286 24	286 32	286 30	286 47	286 55	287 3	287 11	287 19
16	287 22	287 29	287 38	287 45	287 57	288 2	288 11	288 19	288 28
17	288 27	288 34	288 43	288 51	289 0	289 9	289 18	289 27	289 36
18	289 31	289 39	289 48	289 57	290 6	290 15	290 25	290 34	290 44
19	290 35	290 44	290 53	291 3	291 12	291 22	291 32	291 42	291 52
20	291 39	291 49	291 58	292 8	292 18	292 29	292 39	292 50	293 0
21	292 43	292 53	293 3	293 13	293 24	293 35	293 46	293 57	294 8
22	293 47	293 57	294 8	294 18	294 30	294 40	294 52	295 4	295 15
23	294 51	295 1	295 13	295 23	295 35	295 47	295 58	296 10	296 22
24	295 54	296 5	296 17	296 28	296 40	296 53	297 4	297 16	297 29
25	296 57	297 9	297 21	297 33	297 45	297 58	298 10	298 23	298 36
26	298 0	298 13	298 25	298 38	298 50	299 0	299 16	299 29	299 43
27	299 3	299 16	299 29	299 42	299 55	300 8	300 22	300 35	300 49
28	300 6	300 19	300 33	300 46	300 59	301 13	301 27	301 41	301 55
29	301 9	301 22	301 36	301 50	302 3	302 18	302 32	302 47	303 1
30	302 12	302 25	302 39	302 53	303 7	303 22	303 37	303 52	304 7

Gg

A page from Tabulae directionum, *one of the published works of Regiomontanus.* SSPL/Getty Images

the University of Leipzig at the age of 11 and in 1450 went to the University of Vienna. Regiomontanus was awarded a baccalaureate in 1452, but university regulations forced him to wait until he turned 21 to receive his master's degree. He eventually collaborated with his teacher, the mathematician-astronomer Georg von Peuerbach (d. 1461), on various astronomical and astrological projects,

including observations of eclipses and comets, the manu-
facture of astronomical instruments, and the casting of
horoscopes for the court of the Holy Roman Emperor
Frederick III.

The papal legate to the Holy Roman Empire, Cardinal
Bessarion, during a diplomatic visit to Vienna (1460–61),
asked Peuerbach to write an epitome, or abridgment, of
Ptolemy's *Almagest* to remedy the problems in George
of Trebizond's 1450 translation of and commentary on
that great work. When Peuerbach died in 1461,
Regiomontanus left for Rome as a member of Bessarion's
extended household and completed Peuerbach's half-
finished *Epitome* (*c.* 1462; first printed in 1496 as *Epytoma . . .
in Almagestum Ptolomei*). His demonstration of an alternative to Ptolemy's models for the orbits of Mercury and
Venus with respect to the Sun gave Nicolaus Copernicus
(1473–1543) the geometric key to reorient planetary
motions around the Sun. The *Epitome* is still one of the
best critical introductions to Ptolemy's astronomy.

Although he admired the *Almagest*, Regiomontanus was
keenly aware that its geometric models led to inconsisten-
cies (notably between predictions of planetary position
and predictions of planetary size). To remedy these incon-
sistencies, he tried to eliminate the nonconcentric,
two-dimensional eccentrics and epicycles that were the
mainstays of Ptolemy's models. Three-dimensional models
using concentric spheres would, he believed, yield good
mathematical predictions of planetary positions without
jeopardizing the physical principles of natural philosophy.

In Italy (1461–c. 1465), Regiomontanus perfected his
Greek, lectured at the University of Padua, read widely in
Bessarion's Greek library, and fought in the latter's long
feud with George of Trebizond. The controversy prompted
Regiomontanus to write his longest expository work, the

"Defense of Theon Against George of Trebizond," which later fueled rumours, entirely unsubstantiated, that George's sons had him poisoned.

Regiomontanus thoroughly mastered Hellenistic and medieval mathematics. His own contributions to the subject range from the formalization of plane and spherical trigonometry in *De triangulis omnimodis* (1464; "On Triangles of All Kinds") to his discovery of a Greek manuscript (incomplete) of the *Arithmetica*, the great work of Diophantus of Alexandria (fl. *c.* 250 CE). His writings also show his interest in perfect numbers (numbers equal to the sum of their proper divisors), the Platonic solids, and the solution of quadratic, cubic, and higher-dimensional equations.

From 1467 to 1471, Regiomontanus lived in Hungary as astrologer to King Matthias I of Hungary and Archbishop János Vitéz. In 1471 he moved to Nürnberg, Germany, where he established an instrument shop, set up a printing press, and continued his planetary observations in collaboration with the merchant Bernhard Walther. He announced plans to print 45 works, mostly in the classical, medieval, and contemporary mathematical sciences. However, only nine editions appeared, including Peuerbach's *Theoricae novae planetarum* (1454; "New Theories of the Planets"), his own attack ("Disputationes") on the anonymous 13th-century *Theorica planetarum communis* (the common "Theory of the Planets"), his German and Latin calendars, and his 896-page *Ephemerides* (daily planetary positions for 32 years, which showcase his computational skills). His editions pioneered the printing of astronomical diagrams and numerical tables. Several of the works that he prepared and had hoped to print, including editions of Euclid and Archimedes, his own astronomical *Tabulae directionum* (1467; "Tables of

Directions"), and a table of sines that he had computed to seven decimal places, proved influential when circulated in the 15th and 16th centuries in manuscript and in print.

In 1475 Regiomontanus traveled to Rome to advise Pope Sixtus IV about calendar reform. He died there the following year, probably from the plague precipitated by the Tiber River overflowing its banks.

NASĪR AL-DĪN AL-ṬŪSĪ

(b. Feb. 18, 1201, Ṭūs, Khorāsān [now Iran]—d. June 26, 1274, Baghdad, Iraq)

Muḥammad ibn Muḥammad ibn al-Ḥasan al-Ṭūsī was an outstanding Persian philosopher, scientist, and mathematician.

Educated first in Ṭūs, where his father was a jurist in the Twelfth Imam school, the main sect of Shi'ite Muslims, al-Ṭūsī finished his education in Neyshābūr, about 75 km (50 miles) to the west. This was no doubt a prudent move as Genghis Khan (d. 1227), having conquered Beijing in 1215, turned his attention to the Islamic world and reached the region around Ṭūs by 1220. In about 1227 the Ismāʿilite governor Nāṣir al-Dīn ʿAbd al-Raḥīm offered al-Ṭūsī sanctuary in his mountain fortresses in Khorāsān. Al-Ṭūsī in turn dedicated his most famous work, *Akhlaq-i nāṣirī* (1232; *Nasirean Ethics*), to the governor before being invited to stay in the capital at Alamūt, where he espoused the Ismāʿilite faith under the new imam, Alauddin Muhammad (reigned 1227–1255). (This Ismāʿilite state began in 1090 with the conquest of Alamut by Ḥasan-e Ṣabbāḥ and ended with the fall of the city to the Mongols in 1256.) During this period, al-Ṭūsī wrote on Ismāʿilite theology (*Tasawwurāt*; "Notions"), logic (*Asās al-iqtibās*; "Foundations of Inference"), and mathematics (*Taḥrīr al-Majisṭi*; "Commentary on the Almagest").

With the fall in 1256 of Alamut to Hülegü Khan (*c.* 1217–1265), grandson of Genghis Khan, al-Ṭūsī immediately accepted a position with the Mongols as a scientific adviser. (The alacrity with which he went to work for them fueled accusations that his conversion to the Isma'ilite faith was feigned, as well as rumours that he betrayed the city's defenses.) Al-Ṭūsī married a Mongol and was then put in charge of the ministry of religious bequests. The topic of whether al-Ṭūsī accompanied the Mongol capture of Baghdad in 1258 remains controversial, although he certainly visited nearby Shi'ite centres soon afterward. Profiting from Hülegü's belief in astrology, al-Ṭūsī obtained support in 1259 to build a fine observatory (completed in 1262) adjacent to Hülegü's capital in Mārāgheh (now in Azerbaijan). More than an observatory, Hülegü obtained a first-rate library and staffed his institution with notable Islamic and Chinese scholars. Funded by an endowment, research continued at the institution for at least 25 years after al-Ṭūsī's death, and some of its astronomical instruments inspired later designs in Samarkand (now in Uzbekistan).

Al-Ṭūsī was a man of exceptionally wide erudition. He wrote approximately 150 books in Arabic and Persian and edited the definitive Arabic versions of the works of Euclid, Archimedes, Ptolemy, Autolycus, and Theodosius. He also made original contributions to mathematics and astronomy. His *Zīj-i Ilkhānī* (1271; "Ilkhan Tables"), based on research at the Mārāgheh observatory, is a splendidly accurate table of planetary movements. Al-Ṭūsī's most influential book in the West may have been *Tadhkirah fi 'ilm al-hay'a* ("Treasury of Astronomy"), which describes a geometric construction, now known as the al-Ṭūsī couple, for producing rectilinear motion from a point on one circle rolling inside another. By means of this construction, al-Ṭūsī succeeded in reforming the Ptolemaic planetary models, producing a system in which all orbits are described by uniform circular motion. Most historians of Islamic astronomy believe that the planetary models developed at Marāgheh found their way to Europe (perhaps via Byzantium) and provided Nicolaus Copernicus (1473–1543) with inspiration for his astronomical models.

Today al-Ṭūsī's *Tajrīd* ("Catharsis") is a highly esteemed treatise on Shi'ite theology. He made important contributions to many branches of Islamic learning, and under his direction Marāgheh sparked a revival of Islamic mathematics, astronomy, philosophy, and theology. In the East, al-Ṭūsī is an example par excellence of the *ḥakīm*, or "wise man."

CHAPTER 6
TRIGONOMETRIC TERMS AND CONCEPTS

A n alphabetic compendium of terms and concepts commonly encountered in trigonometry is given below.

ALFONSINE TABLES

The Alfonsine Tables (also spelled Alphonsine Tables,) were the first set of astronomical tables prepared in Christian Europe. They enabled calculation of eclipses and the positions of the planets for any given time based on the Ptolemaic theory, which assumed that the Earth was at the centre of the universe. The introduction states that the work was prepared in Toledo, Spain, for King Alfonso X of León and Castile under the direction of Jehuda ben Moses Cohen and Isaac ben Sid. Although no Castilian version survives, internal evidence—they were calculated for 1252, the initial year of the reign of Alfonso, and at the meridian of Toledo—supports the introduction. The tables were not widely known, however, until a Latin version was prepared in Paris in the 1320s. Copies rapidly spread throughout Europe, and for more than two centuries, they were the best astronomical tables available. First printed in 1483, the Alfonsine Tables were an important source of information for the young Nicolaus Copernicus before his own work superseded them in the 1550s.

ALMAGEST

The *Almagest* is an astronomical manual written about 150 CE by Ptolemy (Claudius Ptolemaeus of Alexandria).

Ptolemy's Almagest, *the frontispiece of which is shown above, is a significant work in both astronomy and mathematics.* SSPL/Getty Images

It served as the basic guide for Islamic and European astronomers until about the beginning of the 17th century. Its original name was *Mathematike Syntaxis* ("The Mathematical Arrangement"). *Almagest* arose as an Arabic corruption of the Greek word for "greatest" (*megiste*). It was translated into Arabic about 827 and then from Arabic to Latin in the last half of the 12th century. Subsequently, the Greek text circulated widely in Europe, although the Latin translations from Arabic continued to be more influential.

The *Almagest* is divided into 13 books. Book 1 gives arguments for a geocentric, spherical cosmos and introduces the necessary trigonometry, along with a trigonometry table, that allowed Ptolemy in subsequent books to explain and predict the motions of the Sun, Moon, planets, and stars. Book 2 uses spherical trigonometry to explain cartography and astronomical phenomena (such as the length of the longest day) characteristic of various localities. Book 3 deals with the motion of the Sun and how to predict its position in the zodiac at any given time, and Books 4 and 5 treat the more difficult problem of the Moon's motion. Book 5 also describes the construction of instruments to aid in these investigations. The theory developed to this point is applied to solar and lunar eclipses in Book 6.

Books 7 and 8 mainly concern the fixed stars, giving ecliptic coordinates and magnitudes for 1,022 stars. This star catalog relies heavily on that of Hipparchus (129 BCE), and in the majority of cases Ptolemy simply converted Hipparchus's description of the location of each star to ecliptic coordinates and then shifted these values by a constant to account for precession over the intervening centuries. These two books also discuss the construction of a star globe that adjusts for precession. The remaining five books, the most original, set forth in detail geometric models for the motion of the five planets visible to the naked eye, together with tables for predicting their positions at any given time.

LAW OF COSINES

The law of cosines is a generalization of the Pythagorean theorem relating the lengths of the sides of any triangle. If a, b, and c are the lengths of the sides and C is the angle opposite side c, then $c^2 = a^2 + b^2 - 2ab \cos C$.

FOURIER SERIES

A Fourier series is an infinite series used to solve special types of differential equations. It consists of an infinite sum of sines and cosines, and because it is periodic (i.e., its values repeat over fixed intervals), it is a useful tool in analyzing periodic functions. Though investigated by Leonhard Euler, among others, the idea was named for Joseph Fourier, who fully explored its consequences — including important applications in engineering, particularly in heat conduction.

HYPERBOLIC FUNCTION

The hyperbolic functions (also called hyperbolic trigonometric functions) are: the hyperbolic sine of z (written sinh z); the hyperbolic cosine of z (cosh z); the hyperbolic tangent of z (tanh z); and the hyperbolic cosecant, secant, and cotangent of z. These functions are most conveniently defined in terms of the exponential function, with $\sinh z = 1/2(e^z - e^{-z})$ and $\cosh z = 1/2(e^z + e^{-z})$ and with the other hyperbolic trigonometric functions defined in a manner analogous to ordinary trigonometry.

Just as the ordinary sine and cosine functions trace (or parameterize) a circle, so the sinh and cosh parameterize a hyperbola—hence the *hyperbolic* appellation. Hyperbolic functions also satisfy identities analogous to those of the ordinary trigonometric functions and have important physical applications. For example, the hyperbolic cosine function may be used to describe the shape of the curve formed by a high-voltage line suspended between two towers. Hyperbolic functions may also be used to define a measure of distance in certain kinds of non-Euclidean geometry.

LAW OF SINES

The law of sines is a principle of trigonometry stating that the lengths of the sides of any triangle are proportional to the sines of the opposite angles. That is,

$$\frac{a}{\sin A} = \frac{b}{\sin B} = \frac{c}{\sin C}$$

when a, b, and c are the sides and A, B, and C are the opposite angles.

TRIGONOMETRIC FUNCTION

The six trigonometric functions (sine, cosine, tangent, cotangent, secant, and cosecant) represent ratios of the sides of right triangles. They are also known as the circular functions, since their values can be defined as ratios of the x and y coordinates of points on a circle of radius 1 that correspond to angles in standard positions. Such values have been tabulated and programmed into scientific calculators and computers. This allows trigonometry to be easily applied to surveying, engineering, and navigation problems in which one of a right triangle's acute angles and the length of a side are known and the lengths of the other sides are to be found. The fundamental trigonometric identity is $\sin^2\theta + \cos^2\theta = 1$, in which θ is an angle. Certain intrinsic qualities of the trigonometric functions make them useful in mathematical analysis. In particular, their derivatives form patterns useful for solving differential equations.

TRIGONOMETRY TABLE

A trigonometry table is a set of tabulated values for some or all of the six trigonometric functions for various angular values. Once an essential tool for scientists, engineers, surveyors, and navigators, trigonometry tables became obsolete with the availability of computers. (The six trigonometric functions in relation to a right triangle are displayed in the figure on the bottom of page 217.)

The Greek astronomer Hipparchus (d. *c.* 127 BCE) was the first to compose a table of trigonometric functions (based on the chords in a circle), which he calculated at increments of 7° 30'. Ptolemy improved on Hipparchus's tables by calculating the values at 30' increments. Ptolemy's *Almagest*, the greatest astronomical work of antiquity, would be unimaginable without his table of chords.

The earliest table of the sine function (although still not with its modern definition) is found in the *Surya Siddhanta*, a Hindu astronomical handbook from the 4th or 5th century CE.

The astronomers of medieval Islam were consummate calculators who constructed tables of all six trigonometric functions as a basis for astronomy and astronomical time-keeping. The crown of this endeavour was Sultan Ulugh

Beg's tables, published in 1440 in Samarkand (now in Uzbekistan). The sine and tangent functions (although still not given their modern definitions in terms of ratios), calculated at 1' increments, were accurate to the equivalent of 9 decimal places.

From Muslim Spain, trigonometric tables spread to Latin Europe. Regiomontanus (1436–76), German astronomer and mathematician, composed the first tables with decimal values. Similarly, Georg Joachim Rheticus (1514–74), a student of Nicolaus Copernicus, prepared a magnificent set of tables of all six trigonometric functions at 10" increments accurate to 10 decimal places. Rheticus also took the decisive steps of defining the trigonometric functions in terms of angles rather than arcs and as ratios rather than lengths.

The French mathematician François Viète published tables of all six trigonometric functions in *Canon Mathematicus* (1579). The value of this work was not, however, in the tables, in which he calculated the functions at 1' increments, accurate to five decimal places. Instead, Viète's work was important because he had discovered various trigonometry relationships with which he demonstrated how to use trigonometry to solve equations of degree three and higher. Henceforth, trigonometric tables were useful not only in surveying, astronomy, and navigation but in algebra as well.

The climax for the construction of trigonometric tables in this period occurred with the German Bartholomeo Pitiscus. It was Pitiscus who coined the word *trigonometry*, and his *Thesaurus Mathematicus* (1615) contained tables of sines and cosines calculated at 10' intervals that were accurate to 15 decimal places. Later, still more accurate tables were constructed with the help of logarithms, invented by John Napier in 1614.

TRIANGULATION

In navigation, surveying, and civil engineering, triangulation is a technique for precise determination of a ship's or aircraft's position, and the direction of roads, tunnels, or other structures under construction. It is based on the

Two surveyors with a theodolite take triangulation readings. J. Baylor Roberts/National Geographic/Getty Images

laws of plane trigonometry, which state that, if one side and two angles of a triangle are known, the other two sides and angle can be readily calculated. One side of the selected triangle is measured; this is the baseline. The two adjacent angles are measured by means of a surveying device known as a theodolite, and the entire triangle is established. By constructing a series of such triangles, each adjacent to at least one other triangle, values can be obtained for distances and angles not otherwise measurable. Triangulation was used by the ancient Egyptians, Greeks, and other peoples at a very early date, with crude sighting devices that were improved into the diopter, or dioptra (an early theodolite), and were described in the 1st century CE by Heron of Alexandria.

GLOSSARY

algebra The branch of mathematics in which arithmetical operations and formal manipulations are applied to abstract symbols rather than specific numbers.

automorphism A correspondence that associates to every element in a set a unique element of the set and for which there is a companion correspondence, known as its inverse, such that one followed by the other produces the identity correspondence.

bisect Division of something into two equal or congruent parts, usually by a line, which is then called a bisector.

coefficient A constant multiplicative factor of a specific object.

coordinate A system for assigning an n-tuple of numbers or scalars to each point in an n-dimensional space.

dimension The measure of the size of an object, such as a box, usually given as length, width, and height.

equation Statement of equality between two expressions consisting of variables and/or numbers.

formulation The product of a systematized statement or expression.

function An expression, rule, or law that defines a relationship between one variable (the independent variable) and another variable (the dependent variable).

geometry The branch of mathematics concerned with the shape of individual objects, spatial relationships among various objects, and the properties of surrounding space.

hierarchy A graded or ranked series.

homomorphism A special correspondence between the members (elements) of two algebraic systems, such as two groups, two rings, or two fields.

integer Whole-valued positive or negative number or 0.

irrational numbers Any real number that cannot be expressed as the quotient of two integers.

magnitude A numerical quantitative measure expressed usually as a multiple of a standard unit.

metaphysics The philosophical study whose object is to determine the real nature of things — to determine the meaning, structure, and principles of whatever is insofar as it is.

perpendicular Two lines or planes (or a line and a plane), are considered perpendicular (or orthogonal) to each other if they form congruent adjacent angles.

polynomials An expression consisting of numbers and variables grouped according to certain patterns.

ratio Quotient of two values.

rational numbers A number that can be represented as the quotient p/q of two integers such that $q \neq 0$. In addition to all the fractions, the set of rational numbers includes all the integers, each of which can be written as a quotient with the integer as the numerator and 1 as the denominator.

scalar A physical quantity that is completely described by its magnitude.

tangent Straight line (or smooth curve) that touches a given curve at one point; at that point, the slope of the curve is equal to that of the tangent.

theorem A proposition or statement that is demonstrated; a statement to be proved.

trigonometry The branch of mathematics concerned with specific functions of angles and their application to calculations.

variable A symbol (usually a letter) standing in for an unknown numerical value in an equation.

vector A quantity that has both magnitude and direction but not position.

BIBLIOGRAPHY

ALGEBRA

General History

B. L. van der Waerden, *A History of Algebra: From al-Khwārizmī to Emmy Noether* (1985), is a highly respected classic. Two works that contain selections from original mathematical texts, including many that are directly relevant to the history of algebra, are David Eugene Smith, *A Source Book in Mathematics* (1929, reissued 1959); and John Fauvel and Jeremy Gray (eds.), *The History of Mathematics: A Reader* (1987, reissued 1990).

Ancient and Greek Algebra

Among the books on ancient mathematics, including sections on algebra, the reader may consult O. Neugebauer, *The Exact Sciences in Antiquity*, 2nd ed. (1969, reissued 1993); Richard J. Gillings, *Mathematics in the Time of the Pharaohs* (1972, reprinted 1982); and Jens Hoyrup, *Lengths, Widths, Surfaces: A Portrait of Old Babylonian Algebra and Its Kin* (2002).

The degree to which algebraic ideas do or do not appear in Greek geometric texts has been widely discussed by historians. A comprehensive summary of work on this controversial question appears in Michael N. Fried and Sabetai Unguru, *Apollonius of Perga's Conica: Text, Context, Subtext* (2001).

Indian and Chinese Algebra

Among the few English-language books on the history of algebra in India and China, the following are recommended: C. N. Srinivasiengar, *The History of Ancient Indian*

Mathematics (1967); and Ulrich Libbrecht, *Chinese Mathematics in the Thirteenth Century: The Shu-Shu Chiu-Chang of Ch'in, Chiu-Shao* (1973).

Islamic Algebra

Research on Islamic mathematics has vigorously developed in recent years. Two important works are Roshdi Rashed (Rushdi Rashid), *The Development of Arabic Mathematics: Between Arithmetic and Algebra* (1994; originally published in French, 1984); and J. L. Berggren, *Episodes in the Mathematics of Medieval Islam* (1986).

Algebra in Renaissance Europe

Jacob Klein, *Greek Mathematical Thought and the Origin of Algebra*, trans. from German (1968, reprinted 1992), is one of the most important accounts of the evolution of the concept of number from the ancient Greeks to the 17th century. Paul Lawrence Rose, *The Italian Renaissance of Mathematics: Studies on Humanists and Mathematicians from Petrarch to Galileo* (1975), is a highly respected history of Renaissance mathematics.

Modern Algebra

Leo Corry, *Modern Algebra and the Rise of Mathematical Structures* (1996), traces the emergence of the structural approach, as well as efforts to develop a metatheory of structures.

TRIGONOMETRY

Eli Maor, *Trigonometric Delights* (1998), is a discussion of various topics in trigonometry from a historical perspective. The first five chapters deal exclusively with the history of trigonometry. J. L. Berggren, *Episodes in the Mathematics of Medieval Islam* (1986), contains information on the development of trigonometry in Islam. Barnabas Hughes (ed. and trans.), *Regiomontanus: On Triangles* (1967), is a facsimile edition of Regiomontanus's influential book on trigonometry; pages are arranged so that the English translation appears opposite the original Latin text. George Gheverghese Joseph, *The Crest of the Peacock: Non-European Roots of Mathematics*, new ed. (2000), correcting the notion that modern mathematics is primarily a product of European development, emphasizes the Egyptian, Babylonian, Chinese, Indian, and Arab contributions to algebra, geometry, and trigonometry. Morris Kline, *Mathematical Thought from Ancient to Modern Times* (1972, reissued in 3 vol., 1990), is an exhaustive work on the history of mathematics, with emphasis on the past 300 years.

The following works are comprehensive historical textbooks at the college level, each with a wealth of information on the development of trigonometry: Carl B. Boyer, *A History of Mathematics*, 2nd ed. rev. by Uta C. Merzbach (1989, reissued 1991); David M. Burton, *The History of Mathematics: An Introduction*, 4th ed. (1999); Howard Eves, *An Introduction to the History of Mathematics*, 6th ed. (1990); and Victor J. Katz, *A History of Mathematics: An Introduction*, 2nd ed. (1998).

INDEX

A

abacists, 36–37, 38
Abel, Niels Henrik, 48, 107–110, 117, 123–124, 138, 166
Abel's theorem, 109
Alfonsine Tables, 259
algebra
  branches of, 70–90
  classical, 43–63, 91
  definition of, 23
  elementary, 71–78
  fundamental concepts of modern, 54–57
  fundamental theorem of, 45–47, 61, 75, 173–174
  history of, 23–70
  linear, 60, 78–82
  modern, 83–90
  structural, 63–71
algebraic equations, 163
  solving, 75–78, 89
algebraic expressions, 73–75
algebraic geometry, 87–88
algebraic number, 163–164
algebraic quantities, 71–73
Almagest, 205–206, 207, 238, 244, 246, 247–249, 254, 259–262, 264
analytic geometry, 43–45, 72, 115, 209, 222
analytic trigonometry, 222–223, 230
Archimedes, 32, 237, 255, 257
Argand, Jean-Robert, 61
Aristarchus of Samos, 241

Arithmetica, 96–99
Ars magna (*The Great Work; The Rules of Algebra*), 38, 94, 95, 100
Artin, Emil, 51, 64, 66, 143
Aryabhata I, 93, 106, 206, 227–229
Aryabhatiya, 206, 227–229
associative law, 164
astronomical observations, early, 240–244, 247–250, 253–254, 257–258
automorphism, 164–165
axioms, structural, 84–85

B

Babylon
  contributions to algebra, 23, 26–27, 32, 91
  contributions to trigonometry, 203
  and problem solving, 26–27
Barrow, Isaac, 42
al-Battānī, Abū 'abd Allāh Muḥammad ibn Jābir ibn Sinān, 207, 208, 229
Beltrami, Eugenio, 124
Bernoulli, Daniel, 232
Bernoulli, Jakob, 166, 230
Bernoulli, Johann, 232
Bernoulli, Nicolas, 232
Betti, Enrico, 51
Bhaskara I, 93, 228
Bhaskara II, 31, 91–92

binomial theorem, 165–166
Birkhoff, Garret, 67
Bolyai, János, 123, 124
Bolzano, Bernhard, 110–111
Bombelli, Rafael, 39–40, 41, 42
bookkeeping, use of mathematics
     in early, 35
Boole, George, 60–61, 111–113, 166
Boolean algebra, 67, 111, 113,
     166–168
Borcherds, Richard Ewen, 144
Bourbaki, Nicolas, 68, 144–145
Brahe, Tycho, 249
Brahmagupta, 31, 93–94
Brauer, Richard Dagobert,
     145–146, 157
Burnside, William, 70

C

calculus, 43, 46, 58
Cantor, Georg, 164
Cardano, Girolamo (Jerome
     Cardan), 38–39, 41, 43,
     94–96, 100
Cartan, Élie-Joseph, 146–147
Cartan, Henri, 68, 144, 148
Cassini family, 213
category theory, 68–69
Cauchy, Augustin-Louis, 50–51,
     58, 118, 138
Cayley, Arthur, 53–54, 59–60, 82,
     113–116, 140, 141, 182–183
Chevalley, Claude, 144
China
     contributions to algebra, 23, 76
     contributions to trigonom-
        etry, 203
     and the equation, 31–32

Chuquet, Nicolas, 37
Clebsch, Alfred, 130
Collins, John, 237
commutative law, 168
complex number, definition
     of, 168
computers, for proving and
     formulating theorems, 70
coordinates
     polar, 223–225
     transformation of, 225–226
Copernicus, Nicolaus, 205, 208,
     242, 254, 258, 259
cosines, law of, 219, 220, 222, 262
     spherical law of, 221
Cotes, Roger, 211
Courant, Richard, 131, 155
Cramer's rule, 168–169
Crelle, August Leopold, 109

D

Dantzig, George, 147–148
Dedekind, Richard, 51, 55–57, 65,
     72, 86, 124, 178
degree of freedom, 169
de Moivre, Abraham, 210,
     230–231
De Morgan, Augustus, 60–61, 112
Descartes, René, 43–45, 71, 209
determinants, 57, 58, 170–171
Dickson, Leonard Eugene,
     148–149
Dieudonné, Jean, 68, 144, 149
Diophantus of Alexandria,
     29–31, 32, 41, 96–99, 102, 255
discriminants, 171
distributive law, 171–172
Doctrine of Chances, The, 230

E

Egypt, ancient
 contributions to trigonometry, 203
 problem solving, 25–26, 91
eigenvalue, 82, 172
eigenvectors, 82
Eilenberg, Samuel, 68–69,
  144, 155
Einstein, Albert, 160
Eisenstein, Gotthold Max, 59
Elements, 27, 28, 34, 38, 104, 232
Eléments de mathématique, 68
Engel, Friedrich, 134
equation, definition of, 172
Erdös, Paul, 70
Euclid, 27, 28, 29, 32, 34, 38, 52, 54,
  55, 104, 115, 122–123, 125, 191,
  208, 228, 232, 245, 255, 257
Euler, Leonhard, 108, 210–211,
  231–234, 262
European Renaissance
 contributions to algebra, 23,
  24, 35–42, 91
 contributions to trigonometry, 208

F

factor, definition of, 173
Feit, Walter, 70, 90
Fermat, Pierre de, 43, 95, 99, 133,
  209, 230
Ferrari, Ludovico, 39, 95, 99–100
Ferro, Scipione, 100–101
Fibonacci (Leonardo Pisano),
  35–36
fields, 56, 64, 83–84
 theory of, 65, 68

formal equations, emergence of,
  23–42
 three steps in process leading
  to, 24
Fourier, Joseph, 213–214, 262
Fourier series, 214, 262
Frisius, Gemma, 212–213
Frobenius, Georg, 60, 67, 145,
  146, 149–150
fundamental theorem of algebra,
  45–47, 61, 75
 definition of, 173–174

G

Galileo Galilei, 191, 212
Galois, Évariste, 48–51, 53, 63,
  69–70, 75, 89, 116–119, 135,
  138, 175
Galois theory, 49–51, 66, 89, 120
Gauss, Carl Friedrich, 46, 48, 53,
  54–55, 59, 61, 75, 108, 109,
  119–124, 133, 152
Gauss elimination, 174
Gaussian integers, 54–55
Gelfond, Aleksandr Osipovich,
  150–151
geometry, 43–45, 46, 52–53, 60,
  115, 202–203, 209, 214
George of Trebizond, 254–255
Gibbs, Josiah Willard, 62, 198
Girard, Albert, 46
Gordon, Paul, 87
Gorenstein, Daniel, 70
Great Trigonometric Survey, 213
Greece, ancient
 contributions to algebra, 23,
  24, 32, 34–35, 41, 91
 contributions to trigonometry,
  203–207

and geometric expression,
27–31, 38
Gregorian telescope, 235
Gregory, James, 210, 234–238
Grothendieck, Alexandre, 69,
88, 155
group, definition of, 175
group theory, 51–52, 53, 64,
69–70, 88–90, 116, 119, 175

H

Halley, Edmond, 230
Hamilton, William Rowan,
60, 61–62, 86, 124–128, 133,
136, 192
al-Hasib, Habash, 207
Hasse, Helmut, 157
Heaviside, Oliver, 62, 198
Hermite, Charles, 129
Hilbert, David, 64–65, 67,
86–87, 131, 143, 144, 151–154,
156, 160
Hipparchus, 203–204, 206,
238–245, 248–249, 261, 264
Hodge, William, 176
Hodge conjecture, 176
Holmboe, Bernt Michael, 108
homomorphism, 176–178
Huygens, Christiaan, 230
hyperbolic function, 262–263

I

ideals, 56–57, 178–179
imaginary number, definition
of, 179
India
contributions to algebra, 23,
32, 36, 37

contributions to trigonometry,
203, 206, 207
and the equation, 31
injection, definition of, 179–180
irrational number, definition
of, 180
Islam
contributions to algebra, 23,
24, 31, 32–36, 37, 38, 91
contributions to trigonometry,
206–207, 208

J

Jacobi, Carl Gustav, 110, 116,
123, 127
Jordan, Camille, 51, 60, 119

K

Kamil, Abu, 35
al-Karaji, Abu Bakr ibn
Muhammad ibn al-Husayn,
99, 101–102
Kepler, Johannes, 236, 242
Khayyam, Omar, 34
al-Khwārizmī, Muhammad ibn
Mūsā, 32–34, 102–103
Klein, Felix, 52, 53, 130–131,
134, 156
Kronecker, Leopold, 51, 86,
131–132, 150
Kummer, Ernst Eduard, 55, 86,
131, 132–133

L

Lagrange, Joseph-Louis, 47, 50,
108, 117, 125, 138, 175, 234
Laplace, Pierre-Simon, 112, 125

Legendre, Adrien-Marie, 117
Leibniz, Gottfried Wilhelm, 58
Levi-Civita, Tullio, 160
Lie, Sophus, 53, 130, 133–135, 146
Lie algebras, 53
Lie groups, 53, 146, 149, 156
linear equation, definition of,
    180–181
linear transformations, 81–82
Liouville, Joseph, 51, 119, 135–137
Liouville number, 181–182
Liu Hui, 103–105
Lloyd, Humphrey, 127
Lobachevsky, Nikolay, 123, 124
logarithms, 208, 222

M

Mac Lane, Saunders, 67, 68–69,
    154–155
Madhava, 210
Mahavira, 105–106
Margulis, Gregori
    Aleksandrovich, 155–156
Marinus of Tyre, 251
matrix/matrix theory, 57, 58–61,
    81–82, 86, 115, 182–186
Maxwell, James Clerk, 62, 160, 198
Menelaus of Alexandria, 207–208,
    245–246, 250
Minkowski, Hermann, 152
Moderne Algebra, 64, 67
"Monster, the," 90, 144
multinomial theorem, 186

N

Napier, John, 208, 222, 265
Newton, Isaac, 42, 108, 112, 125,
    166, 210, 230

Nine Chapters, The, 104
Noether, Emmy, 64, 65–66, 67,
    156–158
numbers, concept of, 41–42
number theory, 51, 52, 53–54, 59,
    87, 88, 99, 131

O

On Triangles, 208

P

parameter, definition of, 187
Pascal, Blaise, 42, 95, 187, 230
Pascal's triangle, 101, 165,
    187–190
Peacock, George, 60
Peano, Giuseppe, 201
permutations, 50, 51, 54
Peuerbach, Georg von, 253, 254
Picard, Jean, 213
Pitiscus, Bartholomeo, 265
plane trigonometry, 219–221
Pliny the Elder, 244
Plücker, Julius, 130
Poincaré, Henri, 53
polynomials/polynomial equa-
    tions, 29–30, 43, 45–46, 48,
    49, 57, 63, 64, 67, 73, 74, 75,
    86, 190
prime factorization, 54–57
probability, theory of, 230–231
proportions, theory of, 27–28
Ptolemy, 205–206, 229, 238, 240,
    243, 244, 246–252, 254, 257,
    259–262, 264
Pythagorean theorem, 27,
    202–203, 228, 262

Q

Qin Jiushao, 106–107
quadratic equations, 25, 28, 29,
    31, 32, 34, 35, 40, 92, 191–192
quaternions, 62, 66, 85–86, 125,
    128, 192
Quillen, Daniel Gray, 158–159

R

radical methods, impasse with,
    47–48
rational number, definition of,
    192–193
Regiomontanus, 208, 252–256, 265
Rheticus, Georg Joachim, 265
Rhind papyrus, 25, 203
Riemann, Bernhard, 122, 124,
    152, 160
rings/ring theory, 64, 66, 67,
    84, 85
    in algebraic geometry, 87–88
    definition of, 193
    in number theory, 86–87
root, definition of, 193–195
Rudolff, Christoff, 38
Ruffini, Paolo, 47–48, 50, 117,
    137–138

S

Scheubel, Johannes, 38
Schröder, Ernst, 60–61
Schur, Issai, 67
Seki Takakazu (Seki Kowa), 58,
    138–140
Serre, Jean-Pierre, 150, 159
sines, law of, 219, 220, 222, 263
    spherical law of, 221

Snell, Willebrord van Roijen, 213
Sphaerica, 207–208, 245–246
spherical trigonometry, 221–222
square root, definition of, 195
Steinitz, Ernst, 65, 68
Stevin, Simon, 42
Stiffel, Michal, 38
Stirling, James, 231
Stirling's formula, 231
Stone, Marshall, 67
Sturm, Charles-François, 136
superstructures, 67
surjection, 195
Survey of Modern Algebra, A, 67
Sylvester, James Joseph, 59, 115,
    140–142, 182
synthetic division, 196
systems of equations, 57–61, 197
    solving, 76–78

T

Tait, Peter Guthrie, 62
Tarski, Alfred, 159
Tartaglia, Niccolò, 95, 100
Thomson, John G., 70, 90
Topos theory, 69
triangulation, 266–267
trigonometric functions, 214–219,
    222, 223, 250, 263–264
    of an angle, 216–218
    table of natural functions, 219
trigonometry
    analytic, 222–223, 230
    application to science, 212–214
    classical, 202–208
    definition of, 202
    history of, 202–214
    modern, 209–214

plane, 202, 204, 219–220, 221
principles of, 214–226
spherical, 202, 204, 207,
   221–222
trigonometry table, 264–267
Turán, Paul, 70
al-Ṭūsī, Naṣīr al-Dīn, 208, 256–258

V

van der Waerden, Bartel, 64, 65,
   66, 67, 68, 91
variable, definition of, 197
Veblen, Oswald, 160
vector operations, 200
vectors, 62, 78–81, 82, 197–200
vector space, 200–201
Viète, François, 40–41, 43, 44, 73,
   91, 142–143, 209–210, 265
Vinogradov, Ivan M., 148

W

Weber, Henrich, 51, 63, 175
Weber, Wilhelm, 122
Weierstrass, Karl, 132
Weil, André, 66, 68, 88, 144
Wessel, Caspar, 61
Weyl, Hermann, 67, 145, 155,
   160–161

Y

Yang Hui, 31, 139, 187

Z

Zariski, Oscar, 66
Zelmanov, Efim Isaakovich,
   161–162
zero, concept/use of, 26, 28, 31, 94